Economic Issues of the Eighties

ECONOMIC ISSUES
OF THE EIGHTIES

Edited by Nake M. Kamrany and Richard H. Day

THE JOHNS HOPKINS UNIVERSITY PRESS
Baltimore and London

The Johns Hopkins University Press, Baltimore, Maryland 21218
The Johns Hopkins Press Ltd., London
Library of Congress Catalog Number 79-16772
ISBN 0-8018-2248-3
ISBN 0-8018-2271-8 (pbk.)
Library of Congress Cataloging in Publication data will be found on the last printed page of this book.

Contents

Preface

This volume is based on a series of lectures presented at the University of Southern California in 1977 and 1978 as a part of the Department of Economics' colloquium "Contemporary Economic Issues." The colloquium was open to university students and to the general public; in addition, the lectures were broadcast to some twenty industries through the School of Engineering's Interactive Television Instruction Program.

The colloquium was designed to provide a public forum for leading contributors to modern economic analysis and policy and to present its audience with a spectrum of authoritative views on momentous issues of public concern. The enthusiastic response to the program encouraged us to present the various contributions to a wider audience in the form of the present book.

In bringing this project to fruition we enjoyed the support of John A. Schutz, dean of social sciences and communication at USC, who made possible a generous grant from the Division of Social Sciences of the College of Letters, Arts, and Science. The School of Engineering provided its superb instructional laboratory. Further support was granted by the Atlantic Richfield Foundation.

We want to thank The Johns Hopkins University Press for endorsing the idea of this publication. Special thanks go to Sue Anderson, one of those rare and marvelous individuals, who, with energy and ingenuity, pulled the whole project together and made it an enjoyable experience for everyone concerned. Copy editing and typing were performed in excellent fashion by Ida Abe, Ray Hardesty, Janet Merrit, Carolyn Moser, and Jana Wong. Cyrus Davis assisted in putting the bibliography together. The final proofing and index were the responsibility of Linda Anderson.

Economic Issues of the Eighties

Editors' Introduction

We live in an age of unprecedented affluence and opportunity. Yet economic problems continue to bother the ordinary citizen and challenge statesmen. The particular problems that plague us come and go, sometimes appearing or disappearing with amazing rapidity. Old problems diminish as effective means for their solution are found. Sometimes they simply recede into obscurity as the ongoing process of economic change absorbs their consequences. One example of such an apparently temporary problem was that of the agricultural surpluses of the fifties and early sixties.

But new problems always seem to emerge and march to the forefront of public attention. Sometimes they are unexpected. Even when a few prescient individuals anticipate them, advance preparations to abate or eliminate their bad effects are often inadequate. More often than not economic problems are not well understood, even by expert social scientists and leading people of affairs. As a result, the formulation of policies to deal with them is fraught with difficulty. To make matters worse, basic values differ among individuals and groups, so that agreement about the nature, scope, and importance of economic problems—and thus, about their solutions—is hard to achieve. Consequently, policy formulation involves debate, argument, and even coercion or attempted coercion as various interests contend for influence.

Some economic problems seem to be implacable, enduring for decades or even centuries. For example, starvation and poverty still enslave a large portion of humanity, and many countries seem unable to escape the overpopulation, underdevelopment trap. Other problems are recurrent. They disappear or go into abeyance, only to reemerge later, sometimes with increasing severity, so that their control becomes a chronic challenge generation after generation. Examples are provided by inflation and depression. Each has occurred again and again in the course of economic development since early times. Sometimes they occur simultaneously, as we know from recent experience. Often one or the other or both are dormant, and public attention shifts to other matters.

The enduring or chronic economic problems constitute major issues which occupy important places in the history and development of economic thinking and may be distinguished from less important problems of temporary interest. This book deals with several such issues. These are

1. The general level and fluctuation of income, employment, and prices;
2. The distribution of income, opportunity, and welfare;
3. The relationship of technology and energy to labor productivity, welfare, and economic growth; and
4. The relationship of nations within the emerging world economy.

Certain characteristics of these issues set them apart from transitory problems. First, they are exceedingly complex, and do not lend themselves to clear-cut or easy solutions. Problem definition is of extreme importance because policies based on faulty understanding are often counterproductive. One of the main constraints in problem definition is the availability and accuracy of information. Once an error comes to be regarded as fact, it is hard to alleviate the consequences of the actions based on that error. Issues generally involve dissonances between the way things are and the way decisionmakers (private or public) wish them to be. In the light of new experience or information, perceptions and prescriptions concerning economic issues change. It follows that issues require examination and reexamination, assessment and reassessment, managing and weighing of alternatives, for better choices on a continuing basis. For instance, the coexistence of inflation and high unemployment has caused economists to reexamine their understanding of the trade-off between price and employment changes. New attempts are underway for a better definition of the problem and a better explanation of stagflation.

Second, economic issues have a dynamic character that influences and is influenced by how the economy evolves over time. The classic example is again the macroeconomic issue connected with aggregate employment, income, and the price level, which has led to various theories of business cycles and growth. Dynamic interdependencies characteristic of the big issues may be subtle and counterintuitive too. When policy prescriptions fail to take account of these effects, they may lead to unintended and undesirable consequences. One example, discussed in Chapter 8 below, involves the welfare distribution issue. Efforts to bring health benefits to the old through Medicaid and Medicare have exacerbated inflation while failing to accomplish the distributional objectives for which they were intended.

Another example, mentioned in Chapter 10 below, involves the effect of technology on labor productivity in agriculture. The remarkable advances in this century have made possible a high standard of living for advanced farmers and relatively inexpensive food for the nonagricultural population. But increased use of technology in agriculture has as its corollary an exodus of farmers to cities, where they have expanded by millions an industrial labor force within which unemployment has remained a chronic and virulent problem. Thus, the problems of rural poverty are shifted over time to urban poverty and underemployment. What appears to be a solution to one set of problems appears later as a contributor to another set of problems.

The unanticipated problems created by national health programs and by agricultural development illustrate another characteristic of major economic issues. This third characteristic is that they are interwoven with each other and with the economic system as a whole. They cannot easily be treated in isolation. The national health program appears to involve not only distributive issues of welfare but the macroeconomic issues of the general price level. Inflation, in turn, contributes to many other problems, such as an unfavorable balance of payments and instabilities in world money markets.

Finally, we need to recognize that major economic issues often transcend national boundaries. We have already mentioned how inflation may affect trading patterns; and all of us are acutely aware of how the pricing and trade policies of the Arab oil cartel impinge directly on our lives. Many other examples follow throughout this book.

To summarize, major economic issues involve complex, dynamic interdependencies with supranational implications. They challenge our best abilities to understand, predict, and control. It is scarcely surprising, therefore, that explanations and solutions are not unanimously endorsed. It may be amusing to be reminded of the old jokes that among any three economists one will find at least four opinions, or that all the economists in the world laid end-to-end would not reach a conclusion. But these old saws disguise a fundamental if unpleasant fact of modern life: the modern economy is only partly understood. The basic economic issues need continued attention, deep research, and analysis. Because alternative values and political opinions influence any possible solution, they need open discussion from various perspectives.

The essays of this book are designed to elucidate the fundamental economic issues listed above. The authors are noted for their contributions to economic theory and research methodology and for their sound use of economic analysis to illuminate basic issues and formulate new or modified economic policies. But while each essay, therefore, offers an authoritative study, none provides a final word on its subject or an unassailable point of view. In fact, we have tried, within our conception of the nature of broad economic issues, to provide a variety of points of view. We have assiduously avoided any appearance of a single theoretical approach or policy perspective. This may be frustrating to readers who want to find *the* answer. But if we are to capture the character of the issues themselves, we must be prepared to make our judgments on the basis of partial understanding and sometimes conflicting prescriptions. We should expect to review these judgments periodically and to modify them in the light of new information and analyses. Thus, the contributions of this volume are merely part of what must be a continuing and unending process.

{1}

The Untidy State of
Macroeconomic Analysis

MICHAEL DEPRANO

Macroeconomic analysis and macroeconomic policy are currently in a state of upheaval. The general public and governmental leaders see this most clearly in the inability of governments to deal with the problems of unemployment and inflation, both of which have been plaguing most of the Western democratic economies in recent years. Policies which are thought to alleviate unemployment appear to be successful only for relatively short periods, and at a cost of intensified inflation. Policies which are thought to slow inflation appear to generate levels of unemployment detrimental to the economic welfare of the public and therefore politically dangerous to elected officials.

The problem confronting those responsible for determining public policies is simply that professional economists are unable to present to them a generally accepted theory or analysis of the process of inflation and unemployment useful for formulating policies which will deal with both phenomena in a politically acceptable way. Complete central direction of our economy is not considered acceptable to any major portion of the public. While some advocate wage and price controls, most deem controls as being beneficial for only a short period of time, at best, and then leading to significant distortions in production, output, and employment. Policies relating to changes in government spending, total tax collections, and the amount of money in the economy are based on theories that were generally accepted at various times in the profession but are now in wide dispute. This unfortunate status of macroeconomic analysis is widely admitted by professional economists. So, for example, Professor Hyman Minsky, in the introduction to his brief but penetrating volume *John Maynard Keynes,* points to the "disarray" currently existing in macroeconomic analysis, and indicates that in such a state of disarray "there are competing theories, and for every competing theory there exist observations [of economic phenomena] which are difficult to explain. Every theory seems to be of limited usefulness; anomalies abound" (Minsky 1975, p. vii).

There have, of course, always been disagreements relating to macro-economic theory and policy within the profession, but there has generally been some primary or predominant view which most professional economists accepted, together with one or more apparently unimportant "minority" positions. Today there is no such predominant view or consensus. Several major positions are contending.

Macroeconomics and Microeconomics

Macroeconomics is the branch of economics which focuses on major aggregated variables in the economy, such as the total amount of output of goods and services, the total level of employment or unemployment, the rate of inflation (the rate of increase of prices of goods and services in general), and the total income earned. This can be contrasted with microeconomics, which focuses on the output and purchase of each specified good, the price of that good, the operation of the market for that good, and even the interaction of that market with other markets (especially those of substitute or complementary goods). So, for example, an analysis of the wage and number hired of electricians, the operation of the market for electricians, the impact of electricians' trade unions, and so on would call for the analytical tools of micro-economics; while analysis of the average wage rate in the whole economy, or its rate of change, the level of total employment in all markets, and similar questions would fall within macroeconomics.

At first glance it might appear that the separation of analysis into macroeconomics and microeconomics is artificial and unnecessary, or at best a convenience with no significant differences in explanation actually required. Indeed, this might very well be the case, but it is not clear-cut. An alternative position can be argued and has many adherents. This position is that principles which are applicable, and which actually appear to hold rather well in the analysis of individual markets for specific goods, will not necessarily hold when applied to the aggregates of goods and services in general, the level of employment in general, and so on.

An obvious example in support of this position is in comparing an increase in the price of wheat by itself with a general increase in all prices, wages, etc. If the price of wheat were increased and people expected it to remain at that new price, most of us would agree that this would lead people to desire to purchase less wheat. It would be more expensive relative to prices of other goods, wages, etc. But if all prices, wages, etc., rose, it would be less simple to claim that this would lead to less buying of goods in general. Each good would not be more expensive relative to other goods, nor more expensive relative to wages. At most, we could say that goods were more expensive relative to money (which now would have less purchasing power) or relative to bonds or other fixed-price assets. Even bonds or other kinds of debts are assets for some and liabilities for others, so their lower "real value" should not have an impact on the purchase of goods.

Despite these comments, we must remember that all economic phenomena—micro and macro—are part of the same environment. Appropriately, therefore, many economists, while recognizing the problems mentioned here, still insist that so long as there is a generally agreed-upon analytic approach to individual markets (that there is a generally accepted microeconomic framework), it should be expected that any macroeconomic analysis should not be inconsistent with it. If the outcomes of the macroeconomic analysis differ from what should be expected from simply adding up the results of analyses of the many individual markets, the critical reasons for the differences should be made explicit and should form part of the overall analysis. That is, these economists want to see, for any macroeconomic theory, an explicit presentation of its *microeconomic foundations*. Such a goal should be recognized as a natural part of any scientific endeavor. Apparent inconsistencies can arise in the various analyses of any kind of phenomena, but the scientist insists that his task is incomplete until he has determined the reasons for those apparent inconsistencies.

Aggregate Demand Management: The Keynesian Approach

During the depths of the major depression in 1936 John Maynard Keynes published *The General Theory of Employment, Interest, and Money,* which attempted to explain situations of significant unemployment. The book, while brilliant in many ways, contained many confusing passages and was subject to many misinterpretations. In using the analysis presented there, most economists employed various simplifications which, over time, became pretty much standardized in the profession. In the first eighteen chapters of the book Keynes' theory focused on an economic situation in which wage and price adjustments had no significant role. Despite unemployment and despite inadequate demand for the economy's output of goods and services, prices did not change in any significant way. Later in the book Keynes attempted to argue that even if wages and prices did fall in this kind of situation, his previous results would have been similar: decreases in wages and prices would have had only small effects if any. In any event, he pointed out, in current industrial economies prices and wages do tend to adjust very slowly when they do fall.

The simplified versions of his work, which formed the basis of most macroeconomic policy recommendations for the past several decades, are based on an analysis in which either the price of output or the wages of workers, or both, would not fall despite inadequate demand. The analysis focuses on the demand side, explaining periods of depression or significant recession—periods of heavy unemployment—as times when the demand for output is lower than that which would be needed to keep labor (and other factors of production) fully employed. The analysis of various parts of this demand attempts to explain how employment can fall to a low level and remain there.

The demands of three or four divisions, or sectors, of the economy are usually considered: households' demand for consumption goods, businesses' demand for investment goods (additions to their stock of capital such as factories, equipment, and inventory), and the government's demands for goods and services for public purposes. Analyses of "open" economies—economies which are engaged in foreign trade—also consider foreign demand for these economies' goods and their demand, in turn, for imports from foreign countries. But let us stay with the analysis of "closed" economies for simplicity. This approach considers the household sector essentially passive: consumers simply demand more or fewer goods according to whether their incomes (and employment) are higher or lower. Very important to the analysis is the question of how much consumption demand will change as income changes; this relation is termed the "marginal propensity to consume." After paying any taxes out of their earned incomes, consumers have left their disposable income, some of which is spent on consumption goods and the rest of which is saved. If disposable income rises by $100 million and people therefore increase their consumption expenditures by $80 million, the marginal propensity to consume is 0.8 or $4/5$; and saving must rise by $20 million. The ratio between the change in saving and the change in income which caused it is called the "marginal propensity to save" and in this case would be 0.2 or $1/5$. Since household saving is defined as disposable income less consumption, the two marginal propensities must sum to unity. In Figure 1.1 an increase of 100 in income leads to a consumption increase of 80, so the first graph has a slope of $4/5$. Since saving rises 20 for the same 100 increase in income, the saving function has a slope of $1/5$. A fall from 700 to 600 of income causes consumption and saving to fall by the same amounts negatively.

Other economic influences, such as wealth or interest rates, could also raise or lower consumption, and these effects would show up in the graphs as shifts in the curves. At unchanged income, a factor which caused a higher consumption would shift the consumption function to a higher position and the saving function to a lower position. In most versions of this approach, however, the other influences are considered

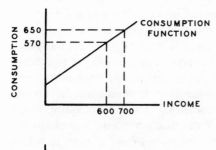

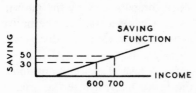

Figure 1.1. The consumption and saving functions

relatively insignificant in their impact on consumption and saving. So, for example, while total wealth (ownership of assets less liabilities) could affect household consumption, it is often assumed that wealth changes rather little in any relatively short period of time, and that what changes could occur would have small impacts on consumption. Interest rates could also have some impact. Consumers often finance some of their purchases (especially of major "durable" goods such as automobiles and refrigerators) by borrowing and incurring interest expense, so that higher interest rates might discourage some purchases. In addition, the more households save, the more they can lend, directly by purchasing corporation or government bonds, or indirectly by depositing cash in financial institutions. High interest rates could therefore encourage greater saving and discourage consumption. Yet this is also considered by many Keynesian economists as a minor influence on consumer behavior. It is a central assumption of the basic Keynesian theory that the relation between consumption and income is rather strong and stable, affected only slightly by other factors.

It is business investment demand that is considered the most volatile element in the analysis. The hypothesis is that this demand depends significantly on business *expectations* of future returns to any new plant or equipment because this stock of capital is rather long-lived. If businesses expect future sales prospects to be favorable, they will expect the new capital to be more profitable than otherwise and will be more likely to order construction of new plant and new equipment. They will also tend to wish to hold higher levels of inventory to meet the higher future sales expected.

Businesses compare the expected future returns with the current price of capital equipment and current rates of interest. If the future prospects are good enough to justify paying the current price for the equipment and incurring the interest expense, they will order more capital goods from firms which produce them. Interest rates can play a significant role in this component of demand. To the extent that purchasing new capital goods involves borrowing, higher interest rates make investment more costly and can discourage it somewhat. Even if borrowing is not involved because a firm already has the funds it needs, a decision not to purchase the capital could permit the firm to make loans to others (e.g., purchase the bonds issued by other companies or by the government) and receive interest. Clearly this is a more attractive alternative when interest rates are high. Again, higher interest rates can discourage the purchase of newly produced investment goods.

As Figure 1.2 indicates, for any specific pattern of expectations about future sales, production costs, etc., the lower interest rate the greater the business demand for investment goods. Any increase in the demand for investment goods means more demand to employ labor and other factors of production to produce them. The demand for the investment goods is part of the demand for the economy's total output. It is a significant part of the theory that the relation in Figure 1.2 is a very unstable one because of its great reliance on expectations about the future. These expectations can, of course, be based only on information which is currently available, and it is thought that small changes in current information can lead to major changes in expectations. [1]

The government demand for goods and services is considered "exogenous," or determined on political grounds (which are not explained by the theory). The government does not look at its income, market interest rates, or similar influences to determine its demand for goods and services. Keynesians point out, however, that by varying its pattern of demand, the government could consciously attempt to offset undesirable changes in other components of aggregate demand to keep total demand at some high but not inflationary level. In addition, by altering the tax laws or the amounts of transfer payments it makes to private individuals, it can influence the private sector's consumption demand or

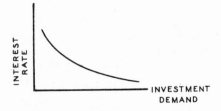

Figure 1.2. Investment demand

investment demand. That is, the government could use *fiscal policy* (policies relating to its budget—expenditures, taxes, transfers, the amount of government saving or deficit) to keep the total level of demand in the economy at about the right level to bring about low unemployment without being inflationary. Too high a level of expenditures or transfers and too low a level of taxes (too great a deficit) would be inflationary. The way the Keynesians suggest this would work is rather straightforward and easy to summarize here.

Let us continue to ignore foreign trade. We can then indicate that the aggregate demand for the society's output is simply the sum of the three domestic sectors' demands:

aggregate demand (AD) = consumption demand (CD)
+ investment demand (ID)
+ government demand for the
economy's output (GD)

If this demand is high enough, the economy could be essentially fully employed (with, at most, a small percentage of reported unemployment of a few people who have seasonal jobs, or who are simply changing jobs and are thus briefly out of work).

Suppose for a moment that the government was spending zero and taxing zero. If the economy is producing an output equal to the aggregate demand for that output, then the total income of the private sectors must equal the aggregate demand. This is because everything that is spent on purchasing the output must end up either as wages for the workers, or as rent, interest payments, or profits for the owners of the businesses. It all ends up as income for the households. Now what if there are government expenditures? The amount that the government spends on the output of the society must also end up in the incomes of the factors of production and therefore in household income (unless businesses are keeping some undistributed profits). To the extent that the government does collect some taxes, however, the disposable income (income after taxes) of households is lower. The total income of *all* sectors (including the government's net taxes—taxes after transfers) equals the value of the total output. One can therefore conclude that if the total *income* of all sectors equals the aggregate demand for the society's output, then the society must be producing an amount of output (*aggregate supply*) equal to that *aggregate demand*. Then there is no reason for the private economy to attempt to raise or lower output. It is producing an amount equal to the total demand. The economy is at rest or in equilibrium:

income (Y) = aggregate demand (AD), or
$$Y = CD + ID + GD$$

The income of the society is simply the sum of the net incomes of each sector (including the disposable income of the household sector). While this sum will equal aggregate demand in equilibrium, this does not mean that each sector must spend an amount equal to its own income. It could save or it could have deficits. Suppose that the household sector did save (had income greater than its consumption). The economy could still be in equilibrium, so long as that saving plus the saving (or minus the deficits) of other sectors equaled the business investment demand. This indicates another way to write the equilibrium condition:

saving = investment demand

where saving is the sum of the saving of each sector (aggregate saving).

When the equilibrium condition (written either way) holds, there is no reason for private economic agents to increase or decrease output or employment. And there is no reason for inflation. There would be no bidding up or down of prices in general. If, at the same time, the economy is essentially fully employed, the economy is rather healthy. If, however, the equilibrium condition holds in a situation in which there is substantial unemployment, there is still no reason for private economic agents to act in such a way as to increase economic activity unless some facets of the economy change in ways which make those agents want to increase their aggregate demand. So, for example, if the government cuts taxes and households have greater disposable income, households are likely to raise CD; or lower taxes might lead businesses to raise ID. (In addition, if interest rates fall, this can raise ID.) The government can act directly to raise aggregate demand by deciding to purchase more goods and services (GD). In these various ways government fiscal policy could be the influence to lessen unemployment.

Some simple graphs can illustrate the points made. Suppose the interest rate is at a certain level so that from Figure 1.2 we can find a specific level of investment demand, which is the same at all levels of income and output. Figure 1.1 shows us the different levels of consumption demand at different incomes. Government demand is the same at all levels of income, unless exogenously changed by policy. We can add these three demands together and get a new curve, the aggregate demand curve in Figure 1.3, with the same slope as the consumption function.

Suppose that in a graphical space similar to Figure 1.3 we also drew the equilibrium condition that $Y = CD + ID + GD$. That would show up simply as a straight line with a 45-degree angle (slope = 1), as shown in Figure 1.4. Putting the two graphs together shows us that there is one level of income and output (Y_o) at which the *AD* coming

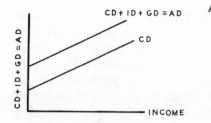

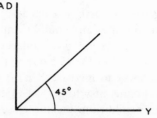

Figure 1.3. Aggregate demand

Figure 1.4. The income-aggregate demand line

from the various sectors (Figure 1.3) does meet the equilibrium condition (Figure 1.4), as shown in Figure 1.5.

Suppose that a statistical analysis of employment in the economy showed us that if we had essentially full employment, the output of the economy would equal Yf, and that this is greater than Y_o. Then, only if the AD line in Figure 1.5 could be shifted up to AD' could we be at full employment. Note that the steepness of the AD line (based on the steepness of the consumption function) determines how much Y will rise for any given shift of AD. If the slope of AD is $4/5$, then a $1 increase in the AD curve will increase Y by $5. (This is called the "multiplier effect.") The fiscal policies mentioned above could apparently do this. A greater GD, for example, would give a greater AD.

According to the principles indicated so far, other ways to raise the AD line would be for business expectations to improve, or for interest rates to fall and increase ID. If ID behaves according to Figure 1.2, we can note that at each lower level of the interest rate the level of AD shifts up, and so the equilibrium income and output can be higher. A graph showing this relation is called an IS line; as interest rates fall, ID rises, and this allows income, employment, and even household saving to rise (since household incomes rise and their increase in consumption is a smaller amount). The IS relation is shown in Figure 1.6.

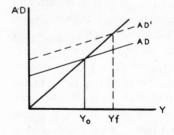

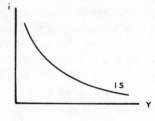

Figure 1.5. Equilibrium income positions

Figure 1.6. The IS curve

Along the *IS* curve at each level of the interest rate (*i*), a point on the curve indicates an "equilibrium" level of income, one at which $Y = AD$ or $S = I$. At any *given* interest rate, the government can increase *AD* (and thus shift the *IS* curve to the right) by increasing *GD*.

Another way to increase *Y* is to get the interest rate to fall, but the question then is how to get it to fall enough to raise *ID* enough so that *AD* gives equilibrium income close to or at *Yf*. Our government does not determine the level of the interest rate: it is determined in the free market by the demand and supply of lending and borrowing (demand and supply for bonds). If the supply of bonds equals the demand for bonds, the interest rate is in equilibrium, and if that interest rate gives an *ID* at which *AD* determines an equilibrium income at Y_o, how can the interest rate be lowered? Either the supply or the demand for bonds must change. The government can at least influence this.

In Keynesian analysis, if there is an excess supply or demand for money on the part of economic agents, they will attempt to adjust this by buying or selling bonds (lending or borrowing). The government determines the supply of money. The demand for money is determined by private decisions about what amount of money is wanted to carry on transactions, hold over for the future, etc. The basic hypothesis is that the higher the level of economic activity (income, output, transactions, employment), the more money economic agents feel they need. At the same time, the higher interest rates are, the more expensive it is to be holding money instead of making loans—buying bonds—and thus earning the higher interest. At any given interest rate, the higher the level of *Y*, the greater the money demand (*Md*), as illustrated in the first panel of Figure 1.7. At any given level of *Y*, the higher the interest rate, the lower the money demand, as illustrated in the second panel of Figure 1.7. (These assume a given price level. If the price level is raised and people expect it to remain at the new level, they will increase money demand.)

Suppose the amount of money in the society is fixed (by the government). Suppose now the level of income somehow rises. The demand for money rises, and money demand is greater than money supply. People will attempt to obtain greater money holdings by borrowing (selling bonds) and thus bid *up* the interest rate. At the higher interest rate the money demand is decreased, and a new equilibrium of money demand and money supply is obtained. In the financial markets, then, higher levels of income and output tend to bring higher levels of interest rates. This relation is represented by an *LM* curve—a curve at which money demand or demand for liquidity (*L*) equals money supply (*M*) and so there is no reason for interest rates to move higher or lower (Figure 1.8).

Figures 1.6 and 1.8 indicate that there would be one level of income and one interest rate at which money demand and supply (and thus

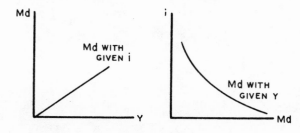

Figure 1.7. The money demand curves

bond demand and supply) would be equal, and also at which the level of *AD* and income would be equal. That, of course, would be where the two curves cross, as shown in Figure 1.9.

Suppose that the level of general equilibrium (equilibrium in the money market and the output market) was at Y_o, and that this was below *Yf*. Then to reach *Yf*, either *IS* or *LM* must shift to the right. A number of very elaborate computer models have been constructed, based on the principles outlined here, to indicate how the government should act to affect output, income, and employment.

The government could push the *LM* curve to the right very easily. It could simply introduce more money into the society (for example, by repaying some of its outstanding debt with newly created money). The higher money supply would mean the old interest rate could not equate money supply and money demand, unless income was higher. That is, the general equilibrium could only be at a higher income or lower interest rate, or both, as Figure 1.10 indicates.

The transmission mechanism is simple. The government prints money (actually, the Federal Reserve banks—the nation's central banking system—"print" checking account type money) and buys government bonds. This bids up prices of the bonds and lowers interest rates (there is less government "borrowing") and at the same time gives larger checking accounts to those who sold the bonds. There is now more

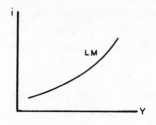

Figure 1.8. The *LM* curve

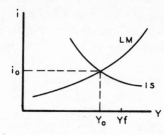

Figure 1.9. Income and interest rate determination

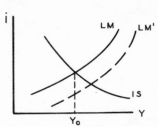

Figure 1.10. Effects of increased money supply

money in the economy. To the extent that the interest rate has not fallen enough to equate money supply with money demand, there is some excess supply of money. Some private economic agents will try to make loans, and thus push interest rates down further. This is indicated by the shift to the right of the *LM* curve. The economy is moving *along* the *IS* curve. Why? Well, the lower interest rate is increasing *ID* (and perhaps even *CD* to some extent), and thus raising *AD*. A new general equilibrium is found at a higher *Y* and a lower interest rate. How did the money market achieve equilibrium? The increase in income and decrease in interest rates raised money demand to the level of the new money supply. The interest rate must keep falling or the level of income must keep rising, or both, until money demand has risen enough to eliminate any disequilibrium in the money market (and therefore in the bond market).

How much the interest rate falls or how much income rises depends on how steep or flat the two curves are. So, one can see immediately that for any given shift to the right of the *LM* curve, the steeper the *IS* curve, the more the interest rate will fall and the less that income will rise. What determines this slope? The underlying relations. If investment is relatively insensitive to interest rate changes, it would take a large drop in interest rates to get any specific increase in *ID*, and so *IS* will be relatively steep. In addition, the lower the marginal propensity to consume, the less impact any specific increase in income (coming from the *ID* increase) will have on consumption demand and thus on further increases in income (the "multiplier effect" seen in Figure 1.5), and so the total increase in income will be smaller and the *IS* curve steeper.

Government attempts to use changes in the money supply to affect aggregate demand through impacts on interest rates or other variables is the government's *monetary policy*. Our earlier discussion of *fiscal policy* suggests that this policy works through affecting the *IS* curve. An increase in *GD* or a cut in taxes would push *IS* to the right, but this would mean a government deficit. How would the government finance the deficit (pay for the goods and services)? It could simply borrow—

issue new bonds—but the greater borrowing would lead to higher interest rates and cut investment demand somewhat. This is why a higher *IS* curve, which cuts the *LM* curve higher and to the right, indicates greater income and also higher interest rates. What is happening is that part of the expansionary effect of higher *GD* is being offset by the higher interest rates, lowering *ID* at least somewhat. One can see that the steeper *LM* is, the worse this offsetting is, and therefore the lower the total multiplier effect. If *LM* is vertical, *GD* increases would be completely offset. What determines how steep *LM* is? Basically, how sensitive money demand is to income and to interest rates. If money demand is extremely sensitive to changes in *income*, a small change in income will bring a large change in money demand, and thus bring a relatively large change in interest rates to offset it. Also, if money demand is very insensitive to *interest rates*, it will take a very large change in the interest rate to affect money demand and offset the impact of an income change. This indicates that large changes in interest rates would be associated with small changes in income.

For a long time the debates about how well Keynesian economics explained real economies centered on questions about the slopes of these two curves, with the slope of the *LM* curve receiving much of the attention. Many critics of the theory argued that money demand was very insensitive to interest rates and so government fiscal policy would be weak or ineffective. With a steep *LM* curve an increase in government spending financed by borrowing would push interest rates up very far, depress *ID*, and thus offset the expansionary effect of the higher *GD*. This "crowding out" of fiscal policies is still argued by many economists on these grounds, but other critics have found more significant reasons for potential offsets to these policies, and these have to do with inflation, to which we will return.

The other way government could finance higher expenditures with the same taxes, or lower taxes, would be by creating greater amounts of money. In principle, the government simply prints the money and buys the goods and services it desires. The actual techniques for doing this are more complicated and involve the Federal Reserve banks. The government actually issues bonds only to finance the purchases. If these bond sales cause interest rates to rise too high, the Federal Reserve banks attempt to offset the higher interest rates by buying government bonds in the "open market," and when they pay for those bonds by check, the people who receive the checks deposit them in banks and so have more money. The *LM* curve shifts to the right. That is, an expansionary government *fiscal policy* would move the *IS* curve to the right. If this government action is financed by money creation, the *LM* curve also shifts to the right. The new equilibrium would be at a higher income and at approximately the same level of interest rate. This would appear to be about ideal. There are no private actions affecting *CD* or *ID* offsetting the greater *GD*. Why not use it? Even critics of fiscal policy—those who claim that the higher *GD* is almost entirely offset by opposing changes in *CD* or *ID* ("crowding out") when that policy action is financed by bond issues—admit that expansionary monetary policy is powerful in affecting *AD*. (Note, for example, that even though the *LM* curve might be nearly vertical, shifting that curve to the right will give a greater level of income. Few economists claim that the *IS* curve is almost vertical.) The critics simply argue that the expansionary effects on income, output, and employment come about because of the monetary expansion, not because of the fiscal policy. So, why argue about it? Use the policy and get the higher economic activity! Right? Not quite. Economists might agree that this set of actions might work if prices and wages are fixed or are extremely slow to change, but the evidence from many countries is that these can change very fast, at least in the upward direction. In a deep recession or depression prices and wages might be slow to fall, and in such an environment the above analysis might be very appropriate. For that matter, in a very deep recession or depression expansionary government policies might be effective without too much upward pressure on wages and prices, and so these policy suggestions might very well be applicable. In most recessions the United States and other industrial economies have experienced in the post-World War II environment, however, the degree of "slack" in the economy has apparently not been enough to prevent inflationary impacts from expansionary government policies, despite a significant degree of undesirable unemployment of resources. Higher prices can tend to push the *IS* curve to the left if, for example, they discourage *CD*. They can also push the *LM* curve to the left as they raise the demand for money to carry on transactions at the higher prices. Either case would cause *Y* to fall to the left and increase unemployment.

Inflation, Monetarism, and Expectations

At one time many Keynesian economists believed that inflation was a serious possibility only if the economy was very close to full employment. Inflation was the result of *AD*'s being greater than output at full employment (or, with some bottlenecks—some significant industries, at least, being at full employment even before the whole economy was). Suppose the economy were in the situation indicated by Figure 1.11. At *Yf*, aggregate demand is greater than income and output, and the economy *cannot* move to the right since it cannot produce much more than *Yf*. The excessive *AD* would lead to a bidding up of prices for goods, and firms would demand more labor (which is fully employed), simply bidding up their wages. The policy implications were clear. If the *AD* curve is so low that it intersects the 45-degree line below *Yf*, the government

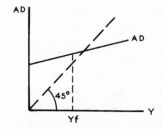

Figure 1.11. Inflationary aggregate demand

should use just enough *expansionary* fiscal and/or monetary policy to get close to *Yf* without exceeding it; and if *AD* is too high, the government might use *contractionary* policy (an approach called "fine tuning"). In the 1950s and 1960s there were some debates concerning how well the government was equipped to engage in such fine tuning. It takes time to implement such policies, and it takes time for the policies to work (lags in the implementing of policy and in the impacts of policy), and the policy impacts might be felt after the economy had already moved to a new situation. This was a serious matter, but more fundamental objections have since arisen.

It was seen early that the expansionary policies started to have inflationary implications before the economy got close enough to *Yf* to achieve desirable levels of employment. The relation between inflation and income levels was seen to be about as in Figure 1.12. The problem was not simply that inflation began before *Yf*, but that inflation started to become significant *well* before *Yf* was reached. Evidence suggested that the flat portion of the curve in Figure 1.12 was actually steeper, and some economists thought they saw a pretty definite relation between unemployment and inflation, as in Figure 1.13. This was seen by some to be another way to illustrate the idea in Figure 1.12, that as the economy approached "full employment," demand for labor in some or all

Figure 1.12. The income-inflation curve

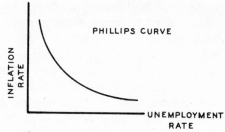

Figure 1.13. The unemployment-inflation ("Phillips") curve

markets would tend to outrun supply and cause wages and prices to rise.

The inflation rate is the annual percentage increase in money wages or in goods prices. The relation between the inflation and unemployment rates is named after Professor A. W. Phillips, who presented some evidence for it in 1958. (Professor Irving Fisher had presented some evidence as early as 1926.) Differences among economists in explaining the curve were not too crucial to macroeconomic *policy*, so long as the curve was essentially stable.[2]

The implications of the Phillips curve were a "good news–bad news" type of thing. The bad news was that macroeconomic policies could not cut unemployment too much without bringing on inflation. The good news was that apparently policymakers at least had a clear-cut choice: they could pick what they considered the "best" combination of unemployment and inflation on the curve and achieve that combination through their policy actions. So, for example, if the curve showed that 5 percent unemployment was associated with 3 percent inflation, the government could pick that combination. Or it could choose slightly less unemployment and perhaps 3.5 percent inflation. In addition, certain kinds of micro policies (job-training programs, subsidies for certain programs, etc.) might be able to shift the curve to the left somewhat.

From the standpoint of economic theorists—specifically Keynesians—there was another benefit from adopting the Phillips curve. The basic Keynesian analysis, although able to indicate inflationary pressure along the lines suggested in Figure 1.11, could not explain or "predict" the specific inflation rate. There is nothing in Figure 1.11 to indicate how high the inflation rate will be. The answer was thought to be simply to attach the Phillips curve to the rest of the Keynesian theory. The basic theory would explain or predict the level of output and therefore the level of labor employed. Labor market statistics would tell how much Yf would be if it was attained. The difference between the Keynesian "equilibrium" level of employment and the employment at Yf was the predicted unemployment, which could show—using the Phillips curve—how much inflation would be forthcoming at that Keynesian "underemployment equilibrium" of labor.

There were two major shortcomings of this fine apparatus, one theoretical and the other empirical. First, although some rather ingenious "micro foundations" were offered to explain the Phillips relation, the basic Keynesian structure still had no generally accepted basis in microeconomic theory. Why did prices and wages not simply adjust upward or downward whenever there was excess demand or supply (especially downward with excess supply) in the markets, thereby eliminating that excess demand or supply, and keep the economy at Yf? The empirical shortcoming was extremely damaging. The Phillips relation simply was not stable. It appeared to change in a very definite way. Each time the government attempted to cut unemployment and was ready to settle for the predicted inflation rate, the actual inflation rate associated with the acceptable unemployment rate appeared to be higher and higher. That is, the curve appeared to shift to the *right* over time as the government attempted expansionary policies.

One other body of evidence, while not conclusive to all economists, at least kept satisfying more and more economists. This evidence was being accumulated by a group of economists who have been labeled "monetarists" or "modern quantity theorists" and were early led by Professor Milton Friedman, who was at the University of Chicago. Even in the early days of the high popularity of Keynesian economics Professor Friedman, his students, and his colleagues attempted to show that the Keynesian consumption function was actually quite unstable and a poor basis for justifying fiscal policy; that fiscal policy was also relatively ineffective for several other reasons; and that to the extent that there might be some small impacts from fiscal policy these impacts would be relatively short-lived. On the contrary, it was the *fluctuations* in the growth of money which had major implications for fluctuations in the economy. The monetarists presented significant evidence (much of it controversial, but even then challenging) that changes in the rate of growth of the money stock seemed to precede changes in economic activity, but with rather long and somewhat erratic timing.

Ironically, a major weakness of the monetarist position was that it also appeared to have little in the way of a microeconomic foundation. In fact, while evidence—data—and policy conclusions were being offered, no formal theoretical structure was presented for a very long time. Professor Friedman offered some interesting conjectures. In the late 1960s and early 1970 several economists, notably Professors Karl Brunner and Alan Meltzer, developed some theoretical frameworks which appear promising. A major difficulty was that while early versions of these approaches explained inflation quite well, and even fluctuations in the economy, they did not adequately explain sustained unemployment. (That is, they could not "predict" or explain a level of unemployment below what is essentially "full employment.") The best they could say was that such unemployment is really only "temporary," which, to economists still perplexed about the 1930s, seemed insufficient. What good is an analysis which says unemployment is "temporary" when the problem could exist for almost a decade? The claim that monetary mismanagement by the government was horrid during those years may be correct, but was unconvincing to Keynesians.

The early theoretical conjectures of the monetarists can be summarized rather easily. If there is one basic position that appears dominant, it is that the private sectors of the economy are relatively stable in their be-

havior. The Keynesian conjectures about volatile expectations significantly shifting the investment function were not, in the monetarists'
theories, taken seriously. Pretty definite behavioral relations could be
found for the private sectors, but they were not the simple Keynesian
types. So, for example, consumption was seen by many as being a stable
function, not of current income, but of the stream of expected future
incomes, which could be approximated pretty well by the *pattern* of
recent years' income. At best, the private sectors' behavior functions
might shift by small amounts, causing small and unimportant fluctuations in the economy. It was the government itself, in this view, which
was imparting the major elements of instability in the economy, primarily
via its monetary changes. If the government, for example, expanded the
amount of money in the society, there would then temporarily be an
excess supply of money, and in readjusting their balance sheets, people
would attempt to trade some of this money for other assets. Certainly,
they would attempt to buy bonds; but as opposed to the Keynesian
analysis, they would not attempt to buy *only* bonds, but also other assets
—land, autos, factories, common stock. Since the amount of most of
these are essentially fixed in the short run, their prices would be bid up.
There would at first, however, be little impact on the prices of goods
and services currently being produced. The prices of assets, in shifting,
would not adjust perfectly and would be somewhat out of line with one
another; but more significantly, they would be out of line with the prices
of currently produced goods. This would be likely to stimulate the production of current output (as people felt more wealthy), and there would
be an expansion in economic activity. Over time, the prices of current
output would also increase; and eventually, a new equilibrium pattern
would develop, with quantities of assets, amounts of output, and so on
back at their old levels and money values—wages and prices of goods—
simply higher. But all these adjustments take time, and in the meanwhile the economy would be fluctuating. Some economists even recognized that fiscal policy changes without monetary changes could have
somewhat similar impacts, not basically because of the government
expenditures, but because the government deficit put more government
bonds in the private economy and the private economy had to adjust to
the greater amounts of bonds.

An interesting difficulty with this analysis was that the more it was
refined and formalized into explicit structures the more it appeared
similar to the Keynesian framework, but without an explicit "explanation" of or prediction for long-period unemployment. In fact, when in
the early 1970s Professor Friedman finally attempted to present some
formal version of his hypothesis, even many monetarists objected that
the framework that he presented appeared very different from his earlier
conjectures and delivered predictions more consistent with some Key-

nesian models than with most monetarists' positions (Friedman et al. 1974).

Only in the last couple of years have formal models been presented which could, at least in principle, explain the outcomes conjectured by monetarists; and while not generally accepted by the profession, they at least appear to have some decent microeconomic basis (but still no explanation for long-term, significant unemployment).

Once again, Professor Friedman, along with Professor Edmund Phelps, made the early conjectures. In the late 1960s these two economists pointed to the *shifting Phillips curve* and presented an answer that appears reasonable to many. Instead of thinking of firms and workers as simple "pure competitors" who accept whatever market wages and prices exist (as in the elementary micro theories), consider that economic agents are the economy, prices, and wages. So long as the general level of the economy (prices, wages, etc.) is essentially stable, with only small changes in relative values, the economy will be about at a level of "natural unemployment" (meaning roughly full employment with small frictions due to seasonal factors, people leaving less desirable jobs for more desirable ones, etc.). In this situation a person without a job knows pretty well what his market wage is, and will rather quickly accept a job at that wage, unless it is deemed too low to justify employment.

Suppose that the government thinks that this "natural" level of unemployment is too high and attempts expansionary policies to lessen unemployment. If those policies do not significantly change the general level of wages or prices, they will tend to have small or insignificant impacts on unemployment. Suppose, however, they are inflationary (reflect expansionary monetary policy). Then some workers who are not willing to work at the old level of wages and prices may note there are jobs at higher wages than they thought existed, and some would be willing to take those jobs, not realizing that prices they would soon be paying for goods would also rise. The result would be that the number of people reported to be unemployed would now be lower, and the Phillips relation would indeed show lower employment associated with the new inflation.[3]

Other versions of the same analysis were more detailed and suggested that people who were reported to be unemployed were really "voluntarily unemployed" in "job search activity" looking for the best wages. An unexpected inflation would present them with jobs at wages higher than they had seen earlier, and they would take these jobs. In effect, people would be "fooled" into accepting employment on terms less favorable than they wanted because they immediately saw the higher wages and did not yet see the higher prices of goods. Over time, however, people would come to realize that prices were rising faster, and that their "real wages" (wages divided by the prices of goods) were no better than before.

When newly unemployed people started in their job search, they would know about the higher inflation rate, and they would want wages which took this into account. Now to cut unemployment, the government in its expansionary policies would have to bring about an even higher rate of inflation in order to fool people into becoming employed. In addition, trade unions would recognize the higher inflation rate, take this into account in their bargaining, and raise wages, making it less attractive for firms to hire more people at the old inflation rate. Each time the government increases the percentage rate of inflation, people soon come to *expect* the new rate and will adjust their actions to this new rate, bringing the level of unemployment back to the natural rate but at the new level of inflation. The Phillips curve has shifted to the right, as in Figure 1.14.

Suppose, as in Figure 1.14, the Phillips curve I combination of unemployment at *Un* and inflation at *OA* currently exists. The government attempts a monetary policy to reduce unemployment to *OC* (a more desirable level politically—there are elections coming up the next year). The government implicitly accepts that this will bring inflation up to *OB*, but this is thought to be "acceptable." This will work, but only temporarily. For a while people are fooled into taking jobs at what appear to be higher real wages. When they find that prices are also higher by about the same percentage, unemployment grows back to *Un*, but now we have inflation at *OB* instead of *OA*, together with unemployment *Un*. The curve has shifted to II. To again attempt to cut unemployment to *OC* will call for an inflation rate *above OB*, along Phillips curve II. And so on indefinitely. Meanwhile, each time the government attempts this, it is causing the economy to fluctuate up and then down again. The explanation for something like the Depression of the 1930s would be that the very significant decline in the money supply during the early 1930s caused *deflation* much faster than people expected, and so unemployment was to the *right* of *Un*, and the Phillips curve was shifting to the left as people adjusted their expectations. Professor R. E. Lucas has demonstrated in a formal way that in a world of changing relative

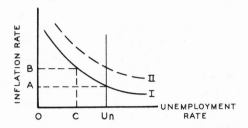

Figure 1.14. The effect of a rise in inflationary expectations

prices, if one also imposes changes in the general level of prices, the information conveyed by the changes in price tags does not convey clear-cut information about relative prices, and so it is optimizing behavior for people to make the best approximations possible (as to how much of the change in price tags is because of, say, relative changes in supply and demand for specific goods and services, and how much is inflation). They therefore act in ways that bring at least temporary "real" changes (changes in quantities of output, in employment, etc.) because of monetary changes that are simply bringing inflationary or deflationary changes in prices and wages. He has suggested that this can be the basis for supposedly "cyclical" fluctuations in economic activity. Of course, that such models can be constructed does not indicate they actually explain our real world; but tests are in order.

In the context of these theories, what can government do? Apparently not very much. It appears that at best it could maintain a low level of unemployment below *Un* only at the price of ever-accelerating inflation (inflation rates becoming ever higher). Even in this way it is doubtful that the government can succeed. As people come to realize what the government is doing, they will even adjust to the ever-accelerating inflation.

Economists who are working with the type of theoretical framework discussed here point out that if one's analysis of private economic behavior incorporates or depends on private expectations of the future, (1) the way those expectations are formed should be made explicit and part of the overall theory, and (2) for the economic theorist simply to postulate some arbitrary (or *ad hoc*) expectations equation which people use continuously, even if it has people generating expectations which are systematically wrong, is to assume people are irrational. (If this were the case, and if the theorist's model was essentially correct, he should be able to become rich by betting in the stock, bond, or commodity markets against those people whose expectations were less than "optimal," or by selling his essentially correct economic information to businesses.)

If the theory being offered by the economist is essentially correct and if people are not using it to form their expectations, they will be systematically incorrect. Over time, they should see that their predictions are not only incorrect, but incorrect in certain systematic ways, and should, if intelligent, correct the way they are forming their expectations. If they cannot be consistently fooled, there is little the government can do in terms of macroeconomic policies to affect real changes in the economy—in output, income, employment, etc.—consistently. In the extreme case, private economic agents are not fooled at all. They simply know what the *goals* of the government are, what policy tools the government has at its disposal, and what theory the government is using to determine its operations. Therefore, private agents should be able to anticipate the government's actions and act in a way that would tend to offset those actions. For example, as trade unions see what the government is doing, they would take this into account in bargaining for wage increases, and so on.

This approach, of course, is not generally accepted by economists, although more and more appear to be attracted by it, or at least to be viewing it as a challenge for further research. To many it appears to be too pessimistic about the prospects for improving the economic environment. We can, according to this approach, eliminate inflation but not bring unemployment down to levels which would seem acceptable to the electorate in a democratic society. What can we do? Nothing, it seems, except perhaps convince the electorate that it is correct and attempt to remove the political pressures on the government to reduce unemployment below *Un*, or perhaps use microeconomic policies involving fine adjustment in relative tax rates, subsidies for specific private actions, etc., which might have small impacts on *Un*.

For that matter, some economists have suggested that rather than having an impact on aggregate demand or on supplier's behavior when they are "fooled," many government micro and macro policies work primarily through their incentive effects on the supplies of labor services, output, and so on. This may especially be the case with tax policies. There would, for example, be increases or decreases in output and labor supply as taxes, unemployment compensation, welfare payments, etc., encouraged or discouraged people from finding jobs quickly or even from wanting to take jobs.

Other economists are still investigating whether the essential concepts of Keynesian analysis and related theories contain elements which overcome the objections raised by monetarists and the "natural rate of unemployment" approach. So, for example, there is some important work being done emphasizing the Keynesian system as an explanation of economies in situations in which markets are not clearing, and focusing on the behavior of individual economic agents when they are so constrained by this situation that they cannot buy or sell all they plan at the going price or wage. How these individual actions result in changes in macroeconomic variables can be so complex and depend on so many factors (including which markets are in excess supply and which in excess demand) that perhaps economic agents can form their expectations only on the basis of predictions of the outcomes when markets are clearing. They could be systematically wrong, then, for long periods of time, and there may be some role for the government in offsetting the outcomes of their behavior. If it is costly to adjust some prices quickly while other prices are adjusting rapidly, price relations can become distorted and become the basis for such a pattern of disequilibrium.

Many economists are quite certain that Keynes was correct that expectations adjust in a very volatile way; and in a world with long-term financial assets such as stocks and bonds, and long-term real assets such as factories and houses, volatility in expectations and profit planning have an impact on balance sheet adjustments, financial interrelations, and thereby on investment demand. If bankruptcies are possible, this volatility will be even more dangerous.

Even just the existence of real capital, which takes a long time to build and a very long time to wear out, can, under various conditions, impart a cyclical movement to the economy. This, together with various shocks (changes in tastes, productive resources, government policy, and international economic relations), can make the economy move in very complicated ways. Because information is costly, it may take a long time for people to form expectations that are not systematically wrong. By the time people have learned to predict and adapt to one situation, essential aspects of the structure of the economy may have changed.

In some of these environments, when employment and output move to unsatisfactory levels, might there be some role for government to remedy the situation? Unfortunately, it is not clear whether any of these or related directions will be fruitful, or whether they will be able to provide adequate grounds for some kind of governmental macroeconomic actions —fiscal or monetary—to achieve better employment and output at lower inflation rates.

Notes

1. Recent reminders of the significance in Keynes of expectations and their potential for volatility, with attempts to deal with these more explicitly in demand-oriented models, have been presented by Davidson 1972 and Minsky 1975.
2. Early explanations generally suggested that when labor markets "cleared," there was still some reported unemployment, since some workers are always in the process of changing jobs; and as the measured unemployment becomes smaller, it actually indicates a developing demand for labor, which would tend to drive wages higher. In addition, "bottlenecks" can occur when some specific labor markets have some excess demand while others are still experiencing unemployment. The government data would only reflect the unemployed in the excess supply markets, and not the excess demand in the other markets which was driving wages up. The natural rate hypothesis, discussed later in this paper, was an explanation casting doubts on the stability of the curve itself, however.
3. Phelps et al. 1970 contains an excellent set of early papers focusing on this and related analyses.

References

Barro, R. J., and Grossman, H. I. 1976. *Money, Employment and Inflation.* Cambridge: At the University Press.
Brunner, K., and Meltzer, A. H. 1972. "Money, Debt, and Economic Activity." *Journal of Political Economy* 80 (September–October): 951–77.
————, eds. 1976. *The Phillips Curve and Labor Markets.* Amsterdam: North-Holland.

Clower, R. W. 1965. "The Keynesian Counter-Revolution: A Theoretical Appraisal." In *The Theory of Interest Rates,* ed. F. H. Hahn and F. Brechling, pp. 103–25. London: Macmillan.

Davidson, P. 1972. *Money and the Real World.* New York: Wiley.

Fisher, I. 1926. "A Statistical Relation between Unemployment and Price Changes." *International Economic Review* 13 (June): 785–92. Reprinted in *Journal of Political Economy* 81, no. 2, pt. 1: 496–502.

Friedman, M. 1957. *A Theory of the Consumption Function.* Princeton: Princeton Univ. Press.

———. 1961. "The Lag in Effect of Monetary Policy." *Journal of Political Economy* 69 (October): 447–66.

———. 1968. "The Role of Monetary Policy." *American Economic Review* 58 (March): 1–18.

———, et al. 1974. *Milton Friedman's Monetary Framework.* Chicago: Univ. of Chicago Press.

Friedman, M., and Schwartz, A. J. 1963. "Money and Business Cycles." *Review of Economics and Statistics* 45, no. 1, pt. 2: 32–64.

Hicks, J. R. 1937. "Mr. Keynes and the 'Classics': A Suggested Interpretation." *Econometrica* 5: 147–59.

Keynes, J. M. 1936. *The General Theory of Employment, Interest, and Money.* New York: Harcourt, Brace.

Lipsey, R. G. 1960. "The Relation between Unemployment and the Rate of Change of Money Wage Rates in the United Kingdom, 1862–1957: A Further Analysis." *Economica,* n.s. 27 (February): 1–30.

Lucas, R. E., Jr. 1972. "Expectations and the Neutrality of Money." *Journal of Economic Theory* 4 (April): 103–24.

———. 1973. "Some International Evidence on Output-Inflation Tradeoffs." *American Economic Review* 63 (June): 326–34.

———. 1975. "An Equilibrium Model of the Business Cycle." *Journal of Political Economy* 83 (December): 1113–44.

Machlup, F. 1967. "Micro- and Macroeconomics: Contested Boundaries and Claims of Superiority." In *Essays in Economic Semantics.* New York: Norton.

Minsky, H. P. 1975. *John Maynard Keynes.* New York: Columbia Univ. Press.

Modigliani, F. 1977. "The Monetarist Controversy; or, Should We Forsake Stabilization Policies?" *American Economic Review* 67 (March): 1–19.

Muth, J. F. 1961. "Rational Expectations and the Theory of Price Movements." *Econometrica* 29 (July): 315–35.

Phelps, E. S. 1972. *Inflation Policy and Unemployment Theory.* New York: Norton.

———, et al. 1970. *Microeconomic Foundations of Employment and Inflation Theory.* New York: Norton.

Phillips, A. W. 1958. "The Relation between Unemployment and the Rate of Change of Money Wage Rates in the United Kingdom, 1861–1957." *Economica,* n.s. 25 (November): 283–300.

Stein, J. L., ed. 1976. *Monetarism.* Amsterdam: North-Holland.

{2}

The Unemployment-Inflation Dilemma
and the Reemergence of Classicism

JOSEPH BISIGNANO

> He bored me a good deal with his science of economics
> and theory of supply and demand, which seemed to me much more
> obvious than he would admit.
> —Italo Svevo, *The Confessions of Zeno*

In a recent debate at the Federal Reserve Bank of San Francisco, Professors Franco Modigliani of MIT and Milton Friedman of the University of Chicago addressed the subject of the role of monetary policy in achieving desired unemployment and inflation objectives. One point regarding inflation on which they agreed was the assessment of its costs. Quoting from a transcript of this debate (Modigliani and Friedman 1977):

Modigliani: "The real costs of inflation are, I think, related to unexpected changes. I believe that steady inflation (and I think Milton would not disagree with this) has almost zero cost. ... So I think that what really is costly about inflation is unexpected deviations of inflation from the anticipated steady state path. This is the problem that I have tried to address. If you find yourself off the long-run Phillips curve, because of unexpected events, ... how do you return to the long-run path?"

Friedman: "I agree, also, with Franco's final point: that steady-state inflation has negligible costs. If you could have inflation at a steady rate, it would not be worth paying much in the form of adjustment costs to move back to a different rate. The fundamental cost, as Franco said, arises from unexpected deviations of inflation from a steady rate."

Another quotation, again drawn from this debate, will help put into focus the subject to which this paper is addressed, the unemployment-inflation dilemma:

The views expressed in this paper represent those of the author and not necessarily those of the Federal Reserve Bank of San Francisco or the Federal Reserve System.

Friedman: "I have been impressed in the past, that the most consistent difference that I could discern between people who tend to favor fine tuning, and people like myself who tend to favor rules, is in the discount rate that they use—a short versus a long perspective."

On the basis of the above quotations, this paper argues that the issue of any dilemma between inflation and unemployment and the existence of any trade-off between inflation and unemployment rests on two elements: (1) the impact of the random, unanticipated components of inflation on real output and employment; and (2) the emphasis of policymakers on the short- and long-run costs of, and returns from, the pursuit of countercyclical monetary policy. Both of these points can be related to basic propositions of classical economic theory.

The first section of this paper reviews a few basic propositions which are considered part of "classical macroeconomics," but which are in fact basic elements of microeconomics, these being the concepts of "neutrality," "dichotomy," and "money illusion." The second section considers how, in a world where prices adjust to eliminate excess supply or demand, any trade-off between unemployment and inflation cannot exist in the classical model. The next section discusses how a short-run trade-off between unemployment and inflation (not necessarily a beneficial one) may exist if the private sector has difficulty distinguishing between absolute and relative price changes. The fourth section briefly examines the recent attack on advocates of countercyclical public policy by the "rational price expectations" school. The final section describes how, the greater the random element in inflation, the greater becomes the difficulty in obtaining any beneficial inflation-unemployment trade-off, assuming the public does *not,* on the average, correctly anticipate what monetary policy will be.

Public Policy in the Classical Model

When the question of public policy is addressed today, the quickest focus is on policies aimed to have some desired effect on demand, as opposed to the supply of some particular good or service. Classical economic policy, on the other hand, with its philosophical origins in the goal of maximizing individual choice, was particularly pessimistic about the ability of the public sector to alter aggregate demand which left relative prices unaffected. (*Relative prices* refers here to the ratio of the prices of any two goods, or to the ratio of an individual price to a price index, and not to the "aggregate" price [index] level.) The reason for this was the proposition that individuals respond to real (price-deflated) economic signals and not nominal (nondeflated) information.

Hence, a doubling of all nominal prices would leave demand behavior unaffected. The notion that individuals respond only to relative (financial unit-of-account free) prices has come to be known as the proposition of economic neutrality, and, as I will show, is quite central to the debate as to whether monetary policy can be appropriately directed to raise the long-run rate of growth of real output or to permanently lower the unemployment rate. (This concept is known in the theory of micro-economics as the proposition that demand functions are homogeneous of degree zero in prices and in income.)

A second proposition of the classical model is that of macroeconomic dichotomy. This dichotomy refers to the proposition that the classical model of the economy could be decomposed, or dichotomized, into two pieces, one subset which determined real magnitudes—e.g., output and employment—dependent only on relative prices (and other real variables), and another subset which, together with the money supply, determined the aggregate price level and all absolute dollar prices. This dichotomization had the result that the money supply played absolutely no role in determining the equilibrium, market-clearing levels of real variables. This basic proposition—that of the neutrality of money—is central to the debate that rages between advocates of countercyclical monetary policy and advocates of monetary rules. The "policy rules" school of thought clings tenaciously in all of its arguments to what are basically classical propositions, those of neutrality and (more or less, depending on the time frame of the argument) of the dichotomy proposition.

The recent revival of strong classical public policy prescriptions in the economic profession admits to the fact that monetary policy is not "neutral" in the short run. To put forth this suggestion, however, does not require the argument that demands for real goods and services are not dependent on relative prices, but rather, that for one reason or another private market participants have some difficulty in determining at the time what the true relative prices are. In the long run, this argument runs, true relative prices are revealed and money returns to its original neutrality role. The simple difference here between the recent revival of classical monetary policy arguments and what might be called "strict" classical arguments is whether the neutrality argument holds in the long run, or holds for both short- and long-run periods of analysis.

If the theoretical neutrality argument regarding the role of relative (vs. absolute) prices in determining individual demand behavior is not empirically supported, the cry resounds that individuals suffer the illness described as "money illusion"—that is, they are foolishly responding to nominal dollar magnitudes and not to real (unit-of-account free or relative) price information. In theory, an equiproportionate change in all prices, money income, and money wealth should leave individual demands unaffected. Thus, the price *level* should not affect individual behavior. There is very little empirical support that the public suffers from money illusion. One paper, by Branson and Klevorick (1969), found some evidence for the existence of money illusion in an aggregate consumption function for the United States; and a later disaggregated study by Cukierman (1972) weakened but did not reverse the Branson and Klevorick conclusion. Branson and Klevorick noted in passing that the empirical existence of money illusion in consumption functions had important implications regarding the behavior of the aggregate supply of labor, implying, one supposes, that if individuals' consumption rose with a rise in the general price level, they might also offer more labor at a higher price level. In this sense one could conjecture that employment would be affected by a rise in prices (a money-illusion-induced trade-off between the price level and unemployment). But little support has been given to the Branson and Klevorick study for the observance of significant negative correlations between unemployment and inflation (the so-called Phillips curve) in recent discussions of why a trade-off might exist, if even only for the short run. To a large extent, most economists assume that money illusion in consumption (nonneutrality) is not a significant empirical phenomenon.

If there has been a coming together of views on macroeconomics in recent years, it could be that this happy event has taken place because of an agreement among many (but certainly not all) economists that classical propositions are reasonable assumptions about conditions that prevail in the long run. This long-run agreement would conclude that individuals do not suffer from money illusion and that the long-run world can be dichotomized into a "real block" and a "monetary block." The latter long-run proposition is identical to the view that inflation is "always and everywhere a monetary phenomenon," a statement made by Milton Friedman in 1966, echoing the sentiments of economists at least two hundred years his senior, David Hume being the most quotable.

Care at this point should be taken to distinguish the source of inflation from the transmission process of inflation, a distinction that becomes particularly clouded when measures to combat inflations are proposed. At the risk of misrepresenting both proponents and opponents of government-sponsored price and wage controls, "neutralists" would argue that rigid control of wages will only affect, for example, relative prices and the aggregate relative wage rate, and will, as a result, have a pernicious effect on the aggregate supply of labor. But nominal wage controls will not have an effect on inflation, which is essentially a monetary phenomenon and requires a monetary stimulus to sustain it. "Nonneutralists" might argue that since wages are really, in an accounting sense, the largest component of aggregate prices, control of wages is equivalent to control of prices. Since the purpose of this paper is not to thread through this debate, I will boldly state my biases: while wages may be the avenue by which inflation is most empirically apparent, varieties of wage controls affect relative prices primarily and affect aggregate inflation only to the extent to which wage controls indirectly result in the pursuit of a less expansionary monetary policy.

Returning to our primary concern with the neutrality-of-money issue, the initial argument advanced against the short-run neutrality-of-money proposition was by A. C. Pigou (1943), and was stated formally by Lloyd Metzler in a seminal article in 1951 (Metzler 1951) which suggested that consumption depended on the real value of government debt held by the private sector. Pigou's suggestion was put forth, however, to argue that with the wealth effect—the variations in the real value of private wealth—the classical model would continue to adjust to restore the full employment of labor. Metzler demonstrated that money was not a "veil," as in the simple classical theory, if saving depends on the real value of private wealth. If this is true, the form of monetary policy would determine whether money is neutral. Specifically, a monetary policy that changes the amount of securities held by the private sector (e.g., open-market operations) will affect the equilibrium interest rate and, in turn, real output and employment. Metzler's argument was, straightforwardly, that a central bank action that reduced the real value of private wealth would increase the propensity to save, thereby resulting in a *permanently* lower interest rate and a *permanently* higher rate of capital accumulation. Since Metzler's 1951 paper, the existence of any nonneutrality of money has, in the long run, usually rested upon wealth effects created by monetary policy. The empirical support for the long-run significance of these wealth effects is mixed, with neutralists often dismissing it and nonneutralists strongly emphasizing it. In fact, even some nonneutralists argue that while these real wealth effects in consumption cause monetary policy to have very significant impacts on real output in the short run, in the long run these wealth effects just about wash out, leaving real output unchanged. In a study of wealth and interest rate effects on consumption in the Federal Reserve-MIT-Penn econometric model, Modigliani (1971) wrote: "Given enough time, our model has very classical properties: to a first approximation, money is neutral (though not 'superneutral') and the quantity theory holds. Hence, in the longest run, neither GNP, nor interest rates, can be affected by the change in M (money). ... But once again, we must stress that these results are of little more than academic interest; what is really important is what happens in the 'short run,' especially the first four to eight quarters."

Note again Modigliani's last statement. It echoes Friedman's earlier concern with "a short versus a long perspective." Although money may have neutral impacts on output in the long run, Modigliani, as a representative of the nonneutralist school of thought, argues that policy ought to concern itself with "especially the first four to eight quarters." Hence, the major issues for aggregate economic policy, might, from these brief illustrations, be considered to be in the evaluation of the short run and of the effects of monetary policy during this span of time. That is, how much does short-run countercyclical policy really buy in terms of gains to output and employment?

Unemployment in a Classical World: Circa 1978

Current controversy within the economics profession and within the political economic policymaking sphere regarding the unemployment-inflation trade-off on balance is not centered on long-run stationary state propositions. Rather, to repeat, the controversy is over short-run concerns, such as what the role of countercyclical public policy should be when, because of short-run impediments to rapid equilibrium adjustment in the labor market, there can be long periods of less than full utilization of the labor force. The answer, from those who—for lack of a better term—might be called "short-run nonneutralists" (or, possibly better yet, the "impatient school"), is usually for aggressive counter-cyclical monetary and fiscal policy. These advocates argue that the real economic and social costs of underemployment are too high to wait for the private labor market to come to full adjustment of supply and demand. "Short-run neutralists" (the "patient school") argue that markets do adjust in time; they bring about the achievement of both efficiency and equity through the market clearing process. Apparently, one fear of the short-run neutralist (patient) school is that government intervention in the marketplace can, if not carefully moderated, result in legislation, edict, or control; this can permanently alter the relative price structure in markets, such as the labor market, and have the effect of institutionaliz-ing (making more permanent) the underutilization of a given factor of production. The example usually given is that of minimum wage legisla-tion, which, some argue, has the intended goal of raising the real wage of those at lower income levels but, in the long run, has the effect of permanently raising the unemployment rate of the group it was originally intended to benefit. Thus, the "patient school" has a pronounced an-tipathy toward aggregate policies that might drive a wedge into the price mechanism and prevent relative price adjustment to occur so as to "clear" product and factor markets.

At this point the reader may be concerned that these rather lofty arguments seem far removed from the real battle lines drawn around any inflation-unemployment dilemma. On the contrary, these arguments are quite central to both the theoretical links and the public policy–political economy links surrounding this debate. Consider, for example, the use of the term *structural* in the unemployment-inflation debate. My colleague Kenneth Froewiss has pointed with interest to the casual use of this term by both the "patient" noninterventionist school and the "impatient" interventionist school. In discussion of the inflation-unemployment problem, "patient school" advocates very often point to the "structural" sources of unemployment, such as the shifting age-sex-skill composition of the labor force, which has tended to raise the equilibrium (noninflationary) unemployment rate, or to legislation, which has prevented the labor market from adjusting to bring about the optimum allocation of labor skills.[1] On the other hand, the "impatient school" often calls attention to such "structural" sources of inflation as automatic price escalator clauses in wage contracts, which tend to make the antiinflation battle more difficult and, as some argue, lead to an attitude of "Let's learn to live with more inflation" or to some form of control over wages and prices. Thus, among professional economists there appears to be strong differences of opinion about whether the "structural economic problems"—implying those not amenable to solution by aggregate demand management (monetary/fiscal) policies—are on the inflation side or on the unemployment side of the issue.

An empirical observation which the "impatient school" often alludes to in an attempt to counter arguments by the "patient school" is that there is a good deal of persistence of unemployment and/or deviations of real output growth below either its historical trend or some desired growth rate. This is often given as evidence that markets are not clearing rapidly enough to bring about equilibrium levels of output, employment, and prices. This observed persistence of employment deviations (how large and how persistent are open to strong debate) from assumed equilibrium values is primarily what the "impatient school" uses as fuel to support its argument for a strong countercyclical policy. Until very recently, the major counterargument of the "patient school" was that policies to alleviate undesired economic disequilibrium (prolong high unemployment) often induced greater variability in real output than would otherwise have been the case. The "patient school" must be admitted to rely (partly on faith) on the belief that (*a*) given little evidence of the empirical existence of "money illusion," the relative price mechanism will ensure the full employment utilization of all resources, and (*b*) the equilibrium achieved will be unique and globally stable. In other words, there cannot be a labor market equilibrium far from full employment if prices are allowed to adjust in order to clear the market. Even the downward rigidity of money wages, many argue, is not sufficient reason to give very broad scope to aggregate demand management policies. The "impatient school" again counters with the empirical observation that "faith in the long run" may be misguided, since the assumed inverse relationship between employment and the real wage rate which is to equilibrate the labor market leads to the expectation that there should be countercyclical movement in the real wage rate—and yet this is not observed.

The substance of the debate on the appropriateness of countercyclical public policy rests largely on what one reads in the observations. The persistence of unemployment above some specified full employment-unemployment rate is enough for the "impatient" nonneutralist school to advocate aggressive countercyclical policy. But like beauty, market equilibrium too is in the eyes of the beholder. The widely different readings of the same set of economic data, very often based on extremely casual empiricism, or, as often, on statistical testing that is not over-whelmingly convincing (either because of questions of economic or statistical methodology), leave many of the central questions of aggregate economic policy open to debate and a wide and equally supportable range of opinions.

As an example of how careful inspection of economic data can sharply change previously held beliefs, consider the hypothesis put forth by Kuznets some time ago, (Kuznets 1961) that there are long swings in economic activity, with an average cycle of about twenty years. To arrive at this, Kuznets transformed the data by taking simple and straight-forward moving averages (first, a five-year moving average, and then a centered first-differencing of the moving-average series). This trans-formation of the data has the effect that even if the original series were a completely uncorrelated sequence (i.e., no lagged dependence), the transformations would be such as to create the appearance of a long cycle, as pointed out by Howrey.[2] Thus, very innocent and modest manipulation of economic data can create or distort patterns of time dependence—cycles if you like—which seriously influence judgments on policy prescriptions. Further discussion of this subject will be treated below. At this point, suffice to say that part of this problem lies, in my opinion, in the construction of economic models which treat very casually the importance of random movements in economic data. The neutralist—nonneutralist debate has been more specifically focused in theoretical and statistical investigations in recent years, partly because more attention has been given to the modeling of stochastic (random) economic variables that are not directly observable, such as price expectations, a subject to which we now turn.

Observed Persistence of Unemployment and the Role of Price Expectations

Let us make a broad jump to the heart of the empirical debate over the existence of a trade-off between unemployment and inflation. The focus of debate is on what has come to be called the "natural rate" of unemployment hypothesis, put forth by Friedman several years ago. It argues that there tends to be some long-run equilibrium rate of unemployment, deviations from which cannot persist for very long: "There is always a temporary trade-off between inflation and unemployment; there is no permanent trade-off. The temporary trade-off comes not from inflation per se, but from unanticipated inflation, which generally means, from a rising rate of inflation. The widespread belief that there is a permanent trade-off is a sophisticated version of the confusion between 'high' and 'rising' that we all recognize in simpler forms. A rising rate of inflation may reduce unemployment, a high rate will not" (Friedman 1968, p. 11).

If unemployment is below that of the natural rate, workers are, during some interim adjustment period, inadvertently accepting a lower-than-equilibrium real wage (resulting in an increased demand for labor). Once workers recognize this mistake, they will bargain for a higher real wage, resulting in reduced demand for labor at the higher equilibrium real wage. The central focus of the natural-rate hypothesis is that labor supply is offered at a real wage, and greater-than-equilibrium employment can result only if workers somehow "misperceive" the real wage.

The focus on workers' "perceptions" of real wages and/or prices has led to the argument that anticipated movements in prices can have no effect on unemployment, since these price expectations would be imbedded in the real wages demanded by workers. Thus, a given rise in workers' price expectations would cause workers to adjust their nominal wage demands in such a way as to keep real wages unchanged, resulting in no labor supply response to the change in price expectations. Here we see the emergence again of the classical neutrality proposition in the supply-of-labor function. A change in a nominal magnitude— the increase in aggregate price expectations—causes nominal wage demands to change in such a manner as to keep the real wage unchanged, with no increase in labor supply. Any supply response by labor must result from some "unanticipated" change in prices. For example, if aggregate prices were expected to rise by 6 percent and nominal wage contracts were negotiated with this increment, but in fact prices actually rose by 9 percent, workers, for some short period of time, could be "fooled" into accepting a lower real wage, resulting in increased demand for labor by business.

Alternatively, consider an argument used by Lucas (1973) and others. If businessmen have limited price information, restricted primarily to their own market, they might interpret a rise in their output prices as an increase in *their* "relative prices" and respond by increasing output in the short run. This increased output would lead to an increased demand for labor and the observance of an inverse relationship between (aggregate) prices and unemployment. But, the argument goes, once businessmen realize that the rise in their output price was accompanied by an increase in other prices (their input prices as well) so that there was no improvement in the relative price of their output, the original increase in output would be reversed. That is, in the longer run, when all aggregate price information is available, the originally observed trade-off disappears. Again, this is a restatement of the neutrality proposition: relative prices adjust, given the full availability of information, so as to clear markets. Nominal variables, such as the rate of change in the aggregate price level, can have no permanent effect on real magnitudes.

Tests of the "Phillips curve" trade-off usually attempt to relate unemployment to movements in anticipated and unanticipated inflation. As an example, consider tests of the following statistical variety:[3]

$$(1) \qquad Un_t = \beta_0 + \beta_1(\pi_t - {}_t\pi_{t-1}^*) + \beta_{2t}\pi_{t-1}^* + \sum_{i=1}^{n} \lambda_i Un_{t-i} + e_t$$

where Un is the unemployment rate, π_t the rate of inflation at time t, ${}_t\pi_{t-1}^*$ the expected (forecasted) rate of inflation for time t made one period earlier, at time $t-1$, and e_t a random error term. The natural-rate hypothesis posits that, given a suitable proxy for the unobservable expected rate of inflation ${}_t\pi_{t-1}^*$, β_2 should equal zero. If there is a "beneficial" trade-off in the short run, the estimated β_1 should be found to be negative. Without going into the econometric question of whether equation 1 is a suitable test of the natural-rate hypothesis, note that lagged values of the unemployment rate are often found in natural-rate tests, included to "clean up" some unspecified problems either with the statistical error term, or as the simple admission that the unemployment rate displays a great deal of serial (time) dependence, one which can carry over into the other explanatory variables if not adequately accounted for. Yet, until very recently, little in the way of theory has been given which would account for the strong dependence of unemployment today on lagged values of the unemployment rate. To deflate the argument of the simple serial interdependence of unemployment, I would like to propose that this dependence can result simply from the use of optimal price forecasts by economic participants.[4] For example, assume that we wish to estimate the relationship between unemployment and anticipated and unanticipated inflation. Assume that the anticipated inflation is the result of an optimal (minimum mean square error) forecast and that the unanticipated (forecast error) component is uncorrelated with (orthogonal to) the anticipated component. Let us write

$$Un_t = \beta_0 + \beta_1(\pi_t - {}_t\pi_{t-1}^*) + \beta_{2t}\pi_{t-1}^* + e_t$$

or

(2) $Un_t = \beta_0 + \beta_1 E_t + \beta_{2t}\pi_{t-1}* + e_t$

where E_t is the inflation forecast error in period t. It can easily be shown that if the inflation forecast $_t\pi_{t-1}*$ is an optimal forecast and the statistical structure of inflation is such that it is a linear combination of a series of uncorrelated random variables, then the optimal forecast, once imbedded into equation 2 in place of $_t\pi_{t-1}*$, will yield an equation in which lagged values of the unemployment rate will emerge as explanatory variables with coefficients that are part of the mechanism used to generate the inflation forecasts. Quite simply, the fact that the unemployment rate displays a good deal of serial (time) dependence in no way implies that the labor market has not cleared to achieve equilibrium or that the labor market is "slow to adjust."

The important point to bring home again is that tests of the natural-rate hypothesis, which provides for the possibility of a short-run trade-off but no long-run trade-off, are in fact tests of the basic neutrality proposition of classical economics that states that demand and supply equations for real goods are unaffected by proportionate (scale) changes in money prices—that is, only relative prices matter. This point, simple and obvious as it may be to economists, is often blurred or ignored in discussions by some policymakers and by the financial press, primarily because of their strong and often overriding concern with the "short run." The equality of the basic neutrality proposition and the neutral-rate hypothesis is reflected in Friedman's statement regarding the efficacy of monetary policy: "To state the general conclusion still differently, the monetary authority controls nominal quantities. ... It cannot use its control over nominal quantities to peg a real quantity— the real rate of interest, the rate of unemployment, the level of real national income, the real quantity of money, the rate of growth of real national income, or the rate of growth of the real quantity of money" (Friedman 1968, p. 11). The debate over whether a trade-off exists, principally a long-run trade-off, is often put in terms of a debate between Keynesians and monetarists, a characterization that grossly distorts the true nature of the debate. In fact, very Keynesian income-expenditure models can be shown to exhibit long-run classical properties, particularly the neutrality property in aggregate output and unemployment equations. The center of the debate needs to focus on how to best test statistically the basic classical neutrality proposition.

The New Classicism: Rational Expectations

As is evident from the above discussion, nonneutrality of the short- or long-run variety must rest to some extent on a breakdown in the relative price mechanism. The question as to why a trade-off between unemployment and inflation should exist at all, even in Keynesian models, is the subject of what has come to be known as the "rational expectations" hypothesis. In order to bring to center stage the basic neutrality position of the classical school, the rational expectations approach defines expectations, primarily price expectations, in their purest form, as mathematical expectations, in which individuals form expectations conditioned on knowledge of the past history of relevant economic variables (e.g., GNP, prices, etc.) and of the structure of the underlying economic system. Combined with the assumption that aggregate supply is dependent on errors in predicting the price level, this results in the theory that (*a*) systematic (i.e., predictable) monetary or fiscal policy will have no impact on real output, and (*b*) the real rate of interest (the nominal rate less the expected rate of inflation) will be invariant to the money supply rule—that is, the systematic movements in the money supply.[5]

The results of applying rational expectations to the problem of optimal monetary policy imply that only unanticipated movements in the price level, and consequently only unanticipated movements in the money supply, can have an impact on real economic growth. Restated, systematic or known monetary policy rules result in the emergence and predominance of the classical neutrality proposition between money and output.

Rational expectations and their effect on the efficacy of monetary and fiscal policy is a broad, technical subject that, when pushed to its limits, questions the entire methodology of empirical economics. It will suffice for our purposes here to refer the reader to recent studies by Shiller (1978), Poole (1976), and Lucas and Sargent (1978) which survey this subject at length. It is important to emphasize, however, that the means by which the rational expectations proposition results in the theoretical validity of the natural-rate hypothesis is by linking behavioral parameters of economic participants to policy parameters established by policymakers. "The natural rate hypothesis restricts the *relationship* of policy parameters to behavioral parameters. It cannot be tested as a behavioral relationship (Phillips curve, supply function and so on) alone" (Lucas 1972, p. 57). Thus, empirical tests of the natural-rate hypothesis require the imposition of identifiable restrictions obtained from specifying the policy behavior of the monetary and fiscal authorities, together with the assumption of rational price expectations formation by the private sector. On the whole, until recently, most tests of the natural-rate hypothesis failed to follow this prescription and hence cannot be said to have satisfactorily accepted or rejected the natural-rate hypothesis.

Is the Short-Run Trade-Off Beneficial?

In a sense, the title of this section is contradictory, coming as it does after a section that says that even if policymakers observed a trade-off in the economic data, they could not exploit it through demand managment policies to improve real economic growth with publicly known policy rules. What, then, is the subject to be considered? Put briefly, if real economic growth can be affected by errors of the private sector in forecasting prices, the question becomes whether these forecasting errors lead to either an improvement or a worsening in real output and employment. The answer is that in certain circumstances it may fall either way. Let us examine a couple of alternative scenarios.

If the major response to price forecast errors is on the supply side of the economy, the output response will be positive—that is, an improvement. The story behind this is the one given earlier. Suppliers of output (and labor) have difficulty distinguishing between changes in *relative* and *absolute* prices. The reason for the misperception may be due to spatial separation (accurate price information available only for the local market) and/or temporal separation (output price information available before input or aggregate price information). Hence, a form of short-run "money illusion" hits the supplier, causing him/her to increase output in the belief that an observed rise in output price means an improvement in relative prices. This response is reversed once accurate price information becomes available and correct relative prices are computed. This stylized story holds, then, that in the short run it is the supply side of the economy that has the problem of distinguishing between relative and absolute price movements. Recent empirical evidence by Parks (1978) shows that the greater the variance in relative price changes, the greater the errors in forecasting the rate of change in the general price level. This evidence would lend support to the argument that the supply side responses would be greater the larger the unanticipated component of inflation.

On the other side of the coin is the negative demand response to unanticipated inflation, which may offset the positive supply response. There is some theoretical evidence that consumers respond to greater uncertainty in the real value of their future income by saving a greater proportion of their current income.[6] Empirically we have observed that in the recent inflationary period consumers responded to greater unanticipated inflation by greatly increasing their personal saving rates. The result was that consumers withdrew their demand for major consumption goods, increasing the severity of the economic downturn. The reverse occurred in the recovery of 1976, when unanticipated inflation fell and personal saving rates fell to abnormally low levels compared with saving rates observed since the early 1960s.[7]

Combining both positive supply and negative demand output responses to unanticipated inflation leads one to suspect that whether we observe a positive or negative short-run trade-off between unemployment and inflation depends on whether the supply response is greater or less than the demand response. Some evidence indicates that the aggregate output and unemployment response may indeed be such that a rise in unanticipated inflation retards short-run economic growth, resulting in greater cyclical instability (Bisignano 1977). While this is still preliminary, greater suspicion ought to be cast on the proposition that in general there is something to be gained from a rise in inflation, anticipated or not. Even if one does not accept the empirical support for the rational expectations' neutrality arguments, even casual empiricism has difficulty revealing any long-run employment benefits to inflation.

Notes

1. See, for example, M. L. Wachter, "The Demographic Impact on Unemployment: Past Experience and the Outlook for the Future," in *Demographic Trends and Full Employment,* A Special Report of the National Commission for Manpower Policy, December 1976.

2. Howrey, 1968. This subject is clearly treated in G. S. Fishman, *Spectral Methods in Econometrics* (Cambridge: Harvard Univ. Press, 1969).

3. For a lucid discussion of alternative tests of the natural-rate hypothesis, see T. J. Sargent, "Testing for Neutrality and Rationality," in *Rational Expectations and the Theory of Economic Policy, Part II: Arguments and Evidence,* Federal Reserve Bank of Minneapolis, June 1976.

4. This crudely abbreviated discussion is meant to focus attention on the need to employ optimal prediction techniques in tests of the inflation-unemployment trade-off, particularly the techniques discussed in Whittle 1963, chaps. 3 and 6.

5. There are a variety of macroeconomic models that result in basic qualitative neutrality with respect to the systematic policy rule when rational expectations are imbedded into their price structure. See, for example, Sargent 1973.

6. For a simple graphical illustration, see Appendix D in Dréze and Modigliani 1972.

7. The response of saving behavior, aggregate output and unemployment to unanticipated inflation is treated more fully in Bisignano 1977.

References

Bisignano, J. 1977. "Savings, Money Demand, and the Inflation/Unemployment Trade-off." *Economic Review,* Federal Reserve Bank of San Francisco, Summer, pp. 6–19.

Branson, W. H., and Klevorick, A. K. 1969. "Money Illusion and the Aggregate Consumption Function." *American Economic Review,* December, pp. 207–10.

Cukierman, A. 1972. "Money Illusion and the Aggregate Consumption Function: Comment." *American Economic Review,* March, pp. 198–206.

Dréze, J. H., and Modigliani, F. 1972. "Consumption Decisions under Uncertainty." *Journal of Economic Theory* 5:308–35.

Friedman, M. 1968. "The Role of Monetary Policy." *American Economic Review,* March, pp. 1–18.

Howrey, E. P. 1968. "A Spectrum Analysis of the Long Swing Hypothesis." *International Economic Review*, June.

Kuznets, S. S. 1961. *Capital Formation of the American Economy: Its Formation and Financing.* New York: National Bureau of Economic Research.

Lucas, R. E., Jr. 1972. "Econometric Testing of the Natural Rate Hypothesis." In *The Econometrics of Price Determination: Conference*, pp. 50–59. Washington, D.C.: Board of Governors of the Federal Reserve System.

———. 1973. "Some International Evidence on Output-Inflation Tradeoffs." *American Economic Review*, June, pp. 326–34.

Lucas, R. E., Jr., and Sargent, T. J. 1978. "After Keynesian Macroeconomics." Mimeographed. July.

Metzler, L. 1951. "Wealth, Saving, and the Rate of Interest." *Journal of Political Economy*, April, pp. 93–116.

Modigliani, F. 1971. "Monetary Policy and Consumption: Linkages via Interest Rate and Wealth Effects in the FMP Model." In *Consumer Spending and Monetary Policy: The Linkages*, Conference Series no. 5, Federal Reserve Bank of Boston, June.

Modigliani F., with discussion by M. Friedman, 1977. "The Monetarist Controversy: A Seminar Discussion." *Economic Review*, Federal Reserve Bank of San Francisco, Supplement, Spring.

Parks, R. W. 1978. "Inflation and Relative Price Variability." *Journal of Political Economy*, February, pp. 79–95.

Pigou, A. C. 1943. "The Classical Stationary State." *Economic Journal*, December, pp. 343–51.

Poole, W. 1976. "Rational Expectations in the Macro Model." *Brookings Papers on Economic Activity* 2:463–506.

Sargent, T. J. 1973. "Rational Expectations, the Real Rate of Interest, and the Natural Rate of Unemployment." *Brookings Papers on Economic Activity* 2:429–80.

Shiller, R. J. 1978. "Rational Expectations and the Dynamic Structure of Macroeconomic Models: A Critical Review." *Journal of Monetary Economics*, January, pp. 1–44.

Whittle, P. 1963. *Prediction and Regulation by Linear Least-Square Methods.* Princeton, N.J.: Van Nostrand.

{3}

An Equilibrium Rational
Macroeconomic Framework

ARTHUR B. LAFFER

The Current Macroeconomic Approach

The basic framework for operational macroeconomic models extant today is based almost exclusively on the analysis of aggregate demand. Supply considerations, if there are any, are merely *ad hoc* attachments. Thus, the role of capacity utilization or employment is solely to yield a division between output growth and inflation (the Phillips curve). Other supply disturbances such as strikes, bad weather, seasonality, and even productivity increases are treated in an *ad hoc* manner through the use of dummy variables, constants, and trend terms.

Nowhere in the development of short-run macroeconomic models are the supply concepts such as total capital, population, and resource endowments employed.[1] Even when one moves to the long-run models, factor supplies are treated as basically exogenous. They are not assumed to be dependent on net factor returns.[2] Thus, savings is assumed solely income-dependent instead of after-tax yield-dependent. Likewise, labor force, labor force skill levels, and average hours worked are considered exogenous or dependent upon exogenous variables (such as population or job availability) as opposed to dependent upon after-tax wage rates.

The principal controversy among macroeconomic persuasions today is focused on just what variables are the prime influences on aggregate demand. Fiscalists place substantial weight on aggregate demand effects of government spending and tax policies. Monetarists focus more on the demand effect of government monetary policy. Neither group pays much attention in their formal analysis to supply considerations. Even the taxonomy of their presentations illustrates a demand orientation. Economists, when describing total output, use demand-exclusive categories such as nondurable and durable goods consumption, residential construction, plant and equipment expenditures, inventory accumulation, government spending, and the trade balance. In the rare instance where income categories are used, they are not used with reference to the net income resulting from the provision of the factor's services. The income figures used are gross of taxes and include the receipt of transfers. They are not the relevant figures to incorporate in an analysis of the supply of factor services.[3]

General Features of a Model Including Supply Considerations

Were one to focus on the supply of factor services, the relevant income variables would be net income received for the provision of the factor's services. As such, all taxes would be netted out, and yet transfer receipts would not be included. For virtually all conceivable supply-side purposes one would want these income figures on a marginal basis. Thus, if transfer payments included "means", "needs," or "income" tests, they too should be included. If, of course, there were wage or work supplements in the form of factor input or product subsidies, then these subsidies should be included in the subsidized factor's income.

In a general equilibrium approach, the appropriate route is to combine the supply of factor services with the aggregate demand for goods and services. The equilibrium demand for goods will exactly equal the total amount of goods produced by the factor services supplied to the marketplace. The supply of factor services to the marketplace, however, depends upon the net income received by those factors for the explicit provision of their services. This, then, is the nature of the macroeconomic model being developed.[4] On the following pages is a description of the major elements of such a model in nontechnical terms. The explicit formulas are given in the notes. Where relevant, the implications of this model will be juxtaposed to those of exclusive demand reliance.

The model takes as basic to economics that if taxes on a product are raised, there will be less of that product. Likewise, if subsidies to a product are increased, in general, there will be more of the now subsidized product. Taxes on commodities discourage them, while subsidies to products encourage them.

Macroeconomic policy in much of the Western world today consists of taxes on work, output, and employment in conjunction with subsidies to nonwork, leisure, and unemployment. Thus, it should come as no surprise that much of the Western world today has little work output and employment and much nonwork, leisure, and inefficiencies.

Government Spending and the Reduction of Output

A firm's decision to hire is based, in part, upon the *total* cost to the firm of the employee's services. The more it costs to hire workers, the fewer workers a firm will hire. Likewise, the less it costs to hire workers, the more the firm will hire. Employees' decisions to work are also, in part, based upon the amount of earnings. The more the employee receives, the more willing he is to work; and vice versa. Employees, it should be noted, do not concern themselves with the total costs to the firm. Employees care primarily about how much they receive *net*. In sum, firms worry about the total wages they have to pay, while employees are concerned with the wages they receive. The difference between the wages firms pay and the wages employees receive is the "wedge." This wedge consists of income taxes, payroll taxes, excises, sales taxes, property taxes, and the market value of the accountants and lawyers firms hire in order to maintain compliance with government regulations.

For a moment imagine a wedge, or tax, of 20 percent on a worker whose gross wages are $200 per week. Also imagine that the employer pays half of the tax and the employee half. Under these conditions, the total cost to the employer is not $200 per week, but $220 per week. The firm's decision to hire is based exclusively on the $220 figure. The employee's net wage is not $200 per week, but $180 per week. Thus, the wedge of $40 is the difference between the wages paid ($220), and the wages received ($180).

It is easy to see what happens if the wedge is increased, say, to 40 percent. Assuming it is still divided evenly, then wages paid by the firm rise from $220 to $240. The firm will hire fewer workers. Wages received by employees will fall from $180 to $160. Employees will be less willing to work. Both the firm's desire to hire workers and the workers' willingness to work will be reduced as the wedge increases. Output unambiguously falls, and the level of total employment falls as the wedge increases.[5]

In the United States, the wedge can be represented either by total government spending, or by the total of transfer payments.[6] Basically, transfer payments are real resource transfers from producers and workers to transfer recipients based upon some characteristic other than work or production. As such, transfer payments reduce the amount of goods and services available to the people who produced them. Transfer payments are a tax on production and work. Likewise, transfers are a payment based upon a characteristic other than work. Some of the transfers may be based on population characteristics, such as age, region of residence, health, sex, and race. In many instances, however, not only are transfers given to people on the basis of a characteristic other than work, but they are often given out only if there is an absence of work. That is, transfers are often a payment explicitly for nonwork. Examples of this are agricultural subsidies, food stamps (income requirement), social security payments (retirement test), housing subsidies

235–236 (means test), and, obviously, unemployment compensation itself.

Countercyclical Government Spending and the Economy's Cyclicality

Viewing the cyclical nature of the economy from this vantage point also gives us a perspective on the role played by fiscal policy slightly different from that found in most economic scenarios today. Let us imagine for a moment an economy that produces, say, 1,000 real units of output and has government transfers and purchases of 500 real units. If this is the case, then the producers and workers who produce the 1,000 real units of output are able to keep 500 of those units. While these producers and workers are paid 1,000 units, they receive only 500 units and, therefore, have a "wedge" of 50 percent. For every two units someone produces, he gets to keep only one. Fifty percent is taxed away and given to someone else.

Viewing the current U.S. economy in this manner, let us see what happens if, for whatever reason, there is a shortfall of income or output down from the 1,000 level to, say, 900 real units. In our economy, as output and employment fall, government spending rises, here almost entirely as a result of increased transfer payments. Increases occur across a whole range of categories, including open-ended, automatic increases such as food stamps, social security benefits, education loans, and unemployment benefits. There may well be newly legislated increases as well. For the sake of the example, let us imagine that government spending rises by 40 real units. Therefore, while output falls from 1,000 to 900, government spending rises from 500 to 540. Now producers and workers receive only four-fifths of one unit for every two they produce, as opposed to receiving the one unit for every two produced previously. By increasing spending during a recession or downturn in production, the government reduces the incentives to produce and work. Far from stabilizing the economy, such countercyclical spending will, in fact, accentuate the cyclical aspects of the economy. The greater government spending is, and the more closely tied to the level of unemployment it is, the more cyclical will be the economy.

Total Taxes and Spending

Suppose one is operating with a Keynesian model. One counter-recession policy would dictate giving the unemployed additional transfers such as was proposed in the original Humphrey-Hawkins bill. The idea here is that the unemployed will spend the money they receive. This spending will result in the employment of people who supply them with goods to buy. In turn, the newly employed will also spend more, resulting in additional employment. This process will raise the level of employment and will increase output. Essentially, the Keynesian model says that giving the unemployed more money leads to a rise in the level of total employment and a reduction in unemployment. According to economic theory, when you pay someone more for doing something, that person does more of it, not less.

If we look at the same situation from the standpoint of the fiscalist interested in supply, the unemployed who are given more money will indeed buy more. But the people from whom the resources are taken to pay the unemployed will spend less. When direct taxes on workers are raised, their real incomes will fall, as will their demand for goods and services. Even when the spending is financed by issuing debt, people will be crowded out of the capital market. In the case of debt issue, resources have been diverted from one form of spending to another. Increased debt is actually just another form of taxes.

President Carter's Proposed National Energy Plan
From a Supply Perspective

In a highly simplified form, the National Energy Plan of 1978 will raise enormous revenues through new and expanded taxes. These receipts will then be put back into the economy in the form of rebates, tax incentives, and transfer payments. A number of economists argue that the destimulative aspects of the higher taxes are offset by the stimulative aspects of the rebates and transfers. They conclude that output, or GNP, will not be much affected. This is clearly the logic put forth by the Carter administration.

If output resulted solely from aggregate demand, one could construe some logic out of the position. Output, however, results from both aggregate demand and aggregate supply. The above analysis totally ignores aggregate supply and, as such, will be off the mark. An increase in tax receipts matched by an equal increase in rebates and transfer payments will unambiguously reduce output and output growth. The bigger the tax increase cum rebate, the greater will be the fall in both output and employment.

To see this point clearly, imagine an increase in U.S. taxes of over $1 trillion, matched by an equal rebate right up to the point where workers and producers receive nothing for their work effort, and nonworkers and nonproducers receive everything. Output will fall to zero. While the example is extreme, the point is clear. Taxes matched by spending reduce output. The administration's energy package, if put into effect, would raise taxes by an enormous amount annually, and would rebate the proceeds. It would result in an enormous loss in incomes in the country and an enormous loss in employment.

Let us examine the key economic aspects of the administration's 1978 proposals.

Taxes. The energy proposals include a number of significant increases in taxes:

i) On gasoline alone, standby authority was requested to start taxing an additional 5¢ per gallon as of January 15, 1978, rising to 50¢ per gallon by 1985.

ii) Automobiles deemed energy-inefficient by their gas mileage would, starting with the 1978 model line, be taxed up to a maximum of $449. This tax would be increased through the 1985 model line, where the maximum tax would be $2,488.

iii) Domestically produced crude oil would continue to be subjected indefinitely to price ceilings. In addition, three yearly tax increases would be imposed on well-head production until the ceiling price plus tax would equal the world price, then $13.50 per barrel. In the case of old oil, the three-stage tax increase would amount to $8.25 per barrel.

iv) The ceiling price on natural gas sold in interstate markets would be raised to $1.75 per 1,000 cubic feet from the $1.45 price. But intrastate natural gas, which previously was uncontrolled, would be subject to the price ceiling.

v) Industrial companies would be taxed at increasing rates on their usage of natural gas. This tax would have started in 1979 at 30¢ per 1,000 cubic feet, and have risen to $1.10 by 1985. The utility tax on the use of natural gas would commence in 1983, until by 1988 it equalized the energy cost between natural gas and distillate oil. Industrial users of petroleum would be taxed at 90¢ per barrel in 1979, and this would rise to $3.00 per barrel by 1985. Utilities that used petroleum would have a flat tax of $1.50 per barrel, beginning in 1983.

vi) Aviation fuel taxes would be raised 4¢ per gallon, and the rebate of 2¢ per gallon on motorboat fuel would be removed. Efficiency targets on appliances would be made mandatory. The U.S. stockpile of oil would be increased by 500 million barrels, to 1 billion barrels. Detailed accounting requirements would be imposed on the energy companies, and antitrust would be more actively pursued.

However one figures it, the program adds up to a massive increase in overall taxes. Estimates of the ultimate revenue from these tax increases range well over $100 billion per year. When one compares these numbers with the total cost of the Vietnam War, of, say, $100 billion over a six-year period, one obtains the proper perspective of the proposal's magnitude. Because of its magnitude, the discrepancy between market values and the amounts workers and producers receive would increase dramatically. If ever enacted, this energy plan would constitute an enormous increase in the wedge and would lead to sharply curtailed production in the market place. Growth rates would be greatly reduced.

While many of us intuitively think of production distortions in terms of factories, machines, or capital equipment, the effect on individual workers' incentives to work could easily be quite consequential. At an additional tax of 50¢ per gallon, a family that drives 20,000 miles per year in a car averaging 20 miles per gallon would have an effective reduction in its income of $500. This figure does not even consider the higher price of the car or the plethora of other taxes and their effect on prices. There is a precise equivalence between product taxes and factor taxes. As such, President Carter's program is equivalent to increased income taxes across a broad range of factors from workers and land to capital investment itself.

To illustrate the correspondence between product taxes and factor taxes, imagine a person who earns $10,000 gross per year. If he pays a flat 50 percent income tax rate on his earnings, he will be left with $5,000 to spend. If, on the other hand, there is a 50 percent tax on the full sales price of all products, he will be able to spend $10,000, but the prices of everything will be doubled. In both instances, his after-tax real income is the same. While the exact associations become far more complicated when we include many products and a multitude of factors, the correspondence principle here remains valid.

Transfer Payments. The administration's energy program also included a substantial increase in either explicit or implicit spending:

  i) All gasoline taxes and crude oil production taxes would be rebated through the tax system (as credits), and to nontax-payers. These rebates, in part, would be biased toward home-heating-oil users.

 ii) Automobiles attaining a specified degree of fuel efficiency would be eligible for rebates up to $473 maximum for 1978 model cars, and increasing over time to $493 for 1985 model cars.

iii) Firms purchasing equipment to generate electricity would receive a 10 percent tax credit on the purchase price.

 iv) Homeowners would receive a tax credit not to exceed $2,000 for investment in solar equipment. Businesses would receive a 10 percent tax credit on solar equipment.

Virtually all of the revenues from the increased taxes would go toward increased government spending, thus mitigating any chances of offsetting tax reductions or reducing national debt. The spending part of the Carter energy program merely consumates the additions to the overall tax wedge. Whereas tax increases in one area, resulting in tax reductions elsewhere, may lead to expanded output, tax increases matched by transfer spending increases will only reduce output and output growth. Overall, the fundamental form of taxation is government spending, irrespective of financing technique used.

To see this, imagine that this year a person does not have to pay taxes. Next year, however, he will have to pay normal taxes plus the taxes he would have paid this year, with interest. How much more would this person spend? Obviously, if he has foresight, he is not going to spend any more. Bond issuance has exactly the same effect as taxation.

Thus, this implication of supply side fiscalism is that if some people are given more money, the demand effects of those who receive more are offset by the demand effects of those who pay the taxes or buy the bonds. Without different distributional characteristics the aggregate demand effect of transfer payments is zero. The full substitution effect remains, however. What we find happening here is that the wedge between suppliers and demanders has increased, so that while the demand curve does not shift, we do move to a different point on the intersection between the demand and supply where the wedge is now larger. Output will actually be reduced if transfer payments increase.

Income and Substitution Effects of Tax Rates

Many economists and economic models make the point that the income effect of a tax rate cut will push people to work less, while the substitution effect will push people to work more. A typical statement would be, "The economic theory of household behavior leaves it unclear whether lowering tax rates will increase or reduce work effort." The economist would go on to say that this is a "question that cannot be answered by theory alone."

These views are widely held in much of the economics profession. They can be found in numerous places, including Joseph Pechman's work on taxes and Lester Thurow's views on a net-wealth tax and full taxation of capital gains. The error of this view originates from trying to aggregate a series of partial equilibrium analyses and, in the aggregate, to ignore the general equilibrium effects of a tax rate change. Theory does answer the question quite explicitly.

The best layman's illustration of the correct general equilibrium statement was given by the *Wall Street Journal*, which states:

M.I.T. economist Lester C. Thurow also speaks favorably of a net-wealth tax and the full taxation of capital gains.

He argues that private capital would still be formed because every tax has an income effect and a substitution effect, and he says the former dominates the latter. If you boost the tax on wealth, people will work harder to achieve their desired level of wealth (the income effect), even as the higher tax discourages them from more work (the substitution effect). But by our reckoning, if you tax $100 from Jones, thus forcing him to work harder, and give the $100 to Smith, Smith is required to work less to achieve his desired level of wealth. The income effect washes out, and all that's left is substitution.[7]

A more detailed response is as follows: (1) For an individual taken by himself, it is clear that at zero or negative take-home wages he will work less than he will at any positive take-home wages. Therefore, over the *entire* range of possible wages the supply of work effort is unambiguously increased by the total increase in take-home wages. (2) Within take-home regions, however, which may cover a wide range of take-home wages, an individual may choose to work fewer hours as take-home wages rise. In such a case, the income effect of higher total take-home wages more than offsets the substitution effect of more take-home pay for the last unit of work.

To see the distinction clearly, imagine the following. A person earns pretax wages of $4,000 per month. He takes one month per year in unpaid vacation. He pays a flat 50 percent tax on all wages, such that his take-home pay is $2,000 per month, or, for the eleven-month year, $22,000. Let us analyze now the following two sets of circumstances.

(a) He wins a once-for-all lottery of an $11,000 after-tax yearly stipend.

(b) He has a permanent reduction in his tax rates to 25 percent.

Under circumstance *a*, the yearly stipend, the general result will be some reduction in the number of months worked. Part of this person's increased income will go into more leisure consumption and thus less work. If he works the same eleven months per year under condition *a*, he will receive $33,000 (0.5 × 44,000 + 11,000) after taxes, and under condition *b* he will also receive $33,000 (0.75 × 44,000). If he works one month less, or ten months, under *a* he will take home $31,000, while under *b* he will take home only $30,000. His lost income is greater if he takes one more month of leisure when tax rates are cut as opposed to when he receives a windfall lottery. Likewise, if he works an extra month under condition *a*, he will have $35,000 take-home pay, and under condition *b* he will have $36,000 take-home pay.

Therefore, if we neutralize the income effect of a tax rate cut, there will be more total work simply because of the substitution effect.

For any *one* person we cannot be sure whether or not the income effect dominates the substitution effect within the relevant range. What *is* clear is that the income effect lowers work effort, and the substitution effect raises work effort. For the economy as a whole, however, the effect of a tax rate cut can be presumed to lead to more work and output. If the income effects across individuals are roughly similar, then the work and output impact of the income effect will net to zero. The higher income accorded the worker whose tax rates are cut must be matched by a negative impact on the income of the spending recipient.

If worker output were unchanged, then a tax rate cut would *pari passu* lead to a spending cut or a negative income lottery. Just as a lottery win lowered work, so a lottery net loss (usually referred to as a poll tax) would lead to increased work. Combining the two always leads to more work. This aggregate effect is equivalent to the work and output effect of our example if he simultaneously had an $11,000 yearly poll tax imposed on him with a reduction of his income tax rate from 50 percent to 25 percent. Income at eleven months of work would be $22,000 $(0.75 \times 44,000 - 11,000)$, but an additional month's work would yield $3,000 net, as opposed to $2,000. Except in obviously perverse cases, he would work more and not less. The theoretical analysis underlying this example can be found in any number of sources.[8]

To my knowledge, with the exception noted earlier, there is not one econometric model today that is consistent with known general equilibrium theory. The most substantial empirical work is that provided by Wanniski.[9]

Total Revenue and Tax Rates

Another implication has to do with the revenue aspects of the wedge model. There are two points on the tax schedule at which the government collects zero revenue. If the tax rate on all income is literally zero percent of everything earned, government revenue will literally be zero. Likewise, if the tax rate is 150 percent of everything earned, the government also collects zero. If, every time a person went to work, he received a bill from the government instead of receiving a check from his employer, sooner or later even the wealthiest and most highly motivated would stop going to his workplace. There would be no earnings, and total government revenue would equal zero. For the sake of argument, imagine the government collects zero revenue at 100 percent tax rates. If we plot tax rates on the horizontal axis and the total revenue on the vertical axis, all measured in real units, what we will find is that at zero tax rates we have zero revenue, and at 100 percent tax rates we also have zero revenue.

If tax rates are increased from 0 percent to, say, 1 percent, total revenue will increase. While output may fall somewhat, there will be a positive tax rate applied to a positive amount of output. Likewise, if the government lowers the tax rate from 100 percent to 99 percent, revenue will also increase. At a 99 percent tax rate, there will be some low level of production and a high positive tax rate. Therefore, if tax rates are lowered from 100 percent, there is an increase in total revenue. If we calculate each point over the whole schedule, we get the relationship shown in Figure 3.1. For each real revenue collected there are two different tax rates. The left part of the curve, which we call the normal range, is characterized by the fact that if the tax rate is increased, so is revenue, and if the tax rate is lowered, so is revenue. The right part of the curve is called the prohibitive range. If tax rates are raised in this range, revenue will fall, while if tax rates are lowered, revenue will increase. No rational government will ever knowingly be in this prohibitive range, it would be necessary that the government simultaneously hate taxpayers and transfer recipients. If tax rates are lowered, the taxpayers have more after-tax income, and the government also collects more real resources to transfer to the truly needy in society.

On a more realistic level the relevant question is not whether revenues actually rise or not but whether a change in tax rates is "self-financing." Therefore, one should focus not only on the specific receipts for which the rates have been charged but also on other receipts, on spending, and on savings. Other receipts must rise if a rate is reduced. The expansion of activity will elicit a greater base upon which all other exchanged rates will obtain greater revenue. Government spending at all levels, will fall because of lowered unemployment, increased poverty, and thus less welfare. Likewise, government employees will require less in real wages because with lower tax rates the same real wages will yield greater after tax wages, and so on. Finally, a cut in tax rates will yield greater savings in order to finance any deficit. Using a broader interpretation these tax

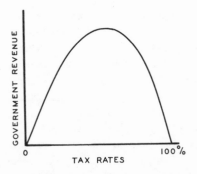

Figure 3.1. The "Laffer curve"

rates and revenue positions should refer basically to the self-financing nature of tax rate changes.

Investment Tax Credit and Corporate Tax Rate Cuts

Perhaps the single most popular corporate tax measure in lieu of a corporate tax rate reduction is the investment tax credit. Dollar for dollar, a corporation tax rate reduction can never be inferior to an investment tax credit and, save in the limit, is always superior. The surprising result is that it is quite conceivable over some ranges that an investment tax credit may actually be inferior to a policy of doing nothing.

There are three categories of firms: firms which have no tax liabilities with or without the investment tax credit; firms which in the absence of an investment tax credit would not have tax liabilities; and, finally, firms which have tax liabilities with or without an investment tax credit.

For any firm that does not pay taxes, the investment tax credit does literally nothing. If the firm is losing money, these losses reflect a tax carry-forward which enhances the sale value of the firm. Depending, of course, upon the specifics of any investment tax credit legislation, it is unlikely that these credits could be carried forward as can operating losses. Therefore, under these circumstances, the investment tax credit will have no effect. A reduction in the rate of tax on corporate profits would make loss operations more unprofitable. If the investment tax credit were able to be carried forward, then loss operations would become less unprofitable—a move clearly in the wrong direction.

In the case of a firm whose annual tax liabilities are less than the investment tax credit applicable to its investment, the effect is precisely the same as elimination of the corporate profits tax. Such a corporation will find any market activity more profitable on the margin and, therefore, will engage in expanded market activity. The expansion of market activity will, in itself, lead to additional tax revenue. The net effect may well be to lead to a *net* expansion of revenue and a lowering of other tax rates.

In the case of a firm whose annual tax liabilities substantially exceed any potential investment tax credit, there will be no incentive for the firm to expand market activity, and there will be two effects, each of which leads to less efficiency. By still incurring a net tax liability per period, the firm will find the marginal tax rate on profitable activities to be literally unaltered. On the margin, therefore, there will be no added incentives to market activity. Market activity will not expand. With no added market activity—assuming government spending stays the same—and with lessened government revenue from profits taxes, there must be an increased tax burden on existing market activities located outside this firm. As such, total market activity will fall. This effect on output and market activity is identical to an increase in marginal tax rates with no reduction in total taxes. Under the circumstances described above, the firm will tend to misallocate societal resources toward excessive use of new investment (because its purchase is subsidized below cost) and underuse of other resources available to the firm, such as old capital, labor, and raw materials.

In sum, therefore, an investment tax credit will have either no effect on unprofitable firms; the beneficial effect of eliminating the corporate profits tax on firms which would pay taxes in the absence of the investment tax credit and which would not pay taxes in its presence; or the deleterious effects of increasing marginal tax rates and distorting relative factor prices for firms which would pay taxes with or without an investment tax credit.

Incidence of a Tax versus Tax Burden

Often the incidence of a tax is very different from the burden of a tax. Raising tax rates on upper-income and wealthy people may actually have the effect of lowering the after-tax incomes of poor and working-class people. Given the level of spending in New York City, if the city were to tax all incomes over $100,000 per year at a 100 percent tax rate, it would get next to nothing in revenues. Those people with incomes in excess of $100,000 per year would either move or find ways not to report the excess. Given the need to finance its spending, the city would have to raise taxes, either explicit or implicit, on lower incomes. Therefore, lowering tax rates on upper-income groups may actually reduce the burden of the tax on lower-income groups. I believe we are well within this range at present. Any increase in the progressive incidence of taxation actually places a heavier burden on poor and low-income people.

Notes

1. An exception to this statement is the econometric model recently developed by Norman Ture under the auspices of the National Association of Manufacturers.

2. In regard to savings and investment, Michael Boskin has found interest sensitivity, as reported in his article "Taxation, Saving, and the Rate of Interest," *Journal of Political Economy,* April 1978.

3. The efforts of P. Craig Roberts are worth separate note. See especially his "Breakdown of the Keynesian Model," *Public Interest,* July 1978, and his "Economic Case for Kemp-Roth," *Wall Street Journal,* 1 August, 1978 (editorials). One should also note the early piece by R. A. Mundell, "Inflation from an International Viewpoint," in *The Phenomenon of Worldwide Inflation,* ed. David Meiselman and Arthur B. Laffer (Washington, D.C.: American Enterprise Institute, 1975).

4. On a more formal scale we assume two productive factors, capital (K) and labor (L) which combine to yield output (Q). Therefore, $Q = K^{\alpha}L^{1-\alpha}$ where α is capital's share of total output and $1 - \alpha$ is labor's share. The demand relationships for both capital and labor depend on each factor's marginal product. Thus:

$$\frac{dQ}{dK} = r_p = \alpha K^{\alpha-1}L^{1-\alpha} \text{ and } \frac{dQ}{dL} = W_p = (1 - \alpha)K^{\alpha}L^{-\alpha}$$

where r_p and W_p are the marginal products of capital and labor, respectively. Supplies of each factor depend upon net wages received of

$$K_s = K_s(r_r)$$

and

$$L_s = L_s(W_r)$$

where

$$\frac{\partial K_s}{\partial r_r} > 0 < \frac{\partial L_s}{\partial W_p}$$

The taxes on each factor are $t_k = r_p - r_r$ and $t_L = W_p - W_r$ and the budget constraint in a rational model is

$$G = t_kK + t_LL.$$

For the full derivations see V. Canto, A. Laffer, and O. Odogwu, "The Output and Employment Effects of Fiscal Policy in a Classical Model," mimeographed (University of Southern California).

5. Equations 40 and 41 of the Canto, Laffer, and Odogwu paper cited above show

$$\frac{\partial Q}{\partial t_L} < 0 > \frac{\partial Q}{\partial t_k}$$

holding the other tax rate constant.

6. As a point, different forms of spending will elicit different output effects. These aspects are beyond the scope of this paper.

7. "A New 'Soak-the-Rich' Theory," *Wall Street Journal,* Review and Outlook, 15 April, 1976, p. 14.

8. See, for example, A. C. Harberger, *Taxation and Welfare* (Boston: Little, Brown, 1974), or J. R. Hicks, *Value and Capital: An Inquiry into Some Fundamental Principles of Economic Theory* (London: Oxford Univ. Press, 1939).

9. J. Wanniski, *The Way the World Works* (New York: Basic Books, 1978).

{4}

How the Domestic Business Cycle Is Affected by the Rest of the World

MICHAEL W. KERAN

The main point that I wish to make in this chapter is that the stabilization policies which are desired by policymakers to influence the level of employment, prices, and output in any one country can be complicated and made more difficult to achieve because of stabilization policies being conducted in other countries. This conclusion is based on the events of the first half of the 1970s. That half-decade had episodes which are unprecedented in modern economic history. There was a breakdown in the international monetary system in 1971-73. The U.S. dollar was the center of the Bretton Wood system established in 1944. The dollar was tied to gold, and all other currencies were tied to the dollar on a fixed and known exchange rate. But in 1971-73, the dollar lost its role as centerpiece as private speculators and private investors massively moved out of holdings of dollars into other currencies. The fixed exchange rate system broke down under this shifting of portfolio preferences away from dollars into German marks, yen, and other currencies. As a result, we went from fixed exchange rates to flexible exchange rates; we went from a world tied to the dollar and U.S. economic hegemony, to one that was more decentralized.

Then in 1973-74, we had another event, one which had a much broader impact on individuals—double-digit inflation. In the United States in those two years, the inflation rate averaged 12 percent, measured by the consumer index. And the inflation rates in other countries were even higher. The third major economic event of the seventies—one with which we are still living—is the historic high unemployment rates which emerged in 1975. The startling, and from the economist's view, troubling nature of these phenomena is that they are worldwide. That is, every major industrial country of the world, and most of the underdeveloped countries too, have suffered with the inflation and recession of the last several years. Some analysts even claim that it has affected social values. People are much more interested in work-oriented rather than leisure-oriented activities when work is a relatively scarce commodity.

Economists did not anticipate the double-digit inflation or the recession. This has created an incentive to try to find out why our profession was unable to anticipate these problems, and what this professional failure tells us about the future. For example, Keynesian models, which base most of their price equations on wages and mark-up on wages, did not anticipate the double-digit inflation because the wage rates did not expand sharply before or even coincidentally with the sharp rise in the general price level in 1973–74. So, in spite of a good deal of rhetoric to the contrary, the inflation was not a cost-push phenomenon. Monetarists also did not anticipate this inflation. That is, the rate of growth in the U.S. money supply was much slower than the rate of inflation. Thus, neither the monetarists nor the Keynesians were able, prior to the event, to explain the inflation phenomenon of 1973–74.

Let us turn to another related issue: the Phillips curve. This is one of the most convenient if not one of the most theoretically elegant theorems in economics. It suggests that inflation and unemployment should move in opposite directions. In the first half of the 1970s they moved together. This has also been an embarrassment for the Keynesian model. Given the fact that Keynesian and monetarist economic models have not been able to explain this phenomenon, what have been the ways in which we have tried to explain the double-digit inflation and, in some cases, double-digit unemployment? There are two ways in which economists have dealt with it, one *ad hoc* and the other what we might call "systematic." To examine these, we must make a distinction between problems and issues. A problem is an event which is unique and which, therefore, requires a unique set of tools to solve it. An issue, on the other hand, is a systematic set of relationships in which one problem observed in the past is simply a forerunner of similar problems in the future.

This is a useful distinction because most economists have treated the double-digit inflation and recession as a problem and not as an issue. By that I mean that most analyses of this phenomenon have treated it as a unique event, one that is unlikely to happen again. If it is unlikely to happen again, then there is no reason for us to worry about developing new economic models to deal with it. The event is behind us, and though we have all suffered, it is not an issue that is amenable to the application of stabilization policy.

The Keynesians, in attempting to develop a unique explanation, talk about so-called supply shocks. It is very easy to illustrate a supply shock. In Figure 4.1, supply and demand schedules represent, not an individual market, but the entire marketplace. The demand curve represents aggregate demand in the economy, the supply curve represents the

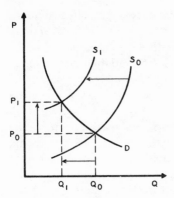

Figure 4.1. Economic response to a supply shock

aggregate supply. The supply curve is vertical at approximately full employment. Now, let us examine the Keynesian argument.

We had a series of events in 1972–74 which sharply, but temporarily, reduced the available supply of goods and services. There was the oil embargo and price increase; there were bad harvests; there was the removal of the anchovies from the Peruvian Coast. There were a whole range of supply shocks. These situations were uncoordinated, yet all occurred in a relatively short period of time. As a result, the supply curve shifted to the left (from S_0 to S_1), and we had higher prices and lower real output. When the shock is over, according to the Keynesians, the economy will revert to the old supply curve and the old relationships.

This type of explanation is internally consistent with the observations of simultaneous inflation and recession. It is also consistent with the fact that we have, in fact, had those type of supply shocks. A problem with this explanation is that under the most pessimistic assumptions about the impact of oil, wheat, and anchovies, the result is not double-digit inflation and 9 percent unemployment. The degree of the shock simply was not big enough to create the size of the impact that it is supposed to explain. So while it is in the right direction, it does not seem to be of the right magnitude.

Monetarists also have a problem-oriented explanation for the inflation. Milton Friedman described this in considerable detail in a number of pieces in *Newsweek* and in other journals. The monetarists' explanation is as follows: In 1971, President Nixon imposed price controls on the U.S. economy. Those controls, which lasted in various degrees of severity until the end of 1972, understated the rate of inflation in the United States from what it otherwise would have been. Then, in 1973–74, those controls were removed, the price level moved back to what it would have been, and during the temporary, or interim, period, the rate of inflation was higher than it otherwise would have been. Now, Friedman supports this proposition by saying that the money supply over the whole period

(1971-74) does a reasonably good job of explaining the average rate of inflation. The growth in money overstates the inflation rate in the first half of that period, under price controls, and understates the inflation in the second half, when the controls were lifted. He does acknowledge that the price level is approximately 4 percent higher than monetary growth over that entire period would suggest. He attributes this to the fact that with a higher rate of inflation in the second half of the period, people desired to hold lower cash balances, and this has increased the rate of money turnover, or velocity.

Again, this observation is consistent with the facts about the U.S. economy. But it fails to explain why the rest of the world has also experienced double-digit inflation at the same time, since the price control explanation does not apply in these other countries.

The second class of explanations is the systematic approach, which involves treating the problem as an issue. In other words, a systematic development could occur again if the same condition which preceded it occurred again. A number of systematic approaches are being developed. Most challenging to the Keynesian in theory, is the so-called rational expectations approach. A second approach that is also quite challenging to the Keynesians' is the "world monetarist" approach. The one I will suggest is less radical in a theoretical sense in that while it incorporates some elements of the world monetarists' view, it is also closely tied with the traditional Keynesian approach.

In the process, I will offer an insight into an important methodological issue. There are three stages in performing research and reporting on it. First, one observes a phenomenon and is dissatisfied with the theories others have used to explain it. In this case, the phenomenon is double-digit inflation and recession, and the dissatisfaction is with the *ad hoc* explanations of both the Keynesians and monetarists. The second stage is to develop an explanation for the phenomenon which is different from the other explanations. It is here that the art and science of economics comes in—and it is as much an art as it is a science. The third step is to test the hypothesis against new information not available when the hypothesis was formulated. This third step is very important. Unfortunately, a great deal of economic research deals only with the first two steps: that is, a phenomenon is observed and an explanation is developed for that phenomenon, but that explanation is not tested against new data. Indeed, this is the state in which my research stands. I have not proven my hypothesis; I have shown only that it is consistent with the observations of the past. It can be proved only if it is shown to be consistent with observations of events in the future, that is, if it can be used to make forecasts. Forecasting the future is a very tough test, but it is a legitimate test of any economic hypothesis that makes inferences about public policy.

The economic model I suggest here is really an amalgamation of theories which are already available in the marketplace for ideas. I have tried to put them together in a way that is internally consistent and that would tend to explain inflation-recession in terms of an issue rather than a problem.

The first element in my approach is the so-called monetary theory of the balance of payments. This is an important theoretical insight developed recently at the University of Chicago, especially by Harry Johnson and Robert Mondell. Arthur Laffer, of the faculty of the University of Southern California Graduate School of Business Administration, has also made contributions to monetary theory of the balance of payments. The one element of that theory which I have used in my work is the fact that the world price level is a function of the world money supply. Just as the domestic money supply can dominate domestic prices, so the world money supply can affect world prices. I have made some modifications to make the theory more applicable in the real world. World prices in my model are the prices of traded goods, that is, those goods which are actually or potentially tradable in international markets.

$$(1) \qquad P_W = f(M_W)$$

P_W is traded goods prices measured as the trade-weighted average of the export prices of the ten major industrial countries of the world. M_W is the world money supply, measured as the trade-weighted average of the money supply of the same ten major industrial countries of the world.

$$(2) \qquad P_{US} \equiv (w)P_W + (w - 1)P_H$$

P_{US} is simply the weighted average of the prices of U.S. home goods (P_H)—the goods produced and consumed at home which are not tradable —plus the tradable goods (P_W). As these equations indicate, the world money supply, which can affect tradable goods prices, can indirectly affect U.S. prices.

The second element in this model is a standard statement of the Keynesian national income identity,

$$(3) \qquad Y = PQ$$

where nominal income (Y) equals price (P) times quantity (Q), and that in turn is determined by the monetary (M_{US}) and the fiscal policy (F_{US}) variables:

$$(4) \qquad Y = f(M_{US}, F_{US})$$

That is, the policymakers—by controlling the nominal money supply, government spending, and tax rates—can affect nominal income. And nominal income can be divided into different combinations of prices and quantities. That means, going back to the aggregate demand curve in Figure 4.1, that different combinations of prices and quantities described in the demand curve (D) are equal to a constant level of nominal income. For this proposition to hold, the aggregate demand curve must be a rectangular hyperbole; that is, movements along this demand curve must represent the same level of nominal income with different combinations of price and quantity.

Shifts in this aggregate demand curve depend upon changes in the *nominal* money supply. Movements along this demand curve, on the other hand, are related to changes in the *real* money supply. A movement up the aggregate demand schedule means prices are rising; but the real money stock (M/P) is falling, and with some lag, real output is falling. The reverse occurs with a movement down the aggregate demand schedule. In general, a movement along the demand curve is associated with a change in the real money supply; a shift in the demand curve is associated with a change in the nominal money supply. We can derive this rather easily from a standard Keynesian model, defining income in terms of nominal values rather than real values.

The third element in this model is an aggregate supply curve, which simply defines the supply of goods and services as a function of nominal wages, the price level, and productivity. Again, the aggregate supply curve would be vertical at full employment. The positive slope is very Keynesian. In the classical model, the aggregate supply curve would be vertical at all prices. The Keynesian model assumes that nominal wages cannot fall from their current values, even with an excess supply of labor. If nominal wages should rise, that would be equivalent to a leftward shift in the aggregate supply curve. Conversely, if nominal wages should fall, that would be equivalent to a rightward shift in the aggregate supply curve. Cost-push elements in any Keynesian model represent shifts in the aggregate supply curve caused by changes in wages.

The model described above is a combination of monetarist and Keynesian elements and can be used to explain what happened in the U.S. economy and the rest of the world in the first half of the seventies.

We started off with a rise in the world money supply from 1970 to 1973. The world money supply stopped rising rapidly in March 1973. That date is important because it is when most of the major industrial countries went on flexible exchange rates. They stopped trying to peg their currencies to the dollar and therefore stopped accommodating the preferences of private persons who wanted to get out of dollars and into German marks and yen. From 1970 to 1973, central banks were compelled to buy the dollars in order to maintain fixed exchange rates. This expanded the domestic money supply as most of the major industrial countries tried to maintain fixed exchange rates in the face of a large capital inflow into their economy. The expansion of the world money supply from 1970 to 1973 was a unique event. We had not previously had a situation where fixed exchange rates were maintained by many countries simultaneously when there was also speculation in favor of their currency. Finally, in March of 1973, these countries decided they had monetized dollars so long that they were losing control of their domestic money supply. Domestic inflation had already started to rise when the central banks dropped their control of exchange rates.

What are the implications of this two-and-a-half-year period of expansion in the world money supply? It led to a rise in world prices, that is, in the prices of the internationally traded goods, with about a two-year lag. From late 1972 until the end of 1974, the prices of internationally traded goods approximately doubled.

This in return led to a rise in U.S. prices. How big a rise in U.S. prices? Since imports represent only 9 percent of our GNP, it would seem to follow that a big price increase in internationally traded goods would have little impact on the United States. But that turns out to be wrong because it is an inappropriate way of measuring the impact of traded goods prices on the U.S. economy. Exports are also traded goods. Our wheat prices, for example, are determined in a world market rather than in a domestic market, and wheat is a major export. Indeed, there are a whole range of goods which are potential exports and whose prices will be determined in a world rather than a domestic market. Of the goods included in a consumer index, the prices of approximately 25 percent are determined in world markets. For the wholesale price index, close to fifty percent are determined in world markets rather than strictly in U.S. markets. In short, the impact of a rise in traded goods prices on the U.S. economy could be much more substantial than would be suggested by looking at a simple import share of GNP.

Thus in 1973–74, a rise in world prices led to a rise in U.S. prices. Prior to that the United States was at an equilibrium position as described in Figure 4.2 by the rectangle P_1EQ_1O. Suddenly we were thrown out of equilibrium by a rise in P_W which led to a rise in U.S. prices not associated with a shift in either the supply or demand curve in the United States. That is, it was not associated with either a change in monetary or fiscal policy in the United States or an exogenous increase in nominal wages. This initially pushed us from equilibrium position (E) to disequilibrium (F) as U.S. prices rose in weighted proportion to the rise in the prices of internationally traded goods. Because this reduced the value of the real money stock—that is, U.S. nominal money stock divided by the U.S. prices declined—we shifted towards point G. Obviously, that is not an equilibrium position either. If the aggregate supply and demand curves are unchanged, then equilibrium can be restored only by a move back to point E.

What are the forces which would cause equilibrium to be restored by a shift back to point E versus an alternative explanation in which

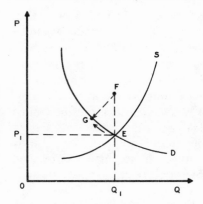

Figure 4.2. Economic response to a rise in traded goods prices

equilibrium could be restored by a leftward shift in the supply curve to some point between E and G? If the equilibrium were restored by our moving back to point E, then the influence of world prices on U.S. prices would have been only transitory. The most important market force operating to reestablish equilibrium in this case is a decline in imports to the United States because of lower real income. The resulting export surplus would lead to an appreciation of the international exchange value of the dollar which would offset the earlier rise in the prices of internationally traded goods.

If equilibrium is restored by the aggregate supply curve's shifting toward point G, then the effect of world inflation on U.S. inflation would be permanent. At this point in the analysis, the role of cost-push and its effect on the aggregate supply curve come into play. If wages respond to the higher prices because of a desire on the part of labor to reverse a decline in real wages, the aggregate supply curve will shift to the left. If the ability of unions to reestablish the nominal wages proportional to the rise in prices (and therefore maintain a constant real wage) is very quick and very sharp, then there will be a leftward shift in the supply curve proportional with the initial movement away from equilibrium position (E). This would reestablish equilibrium at point G with a higher price and lower quantity than we had before the shock. In this case world inflation would have a permanent effect on U.S. prices and quantities. If nominal wages respond slowly and incompletely to a change in prices, then the aggregate supply curve will not shift within the relevant time period, and equilibrium will be reestablished at point E. In this case, world inflation would have only a temporary influence on prices and quantities in the United States.

Which of these two cases operates is an empirical question. Do wages in the United States respond quickly to shifts in prices or do they not? I found that the critical time period was one year. That is, if wages respond to higher prices within a year, then the new equilibrium would be reestablished close to point *G*. If they respond to higher prices with higher wages in a period longer than a year—if it took two or three years—then the equilibrium would be close to point *E*. I looked at the response of wages to prices in three countries—the United States, Germany, and the United Kingdom. I picked Germany and the United Kingdom because these were extreme or polar cases—the United Kingdom being an example where wages appear to respond very quickly to prices, and Germany, a case where wages do not appear to respond very quickly to prices. The United States represents an intermediate case.

Empirical work showed that in the United Kingdom a rise in prices led to a proportional rise in wages within two quarters. That meant when a world price increase shifted the United Kingdom away from equilibrium, the supply curve shifted to the left along with it and reestablished a new equilibrium closer to point *G* at higher prices and lower output than would otherwise be the case. Therefore, the higher foreign inflation was permanently imbedded in the United Kingdom economy, because domestic wages and prices of nontraded goods rose proportionately to prices of traded goods. As a result, the potential export surplus from a decline in domestic income was offset by a rise in prices of nontraded goods.

In Germany, where there was a very sluggish response of wages to changes in prices, aggregate supply hardly shifted at all in the relevant time period, and equilibrium was reestablished at *E*. In this case, an export surplus led to an appreciation of the German mark which in time offset the rise in prices of internationally traded goods. Domestic prices in Germany were only temporarily affected by world inflation. The key difference between the United Kingdom and the German experience is that the natural forces toward equilibrium at point *E* were frustrated in the United Kingdom by a rise in the relative price of nontraded goods, i.e., wages. On balance, the effect of world prices on domestic German prices was temporary because of the appreciation of the German mark resulting from an export surplus. The Germans avoided the permanent impact of this world inflation; that meant that the Germans also enjoyed a lower average rate of inflation over the period.

The United States was an intermediate case, where approximately 60 percent of the higher inflation was imbedded in higher wages in the first year. Therefore, a part of the world inflation was offset by an appreciation of the dollar, and part of it was imbedded in permanently higher prices in the United States.

The model discussed above is consistent with what actually happened during the period of 1970–75. It is also consistent with the period 1955–

75. The combination of high inflation and high unemployment is due to equilibrium output to the left of point E in Figure 4.2. Countries like Germany, where wages did not rise immediately in response to higher prices, had the least amount of domestic inflation and domestic unemployment. Those like the United Kingdom, where wages responded quickly and completely to higher prices, had more severe domestic inflation and unemployment. The United States was the intermediate case, where inflation and unemployment were somewhat higher as a result of higher wages' response to prices.

This is clearly an *ex post facto* explanation of the 1973–74 inflation. To become a really convincing theory, it must be able to account for observations not available when the model was built. Fortunately, I was given a very nice test. The worldwide recession that was created by the deceleration in world money supply after 1973 led to a high rate of unemployment in major countries of the world, and also triggered a renewal of the expansion in the world money supply in 1975 and 1976 to get back to full employment. That would suggest that we would have a return to the same kind of world inflation that we had earlier in the decade. Indeed, this model forecasts that the inflation rate in the United States, as a result of the rise in prices of internationally traded goods, should be between 6 percent and 7 percent for the consumer price index in 1977. I made that forecast in 1976, when most people were forecasting a 5 percent rate of inflation in consumer prices for the United States. The actual U.S. inflation in 1977 was 6½ percent.

I also forecasted that during 1977, prices of internationally traded goods would have to rise by 10–14 percent during the year in order to push up U.S. prices. This seems to have happened. Obviously, this is not complete confirmation of the theory. One observation for one year does not prove an analytical relationship, but it is at least consistent with the theory.

The model would also forecast that the international inflation rate in 1977 would be temporary and that prices of internationally traded goods prices would stabilize because after a very short bout of sharp rises in international money supply in 1975–76, the Germans and the Japanese contracted their domestic money supply, slowing down the world money supply growth. This temporarily will give us a very slow growth in Europe and Japan in real terms, but will set the stage for a much lower rate of internationally traded goods inflation in the future and, therefore, a much sounder base for sustained recovery in the rest of the world.

The policy prescriptions of this model are quite contrary to the U.S. program of urging the Germans and Japanese to follow an expansionary policy to help pull the rest of the world out of recession. Instead, Germany and Japan should continue to follow the slow, moderate expansion policies that they have been following for the last year and a half because that will set the stage for a lower underlying rate of inflation; it will insure that we go back to the conditions of the 1950s, and the first half of the 1960s, when the prices of internationally traded goods were relatively stable. In that context, countries can return to domestic stabilization policies that will be unaffected by developments in the rest of the world. But until that time, we will continue to have domestic economic developments that are strongly influenced by what the rest of the world does.

{5}

The U.S. Economy in the Eighties

WILLIAM A. COX

In contrast to the focus of several other papers in this volume on policy issues in a relatively short-term context, this essay reviews the development of the U.S. labor force over several decades and projects certain fundamental changes in employment conditions and industrial structure that can be foreseen in the 1980s and beyond. In this respect it parallels the contribution by John Hardt dealing with the secular development of the Soviet Union.

The past ten years in the United States have been a period of extraordinary growth in the labor force, as the bumper crop of babies born in the late 1940s and early 1950s has entered the job market. Rapid labor growth combined frequently with poor business conditions has brought soaring unemployment during this period, especially for young people.

Labor force growth probably peaked in 1978 with over 3 million people coming into the job market (3 percent of the previous year's labor force). Because of the declining youthful population, however, labor force growth will drop steadily to about 1 percent annually in the late 1980s, despite the increasing participation of women and a possible rise in immigration. With slower labor growth, unemployment will tend toward lower levels; and, indeed, the emergence of labor scarcity could radically transform America's social and economic problems by the latter 1980s. Allowing for some offsetting productivity gains through greater use of labor-saving methods, potential GNP growth will decline from the recently estimated range of 3.5 percent per year to about 2.5 percent. Some underutilization of highly educated manpower may remain, however, because events over the past fifteen years have catapulted the college-educated share of the labor force upward faster than the number of jobs requiring their training.

This article is based on a lecture delivered at the University of Southern California in November 1977, when the author was a senior economist on the staff of the Joint Economic Committee of the United States Congress.

The evolution of the U.S. economic structure also will be influenced by a number of new factors. Chief among these will be the radical reduction in the size of the American automobile to improve its fuel efficiency; rising relative prices of basic materials and materials-intensive goods because of high energy and environmental protection costs; increasing competition from foreign producers, especially from newly established basic industries in developing countries; and, in the late 1980s and beyond, a decline in domestic demand for consumer durable goods—autos, housing, and household appliances—as a result of demographic developments. Each of these factors will tend to slow the growth of basic manufacturing in the United States and once again to accelerate the shift from manufacturing to the nonmanufacturing sectors, which has been under way for several decades.

Effects of Slower Labor Force Growth

The U.S. economy has been subject to some very sharp changes in demographic conditions over the past generation. Figure 5.1 indicates the rates of population and labor force growth of the past several decades and those foreseen for the 1980s. As the figure shows, population growth soared in the late 1940s and the 1950s and then plummeted in the 1960s and 1970s. The growth rate ranged from 1.2 percent annually

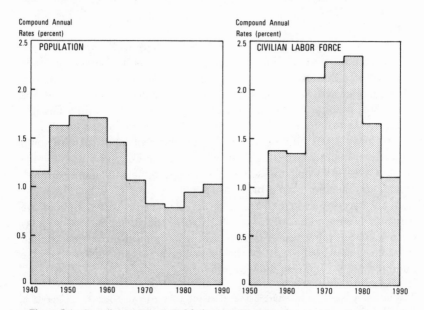

Figure 5.1. Growth patterns of population and labor force

in the early 1940s (indeed, from 0.7 percent in the 1930s) to 1.7 percent in the 1950s; it dropped to 0.8 percent in the 1970s and will remain at about 1 percent in the 1980s. The small rise in population growth projected for the 1980s is an echo of the earlier baby boom, as the large number of people born at that time reach childbearing age.

Because most workers enter the labor force between the ages of 18 to 22, labor force growth reflects the birth rate with a lag of about 18 years. Therefore, labor force growth soared in the mid-1960s, reflecting in part the rise in fertility of the late 1940s and, in addition, a steady increase in the rate of labor force participation among women. The importance of this development in coloring the economic and social conditions of the past decade and the extent to which the coming labor force "bust" affects the outlook for the future have not been adequately appreciated.

Rapid growth in the labor force since the mid-1960s has meant that unemployment has risen sharply whenever the economy's growth has faltered, and even rapid economic expansion has brought unemployment down only haltingly. In contrast to the conditions of the earlier postwar period, there has been a shift in the economy's resource endowment toward relatively more abundant labor and a corresponding relative scarcity of capital and other resources. Macroeconomic policies aimed at reducing unemployment have tended to place excessive demands on productive capacity, creating inflationary pressures, increasing demand for investment capital, and aggravating the balance of trade. While other events have played important roles, this shift in relative factor supplies should not be overlooked in explaining why interest rates soared in the late 1960s and prices of capital goods and natural resources have risen sharply in the 1970s, while labor income in real terms has tended to stagnate. It also cannot be ignored in explaining the sharp deceleration of gains in labor productivity since 1966. The large population of young people, moreover, has made unemployment of youth an especially critical problem and with it other social maladies associated largely with youth, such as vandalism, crime, and drug addiction.

What many people also do not realize is that the drop in births of the 1960s and 1970s will result during the 1980s and 1990s in a drop of labor force growth and a drop in the size of the youthful population.[1] This process is now beginning. As labor force growth falls from an average of about 2.4 percent per year for the 1970s to about 1 percent after 1985, many of the economic imbalances of the present decade will tend to reverse themselves. The unemployment rate will tend to decline more quickly during periods of economic growth and will rise more slowly during recessions. Eventually a condition of recurrent labor scarcity probably will develop. Especially scarce will be applicants for entry-level and other unskilled jobs. Expanding firms will have to use more vigorous methods to attract, train, and retain workers. These methods will include more part-time employment, more flexible working conditions, and more effort to train undereducated job applicants, who today land on the reject heap.

The prospect of changed labor market conditions contains implications for many aspects of economic and social policy. For instance, a tighter labor market will accelerate the absorption into the economy of today's "discouraged workers," people who have given up looking for jobs. It also will smooth the acceptance of minority workers and older workers handicapped today by discrimination. Thus it will lighten the burden on government budgets for unemployment compensation, training programs, and income support programs.

Therefore, employment policies, while providing enough jobs during periods of high unemployment, must be designed to avoid retaining people in jobs with low productivity when more productive work becomes available. Adjustment assistance policies for declining industries also should be devised with this in mind. Welfare policies should be reformed to induce recipients able to work to join the labor force when jobs are available. Potential labor scarcity also implies that present calls for the adoption of so-called appropriate technology, which typically means labor-intensive technology, may not be appropriate except perhaps on a short-term basis.

It may become desirable, in fact, to liberalize immigration policies; and policy analysts will have to rethink the conditions under which a volunteer military force will remain viable during an era with a rapidly declining population of young people. The decline in numbers of geographically mobile young people, moreover, will slow today's migration from the northeastern parts of the country to the South and the West, mitigating the effects of very rapid growth in the latter regions.

The decline in youthful population also implies a dropping crime rate, although law enforcement agencies may try to take credit for this development. The passage of today's large cohort of young people into a phase of greater maturity may end the dominance of youth-oriented culture, for the commercial culture-makers will turn their sights toward the burgeoning market composed of people approaching midlife.

The projected drop of 1–1.25 percentage points in annual labor force growth will constrain the nation's GNP growth potential. Indeed, the growth in labor supplies may be restricted still further by reductions in weekly working hours in some industries and by shifts on the part of some people toward more leisure-oriented ways of life. Increasing relative scarcity of labor, however, implies some increase in labor productivity growth as labor-saving technology is more vigorously exploited. Allowing for this offsetting effect, the long-term potential growth rate of GNP may decline from recent estimates of 3.5–4 percent annually to the range of 2.5-3 percent in the later 1980s. As a result of slower labor and GNP growth, demands on plant capacity may be less prevalent, and the demand for investment capital will grow more slowly, implying reduced inflation and lower interest rates.

The Glut of Highly Educated Manpower

Despite the tendency toward tighter labor markets, underemployment of college-educated personnel may be difficult to eliminate. The over-supply of college-educated people is more severe and probably will be more lasting than oversupply in other segments of the labor force because of a chain of circumstances over several decades that has in the past decade increased the college-educated fraction of the labor force faster than the number of jobs requiring their training.[2]

A critical economic role of highly educated manpower is to facilitate the adoption of new, more productive technology. From 1930 through 1945, however, investment—and with it, the advance of technology—was suppressed by depression and war. After World War II, a wave of innovation took place. Thus, demand soared for employees with up-to-date technical training. As Table 5.1 shows, however, this occurred at a time when the population of college age was declining absolutely (as a result of the Depression's effects on fertility).

Table 5.1 Growth of Higher Education and College-Educated Manpower (Percentages)

| | Growth Rate of | | Fraction of | |
| | Population | College | College-Aged | College-Educated |
Time Period	Ages 18-24	Enrollment	in College	in Population
1920-30	1.7	6.1		
1930			7.2	—
1930-40	0.7	3.1		
1940			9.1	4.6
1940-50	−0.2	*		
1950			*	6.0
1950-60	−0.3	1.9		
1960			20.5	7.7
1960-70	4.5	8.5		
1970			30.6	11.0
Proj. 1980				15-16

Source: Stephen P. Dresch, "Human Capital and Economic Growth: Retrospect and Prospect," in U.S., Congress, Joint Economic Committee, *U.S. Economic Growth from 1976 to 1986: Prospects, Problems, and Patterns,* vol. 11, *Human Capital* (Washington, D.C.: GPO, 1977).

*Both college enrollments and the student age distribution were substantially distorted in 1950 by the deferred college attendance of World War II veterans.

The resulting shortage of college-educated people brought rapid pay increases for starting professionals and a large jump in the fraction of the college-age cohort actually attending school. During this era, in fact, college attendance came to be taken for granted by a large segment of the population. Despite this jump in the proportion of persons of student age attending college, enrollments expanded very slowly during the 1950s because of the small number of people in this age group.

In the mid-1960s, however, the college age group began to grow at unprecedented rates, and the fraction of this group attending college also continued to rise, yielding an enormous increase in the number of college students. The fraction of the labor force having graduated from college—which had risen by only 2.1 percentage points, from 5.6 to 7.7 percent, in the twenty years up to 1960—is expected to reach at least 15 percent of a much larger labor force by 1980. Labor market studies have indicated that the shortage of college-trained personnel relative to the demand for their services turned into a surplus during the early 1970s, and the surplus is more than simply a manifestation of the poor business conditions of recent years. Ironically, the high rate of unemployment among young people has reduced the opportunity costs of going to school and induced some students to remain in college who would not have done so if their current job alternatives had been more attractive. This has aggravated the oversupply.

The consequence of this glut at the highly educated end of the labor market will not necessarily be unemployment for many college-trained people. Instead, it will mean a compression of income differentials between junior managers and technicians on one hand and production workers on the other. This already can be seen in the reduced income spread between college-educated personnel between the ages of 25 and 35 and those with only high school diplomas. There also will be a process of bumping some people down the job status ladder. Many graduates of community colleges and junior colleges will not be recruited for the types of jobs to which they earlier could aspire. The bulge in the age distribution of technicians and managers, moreover, will result in intense competition for advancement among professional people and frustration of the ambitions of many. It will be impossible to invert the organizational status pyramid as the age pyramid becomes inverted in the 1990s.

In summary, the productivity of a rising average education level, which has been an important contributor to rising living standards in the past generation, no longer is being fully exploited today. One result may be a historic reversal in the proportion of student-age persons attending colleges. As the number of college-age persons also drops sharply in the 1980s, the stage may be set for a new shortage of highly educated manpower by the year 2000.

The Evolution of Industrial Structure

It already has been suggested that potential economic growth will slow markedly in the later 1980s because of labor constraints. Several important factors now becoming apparent will curb the share of the basic industries in U.S. economic growth over the longer run.

The first and most immediate of the above-mentioned developments—the well-publicized redesign of the automobile—cuts a broad swath across the basic materials sectors. Since 1975, U.S. automakers have eliminated more than 700 pounds from their average car. This redesign has reduced the demand (or demand growth) for steel, lead, synthetic rubber, zinc, glass, and gasoline. Aluminum and plastics will be substituted for some of these materials in some uses.

The auto's significance becomes clearer when one realizes the degree of dependence of many materials industries on the motor vehicles sector and the extent of the changes that are taking place. As Table 5.2 shows, more than three-fifths of U.S. consumption of synthetic rubber and lead went into motor vehicles uses in 1973, the last year of strong vehicle sales before the design revolution began. Motor vehicles also absorbed one-third of the zinc and one-fifth of the steel consumed in that year. Such uses of these materials, with the exception of zinc, had grown substantially since 1965.

Table 5.3 projects a 38 percent reduction in the average weight of American-made cars from 1973 through 1985, nearly half of which has already been effected; furthermore, it assumes a growth rate in the number of autos sold of 0.6 percent annually (about the same as between 1965 and 1973). Thus, the aggregate weight of autos produced in the United States would drop by 34 percent over these twelve years.

The smaller autos of the future will contain smaller batteries using

Table 5.2 Consumption of Materials in U.S.-Made Motor Vehicles, 1965 and 1973

	Thousand Short Tons			Percent of Total
			Percent	U.S. Usage,
Material	1965	1973	Change	1973
Lead	639	971	52	63
In batteries	—	641	—	42
In fuel additives	—	330	—	21
Synthetic Rubber	1,046	1,631	56	62
Zinc	543	501	−8	33
Steel	20,123	23,217	15	21
Sheet	12,778	15,562	22	42
Bars	3,047	3,285	8	25
Strip	1,031	1,030	0	30
Aluminum	507	860	70	12

Source: Motor Vehicle Manufacturers Association.

Table 5.3 Projected Changes in Automobile Weight, Sales, and Materials Consumption

	1973	1980	1985
Average auto weight			
Pounds	4,220	3,500	2,600
Index (1973 = 100)	100.0	82.9	61.6
Sales of U.S.-made autos			
Thousands	9,658	10,100	10,400
Index (1973 = 100)	100.0	104.6	107.7
Index of aggregate auto weight (1973 = 100)	100.0	86.7	66.3
Change in materials consumption*			
Lead		−7.4%	−15.6%
Rubber		−3.8	−9.9
Zinc		−1.6	−4.1
Steel		−1.4	−3.7
Aluminum		3.3	8.0

Source: Author's projections.
*Percentage of total U.S. usage in 1973.

less lead, and lead additives for gasoline are rapidly being eliminated. Smaller cars require smaller tires, and lighter cars extend tire life, just as the use of the radial tire design already is doing. If auto battery weight declines in proportion to projected auto weight and lead gasoline additives are phased out, then the drop in uses of lead in the automobile from 1973 to 1985 will amount to 15 percent of the total U.S. lead consumption of 1973. A decline in tire weight proportional to the decline in auto weight would mean a reduction in synthetic rubber use of about 10 percent. Because some new batteries and tires go for replacements on older cars, their average size will decline with some lag. On the other hand, recycled materials will be able to supply an increased share of the remaining market.

Most of the reduction in auto weight, of course, will come out of its steel content. A reduction in steel use for automobiles proportional to the drop in aggregate auto weight would signify a decline by 1985 of about 4 percent of total 1973 U.S. consumption. Substitution of other materials may boost this cutback to over 5 percent (about 5 million tons). The decline in automakers' demand for steel may be partly offset, at least for a period, by growth in the demand for steel in construction, machinery, and equipment. Increases in aluminum usage of up to 10 percent of total 1973 U.S. consumption can be foreseen. Thus, the auto sector would become a major aluminum market.

The purpose of the automobile redesign, of course, is conservation of gasoline, and this objective is being achieved. The average 1978 American car gets nearly 60 percent more miles per gallon than a 1973 model. Further rapid advances are programmed by the auto industry, and an average of 27.5 miles per gallon is required by law for new cars produced in 1985. Gasoline demand can be expected to reach a peak in the early 1980s and then to enter a long period of decline. From the standpoint of national policy, this outlook is very welcome, but it will require a steady adjustment in the product mix of U.S. refineries and may mean a growing underutilization of the industry's highly developed capacity to produce gasoline.

Another reason to expect more moderate growth of U.S. basic industries in the future is the sizeable cost being imposed on such industries by measures to protect the environment both inside and outside of the plant. Together with the high prices of energy, these costs raise the relative prices of basic materials and of materials-intensive final products, encouraging substitution of other goods and services. At the same time, these costs make U.S. materials industries more vulnerable to competition from foreign producers, who may not be required to take such stringent environmental protection measures.

Basic industries in a variety of countries now reaching an intermediate state of economic development may become especially keen competitors. Populous developing countries such as Mexico, Brazil, India, Iran, and Korea are erecting metallurgical and metal-working industries. They are competing in an ever-widening array of products, including basic steel, ships, machinery, and standard consumer goods. The oil-producing countries can be expected to develop energy-intensive sectors based on their access to this input at low cost. Countries producing bauxite and other raw materials increasingly are refining and fabricating their resources before exporting them. Most manufactured products of these developing countries, except for those from OPEC members, now can enter American markets under preferential tariffs.

The broad implication of the Third World's industrial drive, together with current U.S. policies, therefore, would seem to be an increasing reliance on foreign suppliers for basic industrial products. Beginning from a high degree of self-sufficiency, this is not necessarily to be regretted. Indeed, the demands of Americans for environmental preservation plus the desire of our highly educated labor force for more creative and less repetitive work may be consistent with the demands of the less industrialized countries for a "new international division of labor." This pattern may also be consistent with growing labor scarcity in the United States, provided that the implied evolution of economic structure is carried out gradually with the aid of effective policies to achieve the adjustment.

The demographic outlook also has important implications for the longer-run evolution of the economy's structure. Just as the declining number of young people in the 1980s will mean a drop in labor force growth, it also will mean a decline in family and household formation. This latter decline, projected graphically in Figure 5.2, is less pronounced

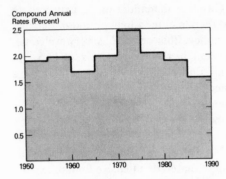

Figure 5.2. Changing rates of household formation

than the drop in labor force because of the tendency toward a greater proportion of single rather than multiperson households due to a rising average age of marriage, more frequent divorce, and other factors.

Young people typically acquire their initial stocks of durable goods (automobiles, housing, and major household appliances) during the first ten years of their adult lives, although high unemployment and high mortgage interest rates in recent years may have retarded this process somewhat. If this pattern of acquisition continues, the demand for these goods will remain high for several years but will begin to decline during the late 1980s, unless advances in technology develop important new products or accelerate the displacement of existing ones. Some of these markets, moreover, are reaching saturation in the sense that the number of units per person or household no longer is growing rapidly. Indeed, the average number (and size) of these durable goods per household may tend to fall with the increasing share of single-person households and of childless and one-child families.

What of the prospects that new technology will evolve products that regenerate the demand for consumer durables? The biggest changes at present are occurring in the automobile. If the auto redesign is successful in appealing to consumers, and if rising retail fuel prices reinforce the exhoration to increase fuel economy, then accelerated replacement of older cars will help to sustain new-car-demand growth in the 1980s. Domestic demand must begin to decline in the 1990s, however, unless a new breakthrough (e.g., an efficient electric car) is achieved, or unless U.S. automakers succeed in competing more effectively against foreign producers at home and possibly abroad.

Greater attention to the fuel economy of other major household apparatus (furnaces, air conditioners, stoves, clothes dryers, etc.), fostered by legal efficiency standards and labeling requirements, may initiate a similar replacement momentum in the markets for these products. Other consumer markets in which demand-stimulating technical breakthroughs are coming are entertainment electronics, home communications equipment, and the application of electronics to existing types of durable goods. Furthermore, the development of medical and telecommunications technology and computerized office systems promises to spur substantial business investment activity. Of course, as in eras past, some major innovations will occur that simply are not foreseen today, as this is the very nature of technical progress.

The energy industries of the 1980s will present a mixed picture. Energy refining, transportation, and distribution will grow more slowly than in the past because of the slower growth of energy demand. The capital-intensive electric power sector also will grow more slowly but probably will benefit from some substitution of electricity for primary energy sources. On the other hand, the boom will continue in domestic extraction of energy products and in producing energy extraction and conservation equipment for the world. This boom will be complemented by growing research and development activity to foster new energy production and conserving technologies.

If an increasing share of income growth takes the form of per capita income, and if the demand for major durable goods tends to decline toward replacement levels, then the composition of demand will tend to shift toward a higher proportion of product fabrication and styling and toward entertainment, travel, education, health care, other services, and leisure. In a labor-scarce environment these services will be provided increasingly with the aid of automated technology.

In sum, therefore, one may foresee a continuation or an acceleration of the already quite advanced shift in U.S. economic structure from the manufacture of goods to the provision of services over the remainder of this century.

Notes

1. Charles Bowman, "The Labor Force, Employment, and Economic Growth," in U.S., Congress, Joint Economic Committee, *U.S. Economic Growth from 1976 to 1986: Prospects, Problems, and Patterns,* vol. 11, *Human Capital* (Washington, D.C.: GPO, 1977).

2. This section draws heavily on an article by Stephen P. Dresch, "Human Capital and Economic Growth: Retrospect and Prospect," in ibid.

{6}

An Alternative Approach to Economic Policy: Macrobehavior from Microstructure

JA Y W. FORRESTER

In recent years the economy has behaved in unexpected ways. Experts disagree in their recommendations for economic policy. Although proven to be ineffective, old policies for stabilizing economic fluctuation and controlling unemployment are continued for lack of persuasive alternatives. The public is losing confidence in economists. In a recent article, Thurow (1977) evaluates the economic profession:

The influence of economists has never been greater ... yet the public esteem of economists has never been lower. ... Economic forecasting has become a multimillion dollar business. ... Yet the economy is widely perceived as out of control with economists having little of value to contribute ... mathematical models and their empirical analogue—econometric models—have now become the standard tools of economics. ... Econometric models proved not up to the task. ... The Phillips curve hypothesis has only one problem. No one has ever been able to find stable price equations in U.S. data. ... [Economics] proceeds in a manner similar to gold mining. Some great, or lucky, prospector strikes a vein of high grade ore in the form of a new paradigm. ... Eventually the vein plays out. ... The last decade has not witnessed a major or even a lesser gold strike. To rejuvenate its internal intellectual growth the profession needs a gold strike, but as with all actual gold strikes, no one knows where, or if, it will occur.[1]

Divergence of Economic Theory from Real Economic Behavior

Why are economists failing to explain real economic behavior? Why are recommendations on economic policy contradictory and unpersuasive? Why does the economy seem too complex to understand? Why do assumptions underlying economic theory seem so unrelated to behavior of people? I believe the answers lie in the way the traditions of the economic profession have led away from the most useful answers.

The plight of economics seems to arise from the very strength of its traditions—traditions that go back 200 years and have been strong enough to prevent a redirection of economics to take substantial advantage of modern computers, of knowledge of managerial behavior, or emerging concepts about the dynamic nature of social systems:

1. The tradition of equilibrium analysis, assuming at each point in the economy an equality of in-and-out flows that implies constant system stocks, has diverted attention from the importance of incorporating variable accumulations (stocks of goods, money, information, men, and equipment) that generate dynamic behavior. The system stocks (accumulations) decouple rates of flow, permit dynamic change, and serve as the system memory of the past to govern action in the present to create change in the future.

2. The traditional perception in economics that proper scientific method follows a deductive logic has led to emphasis on internal consistency in theory rather than on agreement between theory and real-world structure and processes. By contrast, the inductive methods of scientific inquiry, used by other professions, such as management and engineering, give access to rich and relevant observational information about the operating world of business and politics.

3. The tradition of individual personal research, growing from perceiving economics as an academic discipline rather than as practical social engineering, has kept the economic profession a fragmented one. Attention has been diverted from a true systems approach to small studies on bits and pieces of the economic system. Emphasis on personal academic research has precluded multiple research projects along different and competing lines of attack at a scale large enough to be commensurate with the difficulty and importance of economic dynamics.

4. A traditional insistence on simple theory was imposed by the limited tools of discussion, algebra, and two-dimensional diagrams. Simplicity was necessary in a day when only simple relationships could be handled. But simplicity has kept economics from perceiving the extent to which important behavior inherently arises from the complexities of economic life.

5. Traditional theory has focused on restricted concepts of how people presumably should behave in order to optimize results. Assumptions about optimum decisionmaking obscure the

nature of real decisionmaking, in which incomplete information, uncertainty, and lack of understanding of the consequences of decisions dominate behavior.

6. The tradition of assuming that short-term prediction is the ultimate test and objective of economic models—even though such prediction can be demonstrated as unlikely, given the structure of and randomness in economic systems—has obscured the more important and more feasible objective of using models for discovering policies that will improve the inherent behavior of economic systems. [2]

7. The tradition of separating macroeconomics from microeconomics, arising from past inability to handle the complexity of constructing a model of macrobehavior from microcomponents, has led to overconfidence in macroeconomic theory and to creation of a theoretical structure that is inconsistent with the underlying organization and decisionmaking processes of real people.

8. The tradition of separating search for model structure from search for parameters has obscured the possibility of both structure and parameters being drawn directly from observation of real life. Separated search for structure and parameters as two independent processes has apparently resulted from the two-stage development in economics whereby theory came first, followed by econometric parameter selection as a separate process associated with validation. Actually, both structure and parameters can be directly observed in the real-life setting. Such intensive inspection of actual economic processes can bring rich new inputs to economic modeling.

9. The tradition of "validating" models by statistical analysis inadequately recognizes the feedback-loop structures of economic systems. Such feedback structures often introduce ambiguous and misleading results in statistical analysis procedures, in spite of internal checks for reliability of the statistical processes. Dependence on statistical methods has foreclosed the more diverse and demanding forms of validation by which a model is asked to generate a broad range of behavior patterns that can be compared with multiple aspects of actual behavior.

10. The tradition of concentrating on solvable mathematical equations, imposed in the past by the inability to carry out experiments with simulation models, has often restricted models to essentially linear form and has tended to exclude from consideration most of the nonlinear relationships from which important economic behavior arises.

For several years we in the Systems Dynamics Group at the M.I.T.

Alfred P. Sloan School of Management have been working to circumvent barriers imposed by traditional approaches to economic analysis. We believe a successful approach to economic behavior is emerging from

i) Starting, not with limited modification to equilibrium theory, but with an alternative conceptual structure that permits a full range of dynamic behavior;

ii) Adopting a philosophical perception of the scientific method that starts, not with *a priori* principles from which general behavior is deduced, but with broad and careful observation of the real world of economic and managerial practice to determine the structure, organization, physical restrictions, psychological attitudes, information sources, and policies from which actual economic behavior arises;

iii) Organizing a group effort large enough to unify the many aspects of economic structure and behavior and directed toward understanding the economy as a whole;

iv) Giving up simplicity when it stands in the way of reality;

v) Replacing optimization assumptions with representation of decisionmaking based on locally available information and on realistic decisionmaking constraints that impose uncertainty and exclude knowledge of the future except as it is imperfectly deduced from the past;

vi) Abandoning conventional economic prediction as the objective of economic modeling, and substituting the objective of developing alternative policies for improving the character of economic behavior;

vii) Developing the microstructure that generates macrobehavior;

viii) Realizing that no sharp boundary separates structure from parameters, and that both structure and parameters can be drawn directly from observation of real economic activity to form a comprehensive theory of behavior;

ix) Approaching validation as a multidimensional process in which a wide variety of testable assertions can be compared with many different kinds of characteristics of the real world; and

x) Creating an approach that places little restriction on incorporating nonlinear relationships.

System Dynamics National Model

A new approach to economic behavior has been developed to escape the limiting traditions of economics.[3] The effort is yielding the System Dynamics National Model. The National Model integrates major sectors of national activity into a simulation model for investigating how different parts of the socioeconomic system function, how they interact to produce behavior of the entire system, and how alternative policies might yield a more desirable future. The model is designed to simulate a wide range of socioeconomic behavior for evaluating both short-run and long-run consequences of national policy alternatives. Ultimately, the model is intended to show reasons for national social and economic behavior over approximately a 200-year period, from 1850 to 2050.

The National Model, when fully assembled, will consist of six basic sectors: production, finance, household, demography, labor, and government. These sectors describe the major determinants of production, consumption, investment, employment, prices, government policy, and other activities and indices of economic performance. The six sectors of the model are interconnected by flows of information, people, money, goods, services, and orders. In addition to conventional economic variables, the model contains psychological and technical variables such as expectations, level of technology, labor mobility, and social stress.

The National Model contains a range of internal structures spanning from short-term inventory-management and price-setting policies to medium-term capital-investment policies and long-term demographic and environmental forces. By encompassing a diversity of short-term and long-term forces, the National Model can deal with long-range issues of economic growth, resources, energy, population, and capital investment, as well as with shorter-term dynamics of business cycles and economic stabilization policies. The ability to combine long-term and short-term behavior is necessary for comprehensive policy analysis because of the way different modes of economic behavior can affect one another and the way symptoms of different simultaneous modes can be confused with one another.

The National Model treats all major aspects of the socioeconomic system as internal variables to be generated by interplay of mutual influences within the model structure. The model contains production sectors; labor and professional mobility between sectors; a demographic sector with births and deaths and with subdivision into age categories; commercial banking to make short-term loans; long-term commercial and mortgage lending; saving; a monetary authority with its controls over money and credit; government services; government fiscal operations; consumption sectors; and a foreign sector for trade and international payments.

A generalized production sector has been created with a structure comprehensive enough that it can be used, with separate selection of suitable parameters, for each of some fifteen or more producing sectors. Each sector reaches down in detail to about twelve factors of production, ordering and inventories for each factor of production, marginal productivities for each factor, balance sheet and profit and loss statement, output inventories, delivery delay to determine product availability, production planning, price setting, expectations, and borrowing.

The model is formulated for the new DYNAMO III compiler,[4] which handles arrays of equations and makes replication of subparts of the production and banking systems especially easy. For example, an equation in the ordering function need be written only once with two-dimensional subscripts to identify the full array of ordering functions for each factor in each sector.

By reaching from national monetary and fiscal policy down to ordering and accounting details within individual production sectors, the model makes a bridge between macroeconomic and microeconomic structures. Just as major behavior modes in the economy develop from deep within its structure, the model generates the same modes from interactions between elements of the microstructure represented in production, consumption, finance, and government.

Standard Production Sector. A standard production sector is being replicated to form a major part of the model. With appropriate parameter values, the standard production sector can be reproduced to represent sectors for a variety of goods and services—consumer durable goods, consumer soft goods, capital equipment, building construction, agriculture, food processing, resources, energy, services, transportation, secondary manufacturing, knowledge generation, self-provided family services, military operations, and government employment. Such generality focuses attention on the fundamental nature of production of goods and services and simplifies both construction and explanation of the model.

Within each production sector are inventories of some twelve factors of production—capital, labor, professionals, services, new technology, energy, buildings, land, water, transportation, and two kinds of materials. In addition, production is affected by length of work week for labor and length of work week for capital. A Cobb-Douglas production function is used to couple inventories of input factors to output production rate.

For each factor of production in each sector, an ordering function creates an order backlog for the factor in response to desired production rate, desired factor intensity, marginal productivity of the factor, price of the product, price of the factor, growth expectations, product inventory and backlog, profitability, interest rate, financial pressures, and delivery delay of the factor. Ordering functions are far more important than production functions in determining dynamic behavior of production sectors and of the entire model. Ordering functions are policy statements that govern procurement of factors of production and constitute major linkages between sectors. The standard ordering function is far more comprehensive in its structure than the form of investment function that has typically been used in econometric models.

The structure of a standard production sector is essentially the structure of a single firm in the economy. The sector is an aggregation of similar firms. As with a firm, the sector has an accounting subsector that pays for each factor of production, generates accounts receivable and payable, maintains balance-sheet variables, computes profitability, saves, and borrows money. The structure can generate the full range of behavior that arises from interactions between physical variables and money and information variables. A model with such detail communicates directly with people in the real system, where a wealth of information is available for establishing needed parameter values.

A production sector generates product price in accordance with conditions within the sector and between the sector and its customers. For testing governmental control of prices and wages, coefficients can be set to inhibit price changes. A production sector distributes output among its customer sectors. Market clearing, or the balance between supply and demand, is struck not by price alone but also by delivery delay, which reflects availability, rationing, and allocation.

Labor and Professional Mobility. People in production sectors are divided into two categories—labor and professional. For each category, a mobility network defines channels of movement between sectors in response to differentials in wages, availability, and need.

Each mobility network has a star shape with each point ending at a production sector and terminated in a level representing the number of people working in the sector. At the center of the star is a general nonemployed pool, which is the central node for movement of people between sectors. Between the central general nonemployed pool and each sector is a "captive" nonemployed level of people who are not employed but who still consider themselves part of the sector. They are people searching for better work within their sector or on temporary layoff but expecting to be rehired. In a period of rising demand for labor, those in a captive nonemployed level can be rehired quickly, but longer delays are associated with drawing people from other sectors by way of the general nonemployed pool.

The two-tier structure for nonemployed persons simultaneously makes possible rapid responses in layoff and rehiring that occur during a business cycle, and slower responses in movement between sectors that occur as internal balance of an economy shifts.

Demographic Sector. The demographic sector will generate population changes in the model by representing births, deaths, immigration, and aging. Age categories divide people into their different roles from childhood through retirement. The demographic sector divides people between labor and professional streams in response to wages, salaries, demands of productive sectors, capacity of the educational system, and family background.

The demographic sector, by generating a changing age structure of population, will permit examining the stability of Social Security and retirement plans as population growth slows and average age increases.

Household Sectors. The household sectors can be distinguished by economic category—labor, professional, unemployed, retired, and welfare. Each household sector receives income, saves, borrows, purchases a variety of goods and services, and hold assets. Consumption demands respond to price, availability of inputs, and marginal utilities of various goods and services at different levels of income. The household sectors also determine work force participation—the fraction of the population actively seeking work—in response to historical tradition, demand for labor, and standard of living.

The structure of a household sector will be almost identical to the structure of a production sector. A production sector produces goods or services. A household sector produces consumption utility. Both use multiple factor inputs. Both receive money and pay for input factors.

Financial Sector. The financial sector of the model is divided into five parts—commercial banking, long-term business loans, mortgage lending, saving, and the monetary authority. The financial sector determines interest rates on savings, loans, and bonds. It buys and sells bonds, makes long-term and short-term loans to businesses and households, and creates intangible variables (i.e., confidence) in the banking system. The financial sector manages exchanges between money, bonds, deposits, and loans. It monitors debt levels and borrowing capabilities of each business and household sector.

The monetary authority (Federal Reserve System) controls discount rate, open-market bond transactions, and required reserve ratios. In doing so, the monetary authority responds to owned and borrowed reserves of banks, demand deposits, inflation rate, unemployment, and interest rates.

Government Sector. The government sector of the National Model will generate government services, tax rates, government expenditures, transfer payments, and sales of government bonds to finance the national debt. It will manage fiscal policy and government debt. Government services will be generated by purchasing through a standard production sector whose inputs are labor, capital, buildings, energy, and other factors of production, and whose output is government services. An additional replication of the standard production sector may be used to represent military procurement.

Foreign-Trade Sector. The National Model will initially simulate behavior of a single domestic economy. Once the model is developed, parts of it can be replicated to represent foreign manufacturing sectors and foreign resource sectors. Such foreign sectors will connect to domestic assets, energy, resources, and other goods and services. The foreign-trade sector will thus consist of one or more foreign producers and a set of coupling equations linking the foreign and domestic economies. The coupling equations of the foreign-trade sector will generate exchange rates, balance of payments, and flows of imports and exports.

Behavior of the National Model

The National Model is now partly assembled. It already exhibits behavior much like that of the real economy.[5]

In a complex economic structure, many different dynamic modes of fluctuating activity can exist simultaneously. Much puzzling economic behavior arises from superposition of multiple modes. If separate identities of different modes are not recognized, inappropriate or counterproductive policies may be adopted. A model that generates all the modes can reveal the sources of various symptoms and can help in relating each to relevant policy changes.

Assemblies of the National Model in various configurations have included sectors for goods, capital, and energy. The sectors have been operated with pricing and accounting and with labor mobility between sectors. An early simplified assembly will be used here to illustrate behavior that typically emerges.

Figure 6.1 shows a much-simplified diagram of a production sector. For behavior discussed in this paper, financial and pricing parts of production sectors are not active. The labor mobility network is not connected to restrict labor movement, so labor is freely available to a sector on demand. The focus in this limited discussion is on physical changes in inventory and backlog of output, and in stocks of input factors to production. Figure 6.1 shows a very simplified output section of a production sector and two abbreviated ordering functions, one for capital equipment and one for labor.

In the output section of Figure 6.1, orders enter a backlog, and the relationship between backlog and inventory determines ability of the sector to ship product (delivery delay). Inventory is increased by production and decreased by shipments. Generated information includes the conditions of inventory, backlog, shipments, and marginal productivities of factors of production. In the two ordering functions for capital and labor in the figure, ordering of either factor of production is based on multiple inputs. Shown here, symbolically, are information streams from sector output, inventory of factor, and backlog of unfilled orders

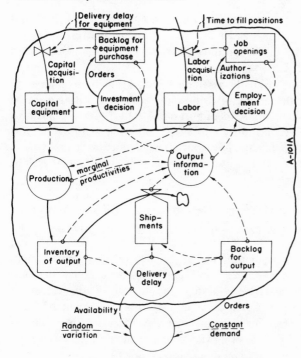

Figure 6.1. Major components of a production sector

for factor. In addition, an ordering function in the actual model uses financial variables, changing availabilities of factors, expectations, and prices.

The structure of a production sector and the interconnecting relationships between sectors are complex enough to cause many different modes of dynamic behavior. In other words, several different tendencies toward cyclic behavior originate from the interactions of inventories, production rate, acquisition of labor and capital, and the supply interconnections between different sectors. We find that interactions within and between typical production sectors can simultaneously generate the major cyclic modes of economic behavior discussed in the literature —business cycles of a 3–7-year period, Kuznets cycles of a 15–25-year period, and Kondratieff cycles of a 45–60-year period. [6]

The several modes of behavior discussed here arise internally within the production sectors themselves and are not induced by broader aspects of the economy, such as changes in consumer income, prices, or interest rates. To observe the inherent characteristics of first one production sector and then a combination of two, the tests described here use a constant demand for sector output modulated by availability of the sector output product. In the short run, as delivery delay increases, the demand generator orders farther ahead in anticipation of need and causes order backlog to arise. In the longer run, as delivery delay increases, unavailability of the product discourages demand and causes a decrease in orders.

The behavior of the partially assembled model will be examined in three stages: first with one sector using only labor as a variable factor of production, in which simple configuration we find that the business cycle is generated; second with one sector ordering both labor and capital, in which the Kuznets cycle appears; and third with two sectors varying both labor and capital, in which the Kondratieff cycle arises out of capital-sector behavior.

The Business Cycle. Business cycles are well-known short-term fluctuations of business activity. Variation appears in production rates and employment, with peaks of activity separated by some three to seven years. Business cycles lie within the experience of most persons and dominate attention in the press and in government policy debates. Figure 6.2 shows the behavior of a single production sector—consumer durables—when capital equipment is held constant and production rate is changed only by variations of employment. A small monthly randomness is superimposed on the otherwise constant demand to induce the sector to respond according to its inherent dynamic periodicities.

In Figure 6.2, the production sector exhibits a sequence of fluctuations typical of normal business cycles. Intervals between peaks vary around five years. Relative timing of backlog, production rate (as shown by labor), and inventory are typical of actual industrial behavior. Backlog tends to peak before production (labor), and production tends to peak

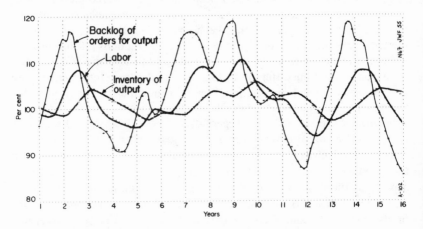

Figure 6.2. Business-cycle fluctuation appearing in labor, inventory, and backlog for a single production sector

before inventory. As in real business cycles, successive peaks show different shapes and spacing.

The significance of the model behind Figure 6.2 lies in its generation of business cycles without variation in consumer income or capital investment. Prices are not changing, demand is constant on the average, money and interest rates are not active, and capital investment is not involved. The cyclic fluctuation in this figure has the major characteristics of business cycles and arises from interaction among backlog, inventory, production, and employment. This is not to suggest that business cycles operate without influencing other activities in the economy. But Figure 6.2 does raise the question of whether changes in consumer income, investment, and monetary decisions are central to generation and control of business cycles or are merely induced by variation arising from employment and inventories.

Fluctuating, business-cycle-like behavior in Figure 6.2 arises from those policies that control employment in response to inventories and backlogs. Such production-control policies tend to amplify disturbances and to convert short-term randomness into an irregular wave that reflects the natural oscillatory character of the system structure.

The reason for amplification and overshoot of employment and production can be seen by tracing an increase in demand through the structure of Figure 6.1. Assume that a constant demand has existed for consumer goods and then that demand suddenly increases slightly. The first consequence is that orders, backlog for output, and shipments all increase, while inventory of output is reduced. Increase in backlog and depletion of inventory continue until management has confidence that the new higher level of business is not an aberration, and until additional factors of production (labor in this example) can be acquired to increase production. Between the time demand increases and the time production increases to equal the new demand, three things occur. First, backlog for output increases to an undesirably high level; second, the inventory of output is depleted below its initial desired level; and third, because demand is now higher, desired inventory (not shown in Figure 6.2) also increases. As a consequence, when production has risen to equal demand, the system is out of equilibrium. Backlog for output is too high, and inventory is too low. With production equal to demand, the new state of disequilibrium could be sustained but cannot be brought back into balance. Production must be pushed higher than the new demand to reduce backlog for output, and to increase inventory, not only back to the old value of inventory but up to the new, higher level of inventory that is appropriate to the new, higher rate of sales. But in further efforts to seek a new balance, when inventory and backlog reach the desired levels, production is apt to be too high, so that inventory continues to rise and further corrections are necessary.

It is from such stock depletions and recoveries that fluctuating modes of economic behavior arise. Disturbances propagate through the system by changing a stock from a desired level, setting up a discrepancy between actual and desired conditions, activating a policy to start a corrective sequence, and progressively working through a cascade of adjustment stages. Time lags in the system delay actions and eventually induce corrections greater than the initiating disturbance.

This preliminary examination of industrial structure suggests that business cycles primarily involve inventories and employment. Capital investment, although it will show fluctuation induced by business cycles, need not be a participant in creating short-term business cycles. Furthermore, business cycles can exist without inputs from money supply, interest rates, or changes in consumer income. Therefore, monetary policy aimed at diminishing business cycles by affecting investment may be coupled only very loosely to primary causes of business-cycle fluctuation. Therefore, monetary policy is likely to provide little leverage for influencing business-cycle behavior.

Although the behavior just described for a production sector was without pricing, accounting, or the labor mobility network, these have all been added in more recent assemblies and do not importantly alter the kind of behavior shown in Figure 6.2.

The Kuznets Cycle. The Kuznets cycle is much less well-known than the business cycle. It exists as a statistical observation that many time series in the economy seem to fluctuate with a periodicity of some 15–25 years. The cause of the Kuznets cycle has been a subject of debate. Other cyclic modes in the economy are of sufficient magnitude to mask the Kuznets cycle from popular awareness.

When realistic parameters for procurement of capital equipment are inserted in a simulation model of an industrial sector, dynamic behavior suggests that investment is primarily a part of the Kuznets cycle, not of the short-term business cycle. Processes of investment are too slow to interact effectively in a cycle of only a few years duration.[7] Conservatism and therefore delay in committing capital funds, the long planning time for new plant and machinery, substantial delays in procuring new physical assets, and the 10–60-year life of equipment and buildings all describe managerial and physical relationships suitable for creating fluctuations of 15–25-year periodicity. Furthermore, the basic processes of production, procurement, and accumulation of capital plant are capable of creating the intermediate cycle without changes in monetary policy, interest rates, or consumption.[8]

Figure 6.3 shows the behavior of the structure in Figure 6.1 when both capital equipment and labor are varied as factors of production. Capital equipment differs from labor in having longer times for planning

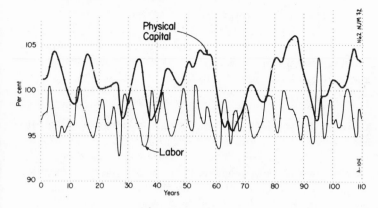

Figure 6.3. Kuznets and business cycles exhibited by capital and labor, respectively, as factors of production

and procurement, and in having a depreciation time much longer than the average length of employment of labor. As before, the sector is supplying to a constant demand that is influenced by availability of the product and perturbed by a very short-term random disturbance. Two curves are shown in Figure 6.3, one for labor as a factor of production, the other for the stock of physical capital as a factor of production. The labor curve in this figure again exhibits a periodicity typical of business cycles; it appears more compressed here than in Figure 6.2 because of the changed time scale. The curve in Figure 6.3 for physical capital in use in the sector also shows fluctuating behavior, but intervals between peaks are clearly longer than those for labor.

Adding procurement of capital equipment produces an additional periodicity of a 15–25-year duration. In Figure 6.3 capital-equipment procurement in a single production sector shows a periodicity typical of that discussed in the literature for Kuznets cycles. In this example there is no active capital-producing sector, so capital is assumed to be available at a constant typical procurement delay. Both the business-cycle-like mode and the Kuznets-cycle-like mode coexist simultaneously. The two modes of behavior arise from different management policies followed for labor and capital in adjusting production to an uncertain demand.

To the extent that interest rates affect investment, they should relate to Kuznets cycles more than to business cycles. But many businessmen would agree that demand, availability, existing plant, and shortage of labor have, over the last 30 years, been much more influential in invest-ment decisions than have interest rates. If interest-rate fluctuations are not necessary for creating Kuznets cycles, and if physical variables have more influence, one is left with the possibility that monetary policy may be inadequate for influencing the capital investment (Kuznets) cycle.

Later model assemblies incorporating labor mobility, pricing, and accounting show behavior very similar to that in Figure 6.3. The implication emerges that physical variables reflecting orders, employment, inventories, and capital equipment, as well as psychological factors, are comparable in importance to price and money in determining economic activity.

The Kondratieff Cycle. The Kondratieff cycle (also known as the "long wave") was forcefully presented in the literature by Nikolai Kondratieff in the 1920s.[9] Kondratieff was a Russian economist who made extensive studies of long-term behavior of Western capitalist economies. His statistical analyses of economic activity showed that many variables in Western economies had fluctuated with peaks about 45–60 years apart. Such peaks of economic activity have been placed around 1810, 1860, and 1920. Kondratieff believed that long cycles are caused by internal structural dynamics of economic systems, but he did not propose a sharply defined set of mechanisms. Most other economists acknowledged that long-term fluctuation had occurred, but that it was caused by events external to pure economics, such as gold discoveries, wars, major technical innovations, and fluctuations in population growth.

Kondratieff cycles are characterized by peaks in economic activity separated by long valleys of stagnation. Such cycles have not been taken very seriously because of lack of a convincing theory of how such long-term disturbances could be caused. After the peak in economic activity around 1920, the Great Depression of the 1930s represented a typical low point in such a cycle. Now, some 50 years after the preceding peak, economic activity has again risen to a high level, but with many signs of faltering. The question arises, Is the Kondratieff wave of underlying structural origin, and does it have significance for current policy?

Recent computer simulations using partial assemblies of the System Dynamics National Model suggest that a long-period cyclic behavior can arise from the physical structure connecting consumer goods sectors and the capital sectors. A sufficient cause for a 50-year fluctuation lies in movement of people between sectors, the long time-span to change production capacity of capital sectors, the way capital sectors provide their own input capital as a factor of production, the need to develop excess capacity to catch up with deferred demand, and the psychological and speculative forces of expectations, which can cause overexpansion in capital sectors.

Figure 6.4 shows two interconnected production sectors of the National Model. One sector has parameters (for inventories and for time required to change production) typical of a consumer durables sector. Parameters in the other sector are typical of those involved in producing capital equipment. The consumer durables sector orders capital equipment

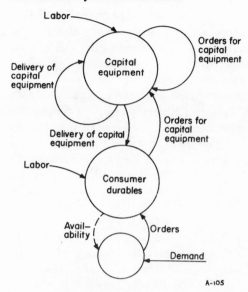

Figure 6.4. A two-sector structure with consumer durables and capital equipment

from the capital equipment sector and has labor freely available. (The labor mobility network for interconnecting labor flows between sectors is not active.) The capital equipment sector also has labor freely available but must order its capital equipment as a factor of production from its own output. An increase in demand for consumer durables would cause the consumer sector to try to increase both of its factors of production. The consumer sector can obtain labor, but when it wants more capital equipment, the capital sector must first expand. But if the capital sector is to expand in a balanced manner, it needs both labor and capital as inputs. A "bootstrap" operation is involved in which the capital sector must withhold output from its customer (the consumer sector) so that it can expand first in order, later, to meet the needs of the consumer sector. Such a bootstrap interrelationship, wherein a sector supplies a factor for its own growth, can create a mode of behavior that does not exist unless the sector is connected in a reentrant way from its output back to its own input.

Bootstrap structures, as when a capital sector must produce capital equipment for itself in order to expand, are common in the economy. Bootstrap structures are of great dynamic importance because they tend to lengthen periods of fluctuation that would otherwise occur, and tend to make those fluctuations more unstable. Another example of a boot-strap structure is found in production of beef. Suppose consumers buy more meat at grocery stores. Inventories decline and prices are pushed up. As inventory depletion and increased price propagate backward along the supply chain through wholesalers, packers, and cattle feeders, they become a signal to cattle ranches to grow more cattle. But how are more cattle produced? Breeding herds must be expanded. To do so, heifers that would otherwise have gone to market for beef must be kept to expand breeding herds. Expansion of production capacity initially diverts beef from the market. Thus, the first response to a demand for more beef is to supply less. Such short-term curtailment of supply in response to an increase in price is just the opposite of that implied by a simple price-supply curve. The reverse reaction drives prices still higher until breeding herds have been expanded. The rise in price is prolonged, herds are overexpanded, and in time, the market is flooded with beef as expansion of herds turns into liquidation and prices collapse. The 14-year cattle price cycle is created out of the bootstrap supply structure, managerial responses to price, and biological delays created by a 9-month gestation period and a two-year maturation delay.[10] The longer delays in procurement and the longer lifetime of capital plant can produce still longer cyclic fluctuations in industrial activity.

Figure 6.5 is taken from a computer simulation using the structure shown in Figure 6.4, in which demand is increased from equilibrium by a small amount and is then held constant. In Figure 6.5 the two-sector industrial structure shows a long, sustained fluctuation in the capital sector of some 50 years' duration. Economic behavior in the capital sector is similar to the classical description of a Kondratieff wave, in which steep peaks in economic activity are separated by broad valleys of depression.

The mode of fluctuation in Figure 6.5 is strongly determined within the model structure and is unstable for small variations and bound by

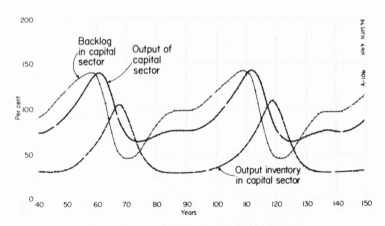

Figure 6.5. A Kondratieff cycle appearing in the capital sector

nonlinearities for large amplitude. Such an unstable mode grows quickly from any triggering disturbance and tends to sustain itself. Unstable modes are especially persistent and not easily influenced unless their nature is well enough understood to discover policies that have strong leverage.

More recent model assemblies show that added structure, such as putting in the labor mobility network, tends to accentuate the unstable long-wave mode. One should expect also that the long wave will be strengthened by a deeper structure of production sectors, as when building construction and energy sectors are added to supply the capital sector, that in turn must supply capital to the building construction and energy sectors. The long lag in changing psychological attitudes, the variable propensity to take risks, and efforts to sustain the upward growth phase by monetary expansion are all expected, when added to the model, to accentuate fluctuation in the long-wave mode. Preliminary tests with more complete structures suggest that the household (consumption) sectors, the banking system, and the Federal Reserve System all contribute to increasing the Kondratieff cycle.

The dynamics of the long wave can be seen by recalling behavior of industrial economies since 1945. After the Great Depression and World War II, every aspect of capital plant was inadequate. Consumer durables, housing, office buildings, factories, transportation systems, and schools were old and inadequate. To rebuild depleted capital stock in a short time, such as 20 years, construction of housing and equipment rose to a rate higher than would be needed in the long run for replacing physical depreciation of capital plant. But when adequate capital plant had been created—a time that may have occurred in the 1960s—tremendous forces persisted to sustain capital accumulation. Labor unions wanted to continue construction, companies in the capital sectors sold their output more aggressively and extended more credit, banks wanted to continue lending on new capital plant, and the Federal Reserve increased money supply and credit in the belief that it could continue to sustain economic growth. The result has been an economic unbalancing, with too much capital expansion and too much debt. Eventually, as capital plant becomes more and more excessive, momentum must falter. It is probable that enough capital plant now exists to sustain consumption output for one or two decades with little new additional investment. I believe excess capital plant explains why capital expenditure was weak in the 1976 recovery. The need for capital plant has become far less than it was 20 years ago.

In more detail, the sequences in the long-wave mode, starting from depression years at the bottom of a cycle, seem to be as follows: slow growth of capital sectors of the economy; gradual decay of the entire capital plant of the economy below the amount required, while capital sectors are unable to supply even replacement needs; initial recirculation of output of capital sectors to their own inputs; progressive increase in wages and development of a labor shortage in consumer sectors that encourage capital-intensive production and still higher demands for capital equipment; overexpansion of capital sectors to a capacity greater than required for replacement in order to catch up on deferred needs; excess accumulation of physical capital by consumers (housing and durables) and by durable manufacturers (plant and equipment); developing failure of capital equipment users to absorb the output of overexpanded capital sectors; sudden appearance of unemployment in capital sectors; relative reduction of labor cost compared to capital, which favors a shift to labor-intensive production and further diminishes the need for new plant; rapid collapse of capital sectors in the face of demand below the long-term average needed by the economy; and slow decline of excess capital stock in all sectors through physical depreciation.

Present economic symptoms are consistent with the top of a Kondratieff wave, if the top is a time of excess capital accumulation. New tankers have been leaving shipyards and going directly to anchorage. Airlines have excess seats and are reducing their fares. For the first time since the late 1920s, many cities have an excess of office space. The U.S. interstate highway system is nearly complete, and another is not needed soon. The financial plight of real-estate investment trusts suggests that we have more commercial space and housing in many places than the economy can support. Most municipalities have built sufficient schools and hospitals.

If we are indeed in a condition of excess capital stock both at industrial and at consumer levels, the implications for business and economic policy are substantial. Under conditions of excess capital plant, increasing money supply will give little incentive for purchasing physical capital. Instead, more money may only feed speculative and inflationary forces.

Model assemblies more recent and comprehensive than those described in this paper suggest that fiscal and monetary policy may be implicated in accentuating Kondratieff-cycle fluctuation. In Figures 6.4 and 6.5 the structure does not include pricing, money flow, or accounting in the production sectors. Without the money-flow subsystem, ordering of factors of production is not restrained by financial considerations. Absence of a liquidity restraint on ordering implicitly means that credit is readily available. When accounting has been added but the banking system has not, the production sector cannot borrow, and falling liquidity restricts ordering of capital plant. Under such circumstances the long-wave mode is reduced in strength. Inactivating the restraint on ordering imposed by low liquidity accentuates the long wave. The tentative interpretation suggests that credit extended from the Federal Reserve through the banking system contributes to overexpansion of capital plant and to creation of the long-wave mode. The National Model is now at a stage where each step in assembly permits examination of additional economic issues.

Life Cycle of Growth. After two centuries of relatively sustained and vigorous growth, the environmental capacity of the United States is becoming heavily stressed. Growth in population, in consumption, in energy usage, in pollution generation, and in the demand for water are triggering strong counterpressures from nature. The process of growing to fill geographic capacity, and eventually being restrained by that capacity, produces the life cycle of growth.

The life cycle of economic growth refers to the S-shaped curve in Figure 6.6. The life cycle can be divided into three phases. First is the period when exponential growth is not inhibited by proximity to geographical limits. Second is the transition region where environmental limits begin to exert enough influence to slow the forces of growth. Third is progression into equilibrium or decline, depending on how the country has managed its balance between population and environmental capacity.

The life cycle of growth can be modeled independently from other dynamic modes in an economy.[11] However, symptoms arising from the life cycle are easily confused with those of long-wave and even business-cycle behavior. It seems important to bring the life cycle of growth into the context of the other modes of economic behavior so that possible

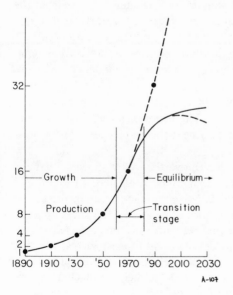

Figure 6.6. Life cycle of economic growth

interactions between them can be studied. The National Model will have structures needed to generate the life cycle of growth. Land is one limited factor of production and will be allocated from a fixed supply. Depletable resources will be tallied to record total extraction of energy and minerals up to any point in a model run so that costs of extraction can increase as more diffuse sources must be exploited. Pollution will be generated and will require an allocation of capital plant for its control. By modeling effects of stress on the environment, we can study gradual shifts in economic costs and constraints and their effects.

A Simulation Model as a Theory

A system dynamics simulation model represents structures governing flows of goods, people, money, and information. A model states observed policies for managing internal interactions. Such a model will respond to noise disturbances by exhibiting modes of behavior inherent in the structure of the model. A model creates behavior that results from its structure. The structure of a model constitutes a definitive theory of causation for the behavior that the model generates.

Unlike a descriptive theory, a system dynamics simulation model is internally consistent. There is no doubt that its structure and policies produce its behavior. The practical question is how well the model, in all its manifestations, agrees with a real-life system that the model is intended to represent.

Multiple tests of validity for a system dynamics model arise from the many ways in which such a model can be compared with the real world. The structure and parameters of a model are subject to verification by those who know the real-life structures and policies. As an entirely separate class of verification procedures, behavior of the model can be compared to real-world behavior.

A system dynamics model may confirm and make more plausible a descriptive theory that already exists. The behavior shown in Figure 6.2 lends support to the inventory-employment theory of causation of business cycles.

A model can cast doubt on a descriptive theory by showing that the theory leads to behavior other than that which is alleged. In Figure 6.3 the curve for physical capital tends to contradict those theories that make capital investment a necessary part of generating business cycles.

A model often reveals behavior that was unknown or neglected in real life but, when explained by the model, is found to exist in real life. My own experience with the Kondratieff wave fell into this class. The long-wave literature was unfamiliar to me, and has been neglected in economics. The production sectors of the model were constructed and interconnected in accordance with an understanding of how corresponding industrial activities necessarily function in real life. Note especially the fact in Figure 6.4 that the capital equipment sector must itself use capital equipment and must be connected from its output back to its own input. We found that the structure in Figure 6.4 produced an unexpected, unstable, bounded-by-nonlinearity, 45–60-year fluctuation. Under such circumstances, one first reviews the model structure to see if the unexpected behavior arises from an oversight in model formulation. Often, as in this case, the structure withstands the examination, and the behavior appears plausible when its cause within the model is understood. One then asks if the same behavior could be happening in the real world. At that point in the investigation, we examined the literature on the Kondratieff cycle. The literature on the Kondratieff cycle is contradictory and confused, yet, even at this early stage, the National Model does much to unify the presumed inconsistencies in the Kondratieff-cycle debate.[12]

Figure 6.7 is from a model simulation using the structure of Figure 6.4. Previously, in Figure 6.5, the exogenous input demand to the consumer-durables sector was noise-free and constant. In Figure 6.7 the demand to the consumer sector has a uniformly rising slope and has imposed on it sixteen small, random variations per year.

Figure 6.7 shows 200 years of simulated behavior for the output production rate of the capital sector. All behavior is internally generated within the model. No time-series data has gone into either construction or operation of the model. Four major peaks appear, at 18 years, 72 years, 126–42 years, and 180 years. On the major fluctuations are superimposed traces of business-cycle and Kuznets-cycle modes. One notes a characteristic shape in which output in the capital sector falls abruptly

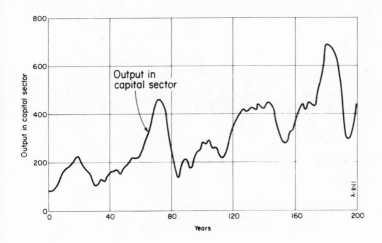

Figure 6.7. Four model-generated Kondratieff cycles

from a major peak, then rises gradually to the next peak with minor oscillations over a time span of some 30 years.

The fluctuation in Figure 6.7 is in units of physical output of the capital sector. On the other hand, several writers have argued that the long wave does not involve real variables in the economy but is only a price and interest-rate phenomenon. What does the model suggest to throw light on the debate? The partly assembled National Model suggests that the long wave is generated by rise and decline of capital-producing sectors and that the effect might be most pronounced in those sectors producing physical capital with longest life. Such might be commercial building construction.

As a result of identifying from model behavior the kind of confirming information we needed to seek, we assembled data for commercial construction, as shown in Figure 6.8. The curve is commercial construction in constant dollars on a per capita basis. The real behavior graphed in Figure 6.8 shows substantial similarity to any of the three interpeak patterns of simulated data shown in Figure 6.7. There is a steep drop from the peak in 1928, a gradual fluctuating climb for 45 years, and another sharp drop starting from the peak of 1973.

Model construction, improvement, and confirmation require multiple comparisons between model structure and real structure and between the resulting model and real behaviors. Real-life behavior suggests ways

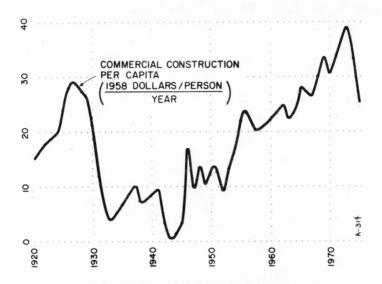

Sources: Statistical Abstract of the United States, 1976;
Historical Statistics of the United States

Figure 6.8. One real-life Kondratieff cycle

to evaluate and question the model. Conversely, the model exhibits behavior that raises new questions and interpretations about what we see in the real world.

Comment

The United States now struggles through a period of growing economic instability. Symptoms of social and economic stress have appeared in such forms as the deepest recession since World War II and in simultaneous inflation and unemployment. Balance of trade and value of the dollar are moving in unfavorable directions. Such economic crosscurrents create political confusion and public disenchantment with national leadership. In troublesome times, causes and remedies are urgently sought. But the economic system is complex; conflicting theories abound; and a desperate search for simple solutions can easily lead to wrong answers.

The conventional search for answers has been concentrated on the most apparent characteristic of national economies—the short-term business cycle. Business cycles are familiar; most people have experienced several; and changes during the business cycle occur fast enough to be readily observed. Consequently, economic research has neglected longer-term economic behavior. But familiarity need not correspond to importance.

As a consequence of overemphasis on business cycles, almost all variations in economic behavior have been attributed to business cycles. The Great Depression of the 1930s is alleged by many to have been just an unusually severe business-cycle recession. Milder recessions since 1945 have been attributed to policies aimed at stabilizing the business cycle. The recent downturn of economic activity has been described as an accentuated business cycle that could have been avoided by wiser countercyclical policies. The public has been promised that present high unemployment can be relieved by expansive fiscal and monetary actions recommended on the basis of business-cycle theory. But all of these assertions may be incorrect. If so, it is because the business cycle is but one aspect, and probably the least important aspect, of present economic turbulence.

Using the long wave and the life cycle of growth as perspectives beyond that provided by the business cycle, the present social and economic environment takes on new meaning.

Monetary Control of Business Cycles. Following World War II, economists began to believe business cycles had been suppressed by skillful management of the money supply. But the evidence was probably misinterpreted. During the rising phase of an economic long wave, capital plant is inadequate, demand presses against supply, capital shortage suppresses the tops of the business cycles, and cyclic corrections in inventories and employment are minor. The rising strength of the long wave can distort the apparent business cycle to produce weak recessions and strong recoveries. Mild business cycles from 1945 to 1970 probably were a natural consequence of how the long wave and the business cycle interact. Nevertheless, in each minor recession, monetary adjustments were made and a business upturn followed. But the monetary actions and economic recovery may only have been coincidental. Business would have had a strong and quick recovery anyway from the buoyancy caused by the underlying wave of capital accumulation. The situation may have been like the ancient Chinese belief in firecrackers as a means to drive away eclipses of the moon. Threat of recession appeared; expansive monetary action was taken; strong recovery would have occurred by itself and did; monetary policy was mistakenly given the credit.

High Unemployment. Present unusual levels of unemployment probably arise more from the long wave than from the business cycle. Unemployment seems most severe in construction and those industries closely associated with capital investment. If so, the problem is not temporary, nor should it be treated by temporary measures. The signals suggest a need for a major shift of people from capital goods and finance probably into consumer products and agriculture. But government-created job programs, motivated by a belief that unemployment is temporary, may trap a generation of people as wards of the government and isolate them from effective participation in the economy. Unless the true nature of economic behavior is perceived, inappropriate and counterproductive actions are likely to be adopted.

Stimulation of National Economies. Conventional wisdom and political expediency combine to exert pressure to increase financial credit when economies falter. Behind such pressures for expansive monetary action lie the beliefs that more capital construction will revive the economy and that more money will induce more capital expenditure. But such ideas, if ever valid, applied to a time of shortage in physical capital, a phase in which we are not now operating. More freely available credit has little leverage to increase investment when equipment and floor space stand idle.

Inflation. But increasing money supply can have an effect. Even if it does not reduce unemployment, it can produce inflation. The idea that a trade-off exists between inflation and unemployment is a hypothesis taken from the context of the short-term business cycle. When transported into the context of the long wave, increasing money supply probably generates inflation to accompany the unemployment, without reducing unemployment. It seems likely that an erroneous belief in a trade-off between inflation and unemployment lies behind policies that are producing inflation to accompany the unemployment. Solutions to the present kind of unemployment probably require an entirely different policy approach.

Bank Vulnerability. Banking is caught in pressures created by peaking of the long wave. Early in the upswing, as in the 1950s, loans were made for high return-on-investment purposes, and there was limited availability of credit-restrained, low-quality loans. As the need for plant and equipment was met, return on investment declined; there were fewer opportunities for secure, high-yielding loans; money supply increased; and loans were made for purposes that did not generate a reliable capacity to pay back debt. In the extreme case, loans were channeled for support of current consumption, as in consumer credit, municipal expenses, and support of social welfare programs in underdeveloped countries. Measures of banking strength have declined because financial institutions have persisted in lending as aggressively in the last part of the long-wave upswing as they had safely been able to do at the beginning of the upturn.

Energy Policy. Confusion over energy policy reflects not only environmental pressures from the life cycle of growth but also technological discontinuities arising from the long wave. Each major upswing of the long wave has had its unique technology, not because changes in technology cause the wave, but because the long wave bunches technological changes. In energy we have had the wood-burning cycle, the coal-burning cycle, and the oil-burning cycle. Each of these has reached a crest, fallen to minor usage, and been replaced by a new energy source and new technology. We are near the end of the oil cycle.

The peak of the next energy technology is probably some 50 years ahead. Our problem today is to look that far ahead and know what to do now. Traditionally the dilemma of exhaustion of a technological era has been solved by struggling through a major depression, letting the old technology wear out, and waiting until sporadic development and experimentation have demonstrated the nature of the road up the next wave of capital investment. If we do not want to go through that traditional process of faltering and recovering, we must succeed in looking across the next 50-year valley, perceive the new technology of the future, and begin to build now. That is far different from the usual industrial practice of building directly on current technology. Ordinarily, existing organizations cannot make such radical changes. Instead, they decline and are replaced by new institutions geared to a changing future.

The present failure to establish an effective energy policy arises from trying to build on a past that cannot survive, while looking no more than a decade or two into the future—where only the decline of the present system is clearly visible. We must think farther into the future in terms of a society with energy of a different kind, built around a new infrastructure of technical support systems and social relationships.

Capital versus Labor. Present industrial enterprises have developed over three decades of sustained emphasis on capital-intensive production that replaced people by machinery. But to believe such capital-intensive emphasis will continue is to have a short view of history. The upswing phase in the long wave is characterized by capital-intensive production. While capital sectors are growing, they attract labor from consumer sectors, produce a labor shortage, and raise wages. Labor shortage and higher wages create incentives for still more capital plant, and the capital sectors grow even faster.

But in time capital needs are met, even overfilled. Excess capital plant develops in consumer sectors, and labor becomes available from decline in capital sectors. After a peak of the long wave, production in consumer sectors can be increased more efficiently by adding labor to existing plant rather than by adding capital. Emphasis shifts to more labor-intensive production. The shift from adding capital to adding labor seems to be happening now in some industries.

Productivity. Much concern is currently expressed because labor productivity is not rising as rapidly as in the past. Productivity has usually risen at the beginning of a business-cycle recovery, but it has not shown much improvement in the present recovery. The answer may lie in the long wave. During the 1950s and 1960s, productivity rose because capital plant was inadequate and added capital increased productivity. But now it is probable that capital needs are mostly satisfied, and in only a few places will more capital plant increase productivity. At the same time, as capacity exceeds demand, the social incentives for more output are weakened. Deliveries are good, backlogs are low, pressure to produce is moderate, and slow production seems desirable to workers to spread work into the future and to protect jobs. Circumstances at the top of the long wave are very different from those in the early phase of an upswing.

An industrial economy is a complex, highly interconnected system. The aggregate behavior of an economy arises from interactions between many subsectors. People working at the many operating positions in companies and governmental institutions have a wealth of knowledge about the structure and policies that govern local action. But few realize how completely knowledge about the parts explains the whole. Within the information available from practical working people lies the key to macroeconomic behavior. But the human mind—using debate, simple diagrams, and deductive logic—is not suited to perceiving the dynamic consequences of the readily available knowledge about the microstructure. Neither can econometric modeling synthesize information about microstructure to explain macrobehavior, because of the degree to which econometric modeling is wedded to macroeconomic theory rather than to microstructure, to statistical correlation rather than to causal relationships, to derivation of parameters from time-series data rather than to observation of parameters in the real operating world, and to internal logical procedures for validation rather than to multiple channels of comparison between a model and the actual economic system.

Only through a comprehensive simulation model can we unify knowledge of the pieces with behavior of the whole. With a simulation model, causal relationships can be traced from policies to their resulting behavior. Because the effect of a policy on both near-term and long-term behavior can be determined with a simulation model, a simulation model becomes a tool for choosing between policy alternatives on the basis of relative effects to be caused within the socioeconomic system.

The Systems Dynamics National Model has now reached a stage of assembly where it is being used and is shedding new light on reasons for puzzling economic behavior. The model is explaining failures of past policies. It is beginning to indicate the direction of more effective policies. Continued assembly of the model will rapidly extend its capacity to explain economic behavior and to evaluate alternative policies. Clearer insights and a better way to anticipate the effect of proposed policies should help in coping with such economic issues as inflation, unemployment, depression, balance of trade, and worsening exchange rates.

Notes

1. Reprinted by permission of *Daedalus*, the Journal of the American Academy of Arts and Sciences, Boston, Fall 1977, *Discoveries and Interpretations: Studies in Contemporary Scholarship*, Vol. 2.

2. Appendix K of J. W. Forrester 1961 emphasizes the importance of designing improved policies for guiding decision, rather than attempting prediction. Random disturbances are shown to preclude accurate forecasting of the future condition of a social system. On the other hand, if two policies are compared, the policy that is less vulnerable to random disturbances is always less vulnerable, regardless of the particular random sequence that impinges on the system. Making an economic system less vulnerable to the unexpected is more feasible than predetermining the unexpected.

3. Description in this section is drawn from Forrester, Mass, and Ryan 1976. For a description of the system dynamics method, see J. W. Forrester 1961, 1968, and 1975 and Goodman 1974.

4. For information on DYNAMO III see Pugh 1976.

5. Material for this section has been drawn from J. W. Forrester 1976.

6. Burns and Mitchell 1946, Gordon 1951, and Hickman 1963.

7. Of course, some earlier authors have also argued that delays involved in movement

of physical capital are too long for the dynamics of capital investment to be an essential cause of business cycles. See Abramovitz 1961.

8. For detailed discussion of an industrial sector simulation very similar to the one used for this paper and for a detailed analysis of business-cycle and Kuznets-cycle behavior, see Mass 1975.

9. See Kondratieff 1935, Garvey 1943, J. W. Forrester 1977, and Duijn 1977.

10. For a general model of dynamic fluctuation in commodity markets and its application to beef production see Meadows 1970.

11. See J. W. Forrester 1971, D. H. Meadows 1972, D. L. Meadows et al. 1974, and N. B. Forrester 1973.

12. See J. W. Forrester 1977.

References

Abramovitz, M. 1961. "The Nature and Significance of Kuznets Cycles." *Economic Development and Cultural Change* 9 (April): 225–48.

Burns, A. F., and Mitchell, W. C. 1946. *Measuring Business Cycles.* New York: National Bureau of Economic Research.

Duijn, J. J. van. 1977. "The Long Wave in Economic Life." *De Economist* (Leiden) 125, no. 4: 544–76.

Forrester, J. W. 1961. *Industrial Dynamics.* Cambridge: MIT Press.

_____. 1968. *Principles of Systems.* Cambridge: MIT Press.

_____. 1971. *World Dynamics.* Cambridge: MIT Press. 2nd ed., 1973.

_____. 1975. *Collected Papers of Jay W. Forrester.* Cambridge: MIT Press.

_____. 1976. "Business Structure, Economic Cycles, and National Policy." *Business Economics,* January 1976, pp. 13–25. Rev. and extended in *Futures,* June 1976, pp. 195–214.

_____. 1977. "Growth Cycles." *De Economist* (Leiden) 125, no. 4: 525–43.

Forrester, J. W.; Mass, N. J.; and Ryan, C. J. 1976. "The System Dynamics National Model: Understanding Socio-Economic Behavior and Policy Alternatives." *Technological Forecasting and Social Change* 9, nos. 1 and 2: 51–68.

Forrester, N. B. 1973. *The Life Cycle of Economic Development.* Cambridge: MIT Press.

Garvey, G. 1943. "Kondratieff's Theory of Long Cycles." *Review of Economic Statistics* 25, no. 4:203–20.

Goodman, M. R. 1974. *Study Notes in System Dynamics.* Cambridge: MIT Press.

Gordon, R. A. 1951. *Business Fluctuations.* New York: Harper & Row.

Hickman, B. G. 1963. "The Postwar Retardation: Another Long Swing in the Rate of Growth?" *American Economic Review* 53 (May): 490–507.

Kondratieff, N. D. 1935. "The Long Waves in Economic Life." *Review of Economic Statistics* 17, no. 6: 105–15.

Mass, N. J. 1975. *Economic Cycles: An Analysis of Underlying Causes.* Cambridge: MIT Press.

Meadows, D. L. 1970. *Dynamics of Commodity Production Cycles.* Cambridge: MIT Press.

Meadows, D. L., et al. 1974. *Dynamics of Growth in a Finite World.* Cambridge: MIT Press.

Meadows, D. H., et al. 1972. *The Limits to Growth.* New York: Universe Books.

Pugh, A. L., III. 1976. *Dynamo User's Manual.* 5th ed. Cambridge: MIT Press.

Thurow, L. C. 1977. "Economics." *Daedalus* 106, no. 4: 79–94.

{7}

Economic Justice

LESTER C. THUROW

Specifying Economic Justice

Until World War II, the problem of economic justice was always phrased in terms of "freedom from want." In a just society no one would "want." A rise in per capita income and an increasing awareness of sociology and psychology caused us gradually to come to the conclusion that economic justice could not be phrased in terms of freedom from want. We discovered that wants were unlimited and that it was not possible, or perhaps even desirable, to satiate them. When we did so, we eliminated the standard solution to the problem of economic justice of both the far right and the far left. Without the ability to satiate wants, economic growth (more for everyone until satiation is reached) cannot serve as a substitute definition of economic justice.

Given that wants were insatiable, the focus of attention swung briefly in the late 1950s and early 1960s to the concept of "needs." We could not satiate wants, but perhaps we could satiate physiological needs. But we discovered that little money was needed to meet physiological needs. For instance, in the early 1960s, $80 could buy a balanced diet for one adult for one year in the form of soybeans, lard, orange juice, and liver. Since almost everyone was rich enough to meet physiological needs, our society had, by this definition, achieved economic justice. But something was still wrong in the real world. What was it?

Basically, economic satisfaction or happiness with one's economic position is not caused by absolute incomes, but by relative incomes. Surveys show that high-income people are happier with their economic circumstances in every country even if a high income in one country would be a low income in a different country. The proportion of the population who are economically satisfied is just as high in India, for example, as it is in the United States. Sociologists use the term *relative deprivation* to explain this phenomenon. Individuals determine whether they are fairly treated by comparing their own income to that of others of their own group and to that of those in nearby reference groups. People have a very strong opinion that rewards should be proportionate to effort and that standards of vertical and horizontal equity should be observed. Hence, I may feel that I am paid too much as well as too little. Our standards of vertical and horizontal equity are heavily conditioned by history and by what actually exists.

Whatever exists is apt to be regarded as fair unless some very strong social forces are unleashed. Some sociologists maintain that standards of relative deprivation and economic justice change only in the midst of the social upheavals of major wars. Interestingly, World War II was the last time that any major changes occurred in the U.S. distribution of market earnings.

While it is no longer possible to specify economic equity in terms of satiating wants, many people try to avoid the equity problem by retreating to the "fairness" of the economic game. We won't worry about the distribution of rewards as such, but we will establish a fair set of rules for the economic game. Whatever distribution of rewards happens to emerge from the fair set of rules will be regarded as fair.

Unfortunately, this option is not open to us either. The reasons are easy to comprehend. Imagine that you were given the task of establishing the game of football. You would have to write down the rules of the game in terms of the size of the field, how the ball can be advanced, the number of men on each team, and so on; and you would also have to establish the initial starting score. Is it 0-0, or something else? While we are used to 0-0 starting scores, every athletic game is not played in this fashion. At Oxford there is a rowing race in which the boats of each college start out in the order in which they finished in the previous race. If a college's boat has a low position, it may take many years to reach the "head of the river," or the number one position.

Similarly, the economic game needs to have a starting score, or an initial distribution of economic resources. There will be a very different distribution of rewards in the market, depending on the starting score. For example, suppose that all of the nation's income was initially given to people who hate the opera. Opera stars would have very low (zero) market incomes. If, on the other hand, all of the money of the society was given to people who love the opera, opera stars would have some of the highest incomes in society. What each of us earns is not independent of where the game begins. As a consequence, each society must, at least once, specify what it considers a fair distribution of economic resources.

As in the game of football, we must establish rules, such as how long the economic game should last and how often it should begin again. Does "equal opportunity" mean that the economic game starts over once every lifetime or once in all of history? If my ancestor clubbed your ancestor back in the cave and my ancestor became a duke, are my ancestors entitled to become dukes, and your ancestors excluded from such? Or, do we have lifetime peerages? Or no peerages at all? In essence, the problem of inheritance taxes is exactly the same. What is the fair starting score? One need not opt for 0–0 to come to the conclusion that there should be limits on the degree of inequality that should be allowed in that starting score.

But before we go on to look at how we might think about the fair starting score, let us look at the current score of the economic game. Obviously, you cannot worry about how to make the economic game better until you know how the current economic game is played and what its outcome will be. As an exercise, let me ask you ten questions about the distribution of economic resources in America. After the questions, I have provided the correct answers.

Questions

1. What fraction of all family income was possessed by the richest 20 percent of all families in 1976?
2. What fraction of all family income was possessed by the poorest 20 percent of all families in 1976?
3. What was the average family income in 1976?
4. If your family income exceeds $50,000, what percentile of the population have you attained?
5. If your family income is below $5,000, what percentile of the population have you attained?
6. What fraction of all of the wealth (physical assets) of the United States is owned by the poorest 25 percent of the population?
7. What fraction of all of the wealth is owned by the richest 19 percent of the population?
8. What is the ratio of black-to-white family income in the United States?
9. What is the ratio of the earnings of full-time, year-round women workers to that of men?
10. What fraction of the United States population lives below the official poverty line?

Answers

1. 41 percent	5. bottom 10 percent	8. 58 percent
2. 5 percent	6. zero	9. 57 percent
3. $15,000	7. 76 percent	10. 14 percent
4. top 2 percent		

Your basic problem is to determine whether or not the distribution of economic resources indicated by these data is fair. If it is fair, obviously no policies are necessary to alter the way in which the economic game is played. If the score is not fair, then there is the problem of determining how the rules of the economic game should be changed in order to create a fair game.

Can Economic Equity Be Discussed?

One often hears it said that although there are economic statements to be made about efficiency, there are none to be made about equity, only personal prejudices. In fact, equity statements stand on the same foundation as efficiency statements. Neither is value-free; both depend on an underlying set of discussable value judgments. Once these value judgments have been made, there are technical studies to be done on economic equity just as there are technical studies to be done on economic efficiency.

Modern analysis of economic efficiency depends on the acceptance of Pareto optimality: state A is better than state B if at least one person is better off in A and no one is worse off. A person is better off in A if he prefers to be in A rather than in B. In a weaker version of the same principle, state A is better than state B if those who are better off in state A could adequately compensate those who are worse off in state A. An economy moves toward Pareto optimality in its weaker sense when scarce resources are used in such a way as to maximize potential output. There are more economic prizes to be distributed. With an improvement in efficiency there is a larger bundle of goods and services (including leisure) from which individuals can choose. More is better.

All analysis of economic efficiency depends upon these postulates, which are all thoroughly ethical in nature. Thus, a value judgment is made that each individual is the best judge of his or her own happiness; and that more choice is always better than less. If productivity goes up, society has a wider range of choices among goods and leisure. It is better off. Without such value judgments, "efficiency" ceases to have any meaning in modern economics.

Paretian efficiency values were easily absorbed into economics because they seemed to be universally held. They are, after all, the values of a liberal-individualistic society. The invocation of universally held value judgments has been the traditional way to avoid discussing values. This occurs partly because we believe what is universally held does not need to be discussed, but also because such values seem to be intuitively true and are often held to be facts rather than values. To many, "more [choice] is better" is a fact and not a value. But it is easy to see alternative postulates. On a survival hike, less is better. In the beginning, the fewer material aids you have, the more you have achieved toward your survival. Many societies are, and have been, founded on the principle that collective judgments dominate individual judgments; in these societies a person is better of in state A if the *group* decides that he is better off.

We may all share Paretian postulates, but this does not alter the fact that they are value judgments or that they elevate us beyond the realm of analysis. Consider the inviolability of consumer preferences. This theory seems sensible, given the nineteenth-century belief in the existence of innate wants within the individual. Given modern sociology and psychology, however, the postulate of innate wants is no longer plausible. We now perceive that every society or culture generates the wants of its population. Moreover, as our knowledge improves of how wants are generated, the activity of generating wants increasingly falls within the domain of deliberate policies. Indeed, a debate concerning our society's attempts to generate traditional economic wants—or other life-styles—is currently underway.

As this example illustrates, various types of beliefs about matters of fact—especially psychological and sociological matters of fact—can force alterations in values. Similarly, many economic beliefs about matters of fact can affect values. Consider statements such as "Income equality is bad because it leads to less work," or "Socialism is good because it prevents an individual from acquiring economic power over other individuals." Before going to the barricades over either of these statements, we must do a lot of hard empirical economic research and tough economic analysis. Does income equality lead to less personal effort? Is economic power less concentrated under socialism? When does the adverse effect on work effort set in? How should economic power be measured?

If "more is better" and the "inviolability of consumers' preferences" are the values underlying any analysis of traditional economic efficiency, what are the values underlying the analysis of economic equity? In the final analysis, the problem depends upon whether you subscribe to Rousseau's belief that all men are equal by nature, or to the Greek belief that men are unequal by nature. It also depends upon how you proceed to define these beliefs on a more precise basis.

To say that men are by nature equal is not the same as saying that men are in fact equal. They are not. This statement means that men are equal until they prove themselves unequal. The burden of proof is on the side of those who maintain that two men are unequal. Conversely, if you subscribe to the Greek belief that men are by nature unequal, the burden of proof lies on the side of those who maintain that two men are equal. Men born into different classes are unequal until proven equal.

Assigning the burden of proof may seem trivial, but it is not. A society that distributes economic resources equally except in those cases where men can be shown to be unequal has a very different distribution of economic resources from a society that distributes resources unequally except in those cases where men can be shown to be equal. The distinction is the same as that made with respect to guilt and innocence in our system of criminal justice. Is a man guilty until proven innocent, or is he innocent until proven guilty?

A belief in the equality of men means that social and economic differences must be justified as functional. They must be shown to lead to something else of merit that legitimates a departure from the norm of equality. Since American society is founded on Rousseauian beliefs rather than on Greek beliefs, equality is the norm. Departures from that norm must be justified.

It is at this point that economic analysis becomes relevant to questions of equity. What departures from equality are economically functional? The answers are not obvious. They depend upon probing more deeply into the concepts of economic equity and into the mechanisms by which the economy actually distributes economic prizes. Only in this manner is it possible to determine the appropriate degree of inequality.

Two Components of Equity

While following these procedures is obviously a complicated task that we are not going to complete at this time, there are a couple of observations which need to be made. First, for a very long time, Western societies have understood the concept of economic justice to include the idea of a minimum economic prize. Any society that does not believe in the minimum economic prize believes in allowing people to starve to death in the streets even when the society has plenty of food in the aggregate. There are societies in the world that tolerate such conditions, but Western societies have not for thousands of years. Thus, for all practical purposes the question is not, Do we believe in a minimum economic prize? but, How high should that prize be and how should it be delivered?

Second, from the point of view of work incentives there is an interesting contrast between the economic game that we ask adult white males to play and that which we ask the rest of the population to play. Adult white males play an economic game in which there is a 4.5-1 ratio between the earnings of the top 20 percent and the bottom 20 percent. The rest of our society plays an economic game in which there is a 28-1 ratio between the top and bottom quintiles. To go back to my burden-of-proof argument, someone would have to be able to show that such a difference in economic games is functional—that is, that it is necessary to provide work incentives for the members of the population who are not adult white males. Although I shall not attempt to prove it at the moment, it is not possible to argue that women, minorities, and young people are that much lazier than adult white men.

As a result, let us look briefly at the public policies for guaranteeing a minimum economic prize and for narrowing income gaps between adult white males and the rest of society. What are they and how can they be improved?

Delivering the Minimum Prize

If one listens to Fourth of July rhetoric, one might think that the United States is the ultimate work-ethic society. Often speakers seem to imply that income from work has an infinite value while income from welfare payments has no value. Yet if one looks at the federal budget, one finds exactly the opposite. In terms of expenditures we are a welfare-ethic rather than a work-ethic society. In 1978, we spent $215 billion for income transfer payments, but only $7 billion for manpower training programs and jobs.

This may, however, be in the process of changing, since the Carter welfare reform proposals contain large job components, and we are gradually expanding public service employment. In addition, the Humphrey-Hawkins bill is being seriously discussed. We are not yet willing to guarantee a job for anyone willing and able to work, but we are increasingly moving in that direction. This is occurring because the private economy has operated at high levels of unemployment during this decade, and there is little indication that it will approach low unemployment levels in the early 1980s. As people lose confidence that the government can or will stimulate the private economy to reach full employment, they increasingly return to direct government employment to solve the problem of unemployment. Nevertheless, income transfer payments are still the primary vehicle for delivering a guaranteed minimum family income. The current system of income transfer payments suffers from three defects. (1) Since it is a federal system in which the states determine benefit levels (the federal government merely offers matching funds), benefit levels differ sharply from state to state. While there is argument as to how many people respond to these incentives by moving from low benefit states to high benefit states (the weight of the evidence seems to be on the side of only small movements), the system does create a set of very perverse incentives. (2) The current system is composed of a large number of overlapping components (food stamps, AFDC, public housing, medicaid, etc.) in which some individuals get very large benefits while other equally needy individuals get very small benefits. Getting into all of the programs for which a low-income family is eligible is a real test of ability and knowledge; many flunk.

(3) Because of the overlapping programs and their individual administration, recipients often end up facing implicit tax rates which exceed
100 percent and are thus a disincentive to work. This could occur, for
example, if the AFDC program said that a family's benefits went down
$0.75 for every dollar they earned while Medicaid raised medical charges
by $0.50 for every dollar earned.

President Carter's 1977 welfare reform proposal attempted to address
all of these problems. Basically it was a two-part negative income tax
with different guaranteed family incomes for those who are not required
to work (the elderly, the disabled, and mothers with children under
seven years of age) and those required to work (everyone else). The
first group was to receive a guaranteed income of $4,200 for a family
of four with a 50 percent tax rate on all earnings (although persons in
this group are not required to work, they may work). Thus, supple-
mentation was to be offered for everyone earning less than $8,400.
The rest of the population was offered a negative income tax with a
guaranteed annual income of $2,300 for a family of four; but those in
this category would be allowed to earn up to $3,800 tax-free before they
started to pay a 50 percent tax on the next $4,600 in earnings. In
addition they were to be offered, and required to take, a government
public service employment job if they could not find work in the conventional economy. In conjunction, these two programs would provide a
higher income floor than that for those not required to work.

In the end these particular proposals may not be adopted, but given
the glaring defects in the current system there is no doubt that some
major reform will be adopted. What is not in the cards is a decision
to quit providing a *de facto* guaranteed minimum income.

Eliminating Discrimination. In the 1960s, the human capital approach
was extensively used to eliminate earnings gaps for women, young people,
blacks, Hispanics, and American Indians. This approach did not achieve
the results expected because most job skills are not learned in formal
education and training but in an informal on-the-job transmission
process from one worker to another. The Labor Department, for example,
found that 40 percent of the labor force reported that they were using
no skills learned in formal education and training and that only 12
percent of the labor force thought that formal education and training
was the best way to learn their current job. In this context manpower
programs can help to provide valuable background characteristics
(good work habits, etc.), but the essence of the problem is getting a job
in which one will receive on-the-job training and opportunities for
advancement.

Whatever the success of manpower training programs in the 1960s, the decade of the 1970s witnessed a diminution of their effectiveness. The high unemployment of the 1970s meant that there were no skill shortages. Employment essentially became a zero-sum game in which every person placed simply displaced someone else who would have had a job without the existence of the government program. Usually the displaced person also came from disadvantaged segments of the population, and the net effect was what I would call "push in; push out:" the government pushed someone into employment and the economy pushed someone out.

Progress requires that we shift the relative demands for labor. Essentially there are two ways to accomplish this objective. One can use government orders (affirmative action and equal employment opportunity regulations) or a system of wage subsidies designed to bribe private employers to alter their hiring patterns. There are real objections to both, but there are no other options. Government orders are essentially reverse discrimination. Someone's opportunities—prime age (25-55) white males—are to diminish in order to make room for other groups. This is the essence of the Bakke case and other reverse discrimination suits. The basic problem is that Bakke is right (he is being discriminated against), and minorities are also right (there is no other technique for ending an equally real history of discrimination). Wage subsidies can also be viewed as discriminatory (some get them and others do not), and they are expensive. Much of the money ends up being spent to encourage the employment of people who would have been employed in any case. With the exception of teenage ghetto blacks, employment rates usually exceed unemployment rates for even the most disadvantaged groups. Workable incremental wage subsidy systems are simply impossible to design.

Perhaps we will move to a system where individuals with a disadvantaged background (white or black) are eligible for help, while those with an advantaged background (black or white) are not eligible for help. But however these legal cases come out, the fundamental problem will not disappear. Some groups make much less than others, and this can be altered only by shifting the relative demand for labor.

An Historic Turning Point

When all else fails, the traditional defense of the U.S. economy is that it works. It may generate more inequality than the other industrialized economies of Western Europe and Japan, but it also generates a higher average income and thus a higher real standard of living for all but the poorest Americans. This argument is dissolving, however, in the post-World War II economic success of the rest of the world. The rest of the industrialized world is rapidly catching up with, and by some measurements, has actually exceeded us. Those who are poor in the United States are no longer wealthy by comparison with the average European or Japanese. They are simply poor.

In the future we will not be able to justify our inequalities on the grounds that they are a necessary component of a high level of productivity. Other economies will have proved that such differences are not necessary. This does not mean that anything will change, however. Inequalities can exist, and have existed, for very long periods of time.

In his Gettysburg Address, Lincoln made a famous but untrue remark. He stated that a nation could not long live half slave and half free. At the time, the United States had already existed in such a state for two hundred years. Large inequities were to remain for the next one hundred years and are still with us. They may never disappear. It all depends upon what type of a society we wish to have.

{8}

Issues in the Economics of Health

MICHAEL D. INTRILIGATOR

Recent Changes in the Economics of Health Care

There have been several important and, in some cases, dramatic changes in the economics of health care in the United States in the recent past that must be taken into account in considering national health policies. The first of these changes has been a very substantial increase in the total cost of health care. For example, in the decade between 1965 and 1975, the real age-adjusted per capita spending on health increased 55 percent, with per capita hospital spending increasing even faster, by 80 percent over this period.[1] This substantial growth in spending on health is even more impressive in view of the relatively large amounts spent at the beginning of the period. The large initial amounts and substantial growth have led to truly remarkable levels of health expenditures, which have made health care the third largest industry in the United States. In 1976 national spending for health amounted to $139 billion, representing $638 per capita and absorbing 8.6 percent of the U.S. gross national product. By contrast, in 1950 health expenditures amounted to $12 billion, or 4.6 percent of the gross national product; and as recently as 1970, $69 billion, or 7.2 percent of the gross national product. Just from 1975 to 1976, national health expenditures rose from $118 billion to $139 billion, or from 8.3 percent to 8.6 percent of the gross national product. Hospital spending alone amounted to $55 billion, or 40 percent of total health expenditures in 1976, making hospitals the subject of considerable attention in terms of national health policies.

A second important change in the economics of health care has been the enormous increase in the price of health services, particularly hospital services. For example, from 1950 to 1976, the average cost of a day of hospital care rose from $15.62 to $175.08, or over 1,000 percent.[2] Average annual increases in the cost of a day of hospital care amounted to 10.3 percent from 1965 to 1967, 13.8 percent from 1967 to 1969, 14.8 percent from 1969 to 1971, and 11.5 percent from 1971 to 1973.[3] These substantial increases have, in recent years, exceeded the rate of inflation for virtually all other consumer goods and services. They have also contributed in a significant way to the overall increase in consumer prices.

A third change in the economics of health care has been the lack of significant increases in the quantities of health services provided the population. While certain groups have certainly received more care and there have been clear improvements in certain areas in the quality of care, the overall quantity of care has increased at only a moderate rate. The total cost of health services can be considered the product of an average price of all health services times an average quantity of health services, where health services include hospital services, physician services, long-term care services, out-patient services, and so on. While the total cost of health services has been increasing at a dramatic rate in recent years, already noted as the first trend, this increase is accounted for largely by substantial price increases, already noted as the second trend, rather than by additional quantities of health services. As a result, the substantially higher health expenditures have not appreciably improved the health status of the population. For example, aggregate measures of mortality and morbidity have not shown significant improvement in recent years, and there has been no increase in life expectancy.[4]

A fourth change in the economics of health care has been the substantial increase in third-party payment of health costs. In third-party payment, the entity paying for health care is neither the recipient of care (the consumer) nor the provider of care (the hospital or physician) but rather a third-party. Traditionally, the third-party payors have been commercial insurance companies, paying for part of the cost of health care of employees covered under group health insurance, or of individuals enrolled in some other health insurance plan. Government has encouraged such private third-party payment via substantial tax subsidies. The individual income tax allows deductions of the cost of health insurance up to a certain amount. Furthermore, employer-paid health benefits are not included in taxable income, while these same benefits reduce the taxable income of the employer. These tax subsidies amounted to over $6 billion annually in 1975. Since 1967, government has also played an increasingly important role as a third-party payor in its own right. Under Medicare, the federal government pays for a substantial part of the cost of health care of individuals over sixty-five; and under state Medicaid programs, federal and state agencies pay for a substantial part of the cost of health care of low-income individuals. Under both the Medicare and the Medicaid programs, providers of health services are reimbursed for all reasonable costs borne in providing health services to program beneficiaries. In 1965, before Medicare and Medicaid, federal, state, and local governments paid 24.5 percent of total health care costs; but by 1976, this government share had risen to 42.2 percent, with the total share of all third-party sources exceeding 65 percent.[5] The change in payment of hospital costs is even more dramatic, with the share of hospital costs paid by the consumer declining from 49.6 percent in 1950, to 8.9 percent in 1976.[6]

The discussion thus far has indicated four important changes in recent U.S. experience in the economics of health care: the dramatic increase in the cost of health care, the enormous increases in the prices of health services, the relative stasis in the quantity of health care provided, and the large increase in third-party payment of health costs. The purpose of this chapter is to analyze these changes using the basic economic tools of demand and supply and to discuss possible national health policies in the light of this analysis.

Demand for Health Care

Health care involves a wide variety of health services, including hospital services (measured, for example, by bed days of care) and physician services (measured, for example, by visits to physicians). An aggregate measure of these services—which would involve appropriate weighting of hospital services, physician services, and other services—is the total quantity of health services provided the population. Multiplying this total quantity of health services by a measure of the price of health services gives us an appropriate average of the cost per hospital bed day, cost per physician visit, and so on.[7]

The *demand curve for health care* indicates the total quantity of health services consumers would purchase at alternative prices. Such a demand curve is shown in Figure 8.1. It shows how the total quantity demanded by all consumers of health services changes as the price of health services changes. It can also be considered the demand curve of a representative, or average, consumer, namely the quantity demanded by this consumer at alternative prices.

At point E, the consumer responds to the price p, which represents certain prices for health services, by consuming the quantity q, representing certain numbers of bed days, physician visits, and so on. (The arrows show the direction of interpretation—from p to q.) The total cost of health services is then price times quantity, or the shaded rectangular area.

Consider now the effect of an increase in the price of health care. The result of a rise in price is a reduction in the quantity demanded, as shown in the figure in the move from E to E'. The result of the rise in price from p to p' is a reduction in the quantity demanded from q to q'.

A frequent objection to this line of reasoning is that health care is a necessity, that people obtaining health care do only what their physician tells them to do, and that the quantity of health care demanded therefore does not depend on price, there being no reduction in the quantity demanded as price rises. There are several responses to this objection.

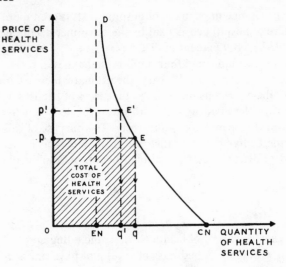

Figure 8.1. The demand curve for health services

First, consumers are constantly making choices at the margin where they are influenced by prices. As a result of rising prices they may not see their physicians as frequently, they may not stay quite as many days at hospitals, they may not undertake certain tests, they may postpone or cancel elective surgery, and in many other ways they may seek less health care. Second, at least some physicians are conscious of prices and will prescribe less extensive care or fewer days of care as prices rise. Third, empirical studies do find a downward sloping demand curve for health services, for which individuals seek less care as price rises and more care as price falls.[8]

The economic analysis up to this point is no different from that for other goods and services, for which there exists a downward sloping demand curve. There are, however, two distinctive features of the demand curve for health services, as shown in Figure 8.1, which are worthy of discussion. First, there is a finite intercept on the quantity axis, which has the interpretation of the amount of health care demanded as the price falls to zero. Second, there is a minimum level of health care which the demand curve approaches in an asymptotic fashion as price increases to very high levels.[9]

The first special feature of the demand curve is the finite intercept, labeled *CN* in Figure 8.1, which can be interpreted as *clinical need*. This is the amount of care that a clinical expert might recommend if there were no charge for care. By the arguments given before, this is larger than the care demanded at a positive price, but the point to be made here is that the quantity demanded at a zero price is nevertheless finite. There is an upper limit to the amount of health care that individuals will seek even when its cost is zero: there are limits to the amount of health care that can be utilized. For example, certain groups that receive free care, such as those in the armed services and veterans, do not utilize infinite amounts of health care.[10] Nor do physicians and their families. Yet another example is extremely wealthy individuals, for whom the price of health care, relative to their income or assets, is very small. While such individuals may demand a large amount of care, it is not an unlimited amount.[11]

The second special feature of the demand curve is the minimum asymptotic level, labeled EN in Figure 8.1, which can be interpreted as *economic need*. This is the amount of care that the individual would seek even if the price were very high (but still affordable given the income of the individual).[12] It is a measure of need, using economic considerations of high price to exclude all health care that is not considered essential by the individual. The level of care provided at this point is, to a large extent, that minimum needed to preserve life and basic health, all other health care having been dispensed with in the face of an extremely high price of care. The amount of health care labeled EN can be interpreted as the *minimum need*, while that labeled CN can be interpreted as the *maximum need*. The former is that level of care chosen as price rises very high, while the latter is that level chosen as price falls to zero.

A demand curve such as the one shown in Figure 8.1 may be relevant at any one time, but over time it can and does shift. It shifts as factors other than price, which also affect the demand for health care, change. In recent years probably the leading cause of a shift in the demand curve for health care has been the growth of health care financing mechanisms, particularly third-party payment, which has already been noted as one of the significant changes in the economics of health care. The result of such third-party payment is a shift of the demand curve as shown in Figure 8.2[13] The effect of third-party payment is to reduce the net price of health services paid by the consumer.[14] Consider, for example, the consumer of health care at E, where price is p and quantity is q on demand curve D_0. Suppose a third-party payment mechanism that paid half the cost of care was established. From the viewpoint of the consumer the cost is cut in half—to $p/2$. The quantity associated with this net price is the new quantity demanded at price p with 50 percent payment by third parties, as shown in the figure. Considering all possible prices and quantities before this establishment of a third-party payment mechanism and locating the quantity associated with price after it is cut in half generates the demand curve $D_{.5}$, where the 0.5 subscript refers to the 50 percent payment by third parties. Similarly, $D_{.3}$ and $D_{.6}$ refer to 30 percent and 60 percent payment by third parties, respectively, and the original demand curve D_0 refers to no such third-party payment.

The recent shift of the demand curve over time has been from $D_{.3}$ to $D_{.5}$ to $D_{.6}$, as there has been greater and greater reliance on private and public

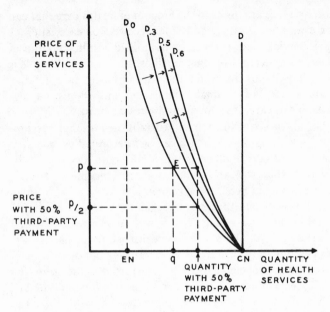

Figure 8.2. Shifts over time in the demand curve for health
services due to third-party payment

third-party payment mechanisms. This shift is shown by the arrows in the
figure. The result of this shift is to increase the quantity demanded at any
price by shifting the demand curve closer and closer to D_1, which is the
limiting case as 100 percent of the cost of care is provided by third
parties.[15] This limiting demand curve calls for purchase of CN as the
amount of health care at any price, since others are paying the full cost of
care.

Another effect of the increase in third-party payment is indicated in
Figure 8.2. The clinical need intercept of the demand curve is unchanged
as the proportion of health care costs paid by third parties increases. The
economic need asymptote of the demand curve shifts, however, as this
proportion increases, shifting to the right and indicating greater economic
need. As third-party payment covers a larger proportion of the total cost
of health care, individuals will increase the minimum level of care they
seek, requiring more and more care at a minimum and, in general, seeking more sophisticated and more expensive care. Eventually, when third-
party payment covers all the cost of health care, at D_1, economic
(minimum) need and clinical (maximum) need are identical.

The Supply of Health Care

The *supply curve of health care* refers to the amounts providers, such as hospitals and physicians, are willing to make available at alternative prices. Figure 8.3 shows such a supply curve. At point *A* providers are making available the quantity *q* at price *p*. As price rises to *p"* the providers will be willing to make available additional amounts, increasing the quantity supplied to *q"*, at *E"*. This positive responsiveness to price is the result of many possible changes, such as physicians' finding it profitable to employ more aides, hospitals' using more nurses, use of more efficient techniques, and greater use of new and improved equipment. While there is a postitive response to price increases, as shown in Figure 8.3, this response is very limited. The supply curve tends to be quite steep because of the difficulty of substituting other inputs for physicians and hospitals, the large expense and long lags in the production of new physicians and hospitals, and the difficulties in using new techniques and equipment. The supply curve is referred to as one that is highly inelastic in not showing large responses to price increases.[16]

Another important feature of the supply curve is that it has tended to be constant, or nonshifting, unlike the demand curve, which has shifted out significantly over the recent past.[17] The enormous expense of new facilities and new health manpower, combined with the substantial political, legal, and economic constraints on the entry of new providers, has led to a supply curve that is both inelastic and constant, exhibiting neither any significant responsiveness to price nor any appreciable change over time.

Demand and Supply

The demand curves of Figure 8.2 and the supply curve of Figure 8.3 are

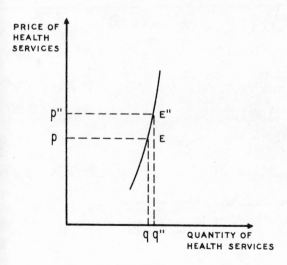

Figure 8.3. The supply curve for health services

superimposed in Figure 8.4. With demand curve D_0 and supply curve S there is an equilibrium at E_0, where the two curves cross. This point of intersection is an equilibrium in that at this price, p_0, the amount that consumers would like to purchase, q_0, is exactly the same as the amount that providers would like to make available. Any other point is a disequilibrium, involving an excess of the quantity demanded over the quantity supplied, or visa versa.

Figure 8.4 also shows the shifting demand curves of Figure 8.2, with the shift based on the amount of third-party payment. Consider the equilibrium at E_0 and assume there has been a shift of the demand curve to $D_{.3}$, based on private and/or public third-party payment of 30 percent of the cost of health care. Assume that the supply curve does not shift. The result of the shift of the demand curve from D_0 to $D_{.3}$ is that at the old equilibrium price p_0 there is an *excess demand*—that is, an excess of demand over supply; given as ED. The result of this demand is that consumers bid up prices to obtain health services and/or providers raise prices to ration the available supply. Thus there is pressure for prices to rise toward the new equilibrium at $E_{.3}$, where price, $p_{.3}$, is larger than the old equilibrium price and where the quantity is slightly larger than the old equilibrium quantity. Similarly, the equilibrium rises to $E_{.5}$ and $E_{.6}$ as a result of a shift of demand to $D_{.5}$ and $D_{.6}$, respectively.

The process depicted in Figure 8.4 is very useful as a way of understanding the recent change in health prices and costs. Given a stable and in-

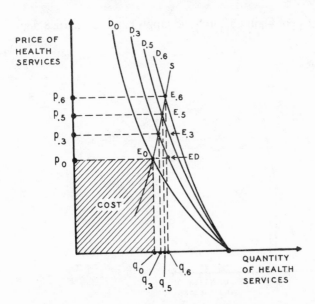

Figure 8.4. Demand and supply curves for health services

elastic supply curve, as demand has shifted out over time, because of increases in third-party payment, prices have risen substantially, quantities have increased only slightly, and total cost has risen dramatically—shown in Figure 8.4 as the area of the rectangle representing price times quantity, such as that for E_0.

An important aspect of this interpretation of the recent history of rising prices and substantial cost increases is its *feedback nature*. As prices and costs increase, there is more pressure for third parties, including the government, to pay a higher share of the cost of health care.[18] Thus, group health insurance becomes a more attractive fringe benefit for both employers and employees, and there is political pressure for government to pay a greater share of the cost of health care for populations already covered, or for new population groups. The result is a further shift outward of demand, as in Figure 8.2, and further increases in price and cost. The system tends, not to correct itself, but to magnify initial price increases, with higher prices leading to greater third-party payment, which leads to yet higher prices. This process keeps boosting prices and costs over time, slowing down only as the percentage of costs paid by third parties reaches some maximum level.

In addition to rising prices and substantial cost increases, other recent major changes in health care are explained by the demand and supply curves of Figure 8.4, coupled with the feedback process of price and cost increases leading to greater third-party payments and to further outward shifts in demand. At $E_{.6}$, for example, where third-party payment amounts to 60 percent of health care costs, there is more health care provided, at a higher price, and at much larger cost than at $E_{.3}$, where third-party payment amounts to 30 percent of health care costs. In addition, however, the demand curve is more inelastic at $E_{.6}$ than at $E_{.3}$, meaning that consumers respond less to price increases.[19] Whereas in the former equilibrium at $E_{.3}$ consumers would reduce the quantity demanded as price increased, at $E_{.6}$, there is a smaller reduction in response to price increases. Consumers at the new equilibrium will seek longer hospital stays, more frequent visits to physicians, use of the latest (and most expensive) medical equipment, and so on. Such behavior, which has become very much a part of current health care delivery, is understandable. Consumers are quite rational in seeking more and higher quality health care when others, the third parties, are paying a substantial share of the cost.

Policy Responses

What are appropriate policy responses to the changes in the economics of health care identified at the beginning of this chapter? These changes have been analyzed in the last several sections using the economic tools of demand and supply, and these same tools can be applied to study policy responses.

One type of policy response is to foster policies that will shift out supply, as shown in Figure 8.5 in the shift from supply curve S to supply curve S'. With this shift in supply, the shift in demand from $D_{.3}$ to $D_{.6}$, as in Figure 8.4, is offset in terms of price increase, price remaining at $p_{.3}$ despite the shift in demand. While total cost of health care is greater at $E'_{.6}$ than at $E_{.3}$, it is less than it would have been at $E_{.6}$, if the supply curve had not shifted as shown.[20] In fact, government policy has in recent years attempted to shift out supply as shown in the figure. Among such policies are substantial subsidies to hospital construction, subsidies for medical school construction and expansion, and various attempts to encourage greater efficiency in the delivery of health care.[21]

Another type of policy response would be a shift of demand *inward*, e.g., from $D_{.6}$ to $D_{.3}$ in Figure 8.5 in order to reduce the price and cost of health care. While this type of policy response has not been as evident as that of fostering an outward shift of supply, there have been some attempts in this direction, such as stricter limits on Medicare and Medicaid reimbursement, the development of Professional Standards Review Organizations (PSROs) to control hospital utilization and so on. There have also been proposals to reverse the mechanisms at work in Figure 8.4 by substantially increasing the share of health care expenditures paid by the patient via increases in coinsurance and in deductables.[22] But such a

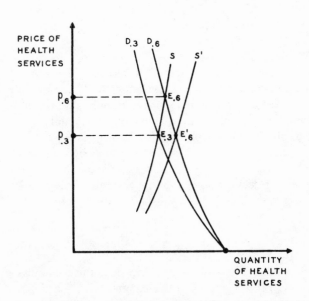

Figure 8.5. Shift in the supply curve for health services

change in the financing of health care would reverse the course of the recent past; could reduce access to health care for precisely those target populations for which government has sought to provide more care, namely the elderly and the poor; and would result in a significant increase in the risk of severe financial loss as a result of major illness, particularly for middle-income families. Such effects are politically unacceptable.[23]

A third type of policy response is that of establishing limits on the prices of health care, such as that of the Economic Stabilization Program, rate setting, rate review, and various prospective reimbursement systems.[24] An interpretation in terms of demand and supply curves is presented in Figure 8.6. If the demand curve shifts from $D_{.3}$ to $D_{.6}$ in the face of a constant supply curve, the equilibrium will shift from $E_{.3}$ to $E_{.6}$, as in Figure 8.4. Suppose the government establishes a ceiling price of p_c, which is, however, below $p_{.6}$. The result will be a disequilibrium situation in which there is an excess of demand over supply, as shown. The shortage of supply relative to demand will lead to nonprice rationing, such as long delays in receiving appointments with physicians, in obtaining a hospital bed, or in obtaining services. Furthermore, to the extent that this limit on price applies to only one category of consumer—e.g., on reimbursement under Medicare or Medicaid—it will lead to a substitution between categories of consumers in favor of those for which no limit has been set, a reduction in the quality of care provided the affected population, and/or a shift of the cost of care from the affected population to other populations (e.g., from

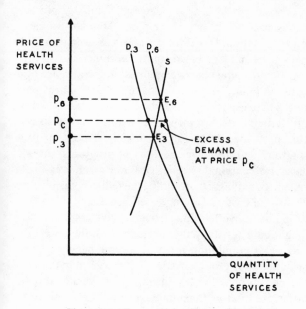

Figure 8.6. The result of setting a ceiling price p_c

the Medicare/Medicaid population to private-paying patients). Finally, price setting (and other forms of regulation) in a sector such as health care—involving many diverse providers and services which are difficult even to define—necessarily entails high cost, many exceptions, extensive case-by-case decisions, and political intervention, all of which tend to aggravate rather than to solve the problem.[25]

A fourth type of policy response is that of establishing a ceiling price, as in Figure 8.6, but using government health services, such as the Veterans Administration hospitals, to handle the excess of demand over supply. This type of policy has not been pursued, since most government health services are intended for specific population groups, such as veterans, Indians, and members of the armed services.

A Comprehensive Policy: National Health Insurance

A comprehensive health policy would take into account demand, supply, and their special features and dynamic behavior. Such a policy could be established through the adoption of a comprehensive system of National Health Insurance, which would affect both the demand for, and the supply of, health care.

A comprehensive National Health Insurance system would recognize that it is in the interest of both individuals and the society at large to provide the entire population with access, at low money and time price, to certain minimal levels of health care. Above these minimums, a system of deductibles and coinsurance would restrain demand. Thus, above the minimum levels the consumer would pay all or part of the cost of care. The traditional objection to National Health Insurance has been that such a system would boost demand and lead to substantial cost increases. In recent years, however, such cost increases have occurred in the absence of a National Health Insurance plan. Given the substantial fraction of cost already paid by third parties, especially the federal government, a comprehensive system of National Health Insurance may in fact restrain, rather than promote, cost increases. For example, if current programs—representing a totally disorganized mixture of programs, private and public—are replaced by a national system that is universal, everyone's access to health care can be equalized, resulting in reduced benefits to some currently highly favored groups, but increased benefits to those currently receiving few, if any, benefits. In particular, low- and middle-income consumers might gain substantially, while those in the lowest income group and in the older population might lose some benefits. Such adjustments between population groups would be possible only under a comprehensive system of National Health Insurance. It would also be more efficient, however, in that with suitable deductibles and coinsurance, all consumers would have an interest in reducing the cost of care.

By contrast, under the present system very few consumers have such an interest, given the substantial benefits under Medicare and Medicaid and under various private group health insurance systems. Thus, far from accelerating health care cost increases, National Health Insurance could restrain such increases.

In addition to possible adjustments in coverage between different population groups, a comprehensive system of National Health Insurance could also make possible adjustments of other types, such as adjustments between catastrophic care, acute care, and preventive care. While there should be some provision for catastrophic coverage, it must be recognized that a few such cases can utilize vast amounts of health resources that could be utilized to provide acute and preventive care to many individuals. The proper balance between various types of care cannot be realized under the present disorganized system, but it could be realized under a comprehensive system. Similarly, the proper balance between long-term and short-term care; between hospitals, nursing homes, and other facilities; and between older and newer medical technologies, which cannot be achieved under the present system, could be realized under National Health Insurance.

Another advantage of a comprehensive National Health Insurance system would be a reorganization of health care delivery. This would have the effect of shifting out supply. Such a reorganization could include, for example, large prepaid units with an integration of health delivery components, which can take advantage of scale economies in health care delivery. Other effects on supply—additional physicians, hospital beds, and so on—could also result from a National Health Insurance plan, which could lead to greater efficiency in the production and use of health care inputs.

Attention should be focused on a *comprehensive* system. Policy directed to health care delivery has thus far been both piecemeal and minimal. For example, some groups receive substantial coverage by the federal government through Medicare and Medicaid, while others receive no such coverage. Other groups receive a great variety of coverage through private insurance carriers, while some have no coverage whatsoever. Similarly, some private groups, such as the Kaiser Foundation, have long provided care via large prepaid groups. There have also been some recent developments along these lines through Health Maintenance Organizations (HMOs). Altogether, however, these providers represent only a very small fraction of health care delivery, and there appear to be substantial political and economic barriers to the development of new HMOs. A National Health Insurance system, to the extent that it is comprehensive in treating all consumers and providers, can avoid the inequities and inefficiencies of piecemeal coverage and lead to more efficient modes of organization and operation.

Overall then, a comprehensive system of National Health Insurance could be an important mechanism for improving both the efficiency and the equity of health care delivery.

Notes

1. See Gibson and Mueller 1977.
2. See Council on Wage and Price Stability 1977. For discussions of the inflation of health costs, particularly hospital costs, see Feldstein 1971a, 1971b, 1974, 1975, Klarman 1970, and Davis 1973.
3. See U.S. Department of Health, Education, and Welfare 1975.
4. Fuchs 1975 points out that health in the United States has little to do with what is spent on health care. Rather it has much to do with heredity, environment, and personal life styles.
5. See Gibson and Mueller 1977. The government share would be even larger if the government subsidies of private health insurance via tax reductions through deductions and exclusions were taken into account.
6. See Feldstein and Taylor 1977 and Gibson and Mueller 1977.
7. To the extent that hospital expenditures account for a significant fraction of total health expenditures, a reasonable proxy measure of the price of health services is the average cost per hospital bed day.
8. See P. Feldstein 1966, Rosenthal 1970, Joseph 1971, Newhouse and Phelps 1974, and Yett et al., 1975.
9. For a further discussion of the first of these distinctive features, see Yett et al. 1970. p. 35. These two features are the opposite of those usually believed or found to exist for demand curves for other goods and services. Specifically, it is typically assumed or found that these goods and services are not purchased above a given price and that, as price falls to zero, they are purchased in unlimited amount.
10. Among other reasons for a finite demand at zero price for such groups is the time price of health care. While the money price may be zero, the time price, involving both the duration of care and waiting for care, may be high.
11. Probably the most extreme case is the president of the United States, with his own personal physician available at all times and with unrestricted access to hospital care. Even in this extreme case the demand for care is finite.
12. Clearly, if the price were large enough, the indiviual would have to reduce the quantity of care, since the price would exceed his total income. The point at which all income is spent on health care is, however, never reached for most individuals.
13. There are, in fact, other factors in addition to third-party payment that have resulted in the outward shift of demand. These include a greater role for physicians as the key decisionmakers in health care delivery, greater consciousness of health care, technical developments in the provisions of health services, and higher income levels. These other factors would result in even greater shifts of demand than those shown in Figure 8.2.
14. See Klarman 1977 for a discussion of the "two-price system," in which the gross price of services exceeds the net price to the consumer. See also n. 18 below.
15. The increase in demand resulting from greater insurance coverage, which reduces the price to the consumer, is sometimes called "moral hazard." See Arrow 1974.
16. The supply curve is inelastic in that any percentage increase in price will lead to a smaller percentage increase in the quantity supplied: a 10 percent price increase will increase supply by less than 10 percent. This concept of elasticity can also be applied to the demand curve, where the demand curve is inelastic if any percentage increase in price will lead to a smaller percentage *decrease* in the quantity demanded.
17. In fact, adjusting for *quality* of health care, the supply curve has, if anything, probably shifted *upward*, with the cost of providing the same level of care increasing as a result of more sophisticated procedures, equipment, and so on. Inflation in the price of goods and services purchased by providers of health care also has the effect of shifting supply upward. These effects, which are ignored in the following section, would further accelerate cost and price increases. Many studies have attributed a large part of the increase in the cost of health

care to the increase in wages and prices paid by hospitals and other providers. These studies, however, tend to ignore the fact that demand for labor and nonlabor inputs by providers is *derived* from the demand for health care. Increases in wages and prices paid by providers may therefore be a *consequence* of shifts in demand for health services. If so, it is the shift in demand, rather than the increases in wages and prices, that should be identified as the cause of the increase in the cost of health care.

18. If third parties pay a higher share of cost, the net price paid by the consumer will not increase as rapidly as the gross price. For example, Feldstein 1975 notes that in 1950, the average cost of a day of hospital care was about $16, but the consumer paid 63 percent of the cost of care, or about $10 as a net price. By 1974, the average cost rose to about $125, but the consumer paid only 23 percent, or about $28.50 as a net price. Adjusting to 1950 prices, the net price rose to only $13, so in real terms the net cost rose only 30 percent in this 24-year period.

19. A 10 percent increase in price may lead, for example, to a 5 percent decrease in quantity demanded at $E_{.3}$, but only to a 3 percent decrease in quantity demanded at $E_{.6}$.

20. This reduction in expenditure due to an outward shift of the supply curve follows from the fact that the demand curve is inelastic.

21. There has been a recognition recently that increasing hospital capacity may not, in fact, increase supply, given relatively low occupancy rates. Whatever the factors limiting supply are, they apparently do not include lack of hospital beds. Thus, policy on hospital capacity has reversed itself from the previous Hill-Burton financing of hospital construction to the present certificate-of-need requirement under which a regulatory authority must issue a permit based on community needs before there can be an increase in hospital capacity. For discussions of the apparent lack of effectiveness of the certificate-of-need requirement, however, see Hellinger 1976 and Salkever and Bice 1976.

22. See Feldstein 1971c. *Coinsurance* refers to the proportion of the cost paid by the consumer. *Deductibles* are the amounts fully paid by the consumer.

23. For example, proposals by the Nixon and Ford administrations to increase cost-sharing by Medicare beneficiaries could not even attract a sponsor in Congress.

24. On prospective reimbursement systems see Hellinger 1976 and Gaus and Hellinger 1976. In such a system, rates are set prior to the delivery of services through budget review, application of formulas, negotiation, or some combination of these methods.

25. For a further discussion of the inappropriateness of regulation of health care delivery, see Noll 1975 and Enthoven and Noll 1977.

References

Arrow, K. J. 1974. "The Economics of Moral Hazard." *American Economic Review* 64: 253-72.

Council on Wage and Price Stability. 1977. *The Rise of Hospital Costs.* Washington, D.C.

Davis, K. 1973. "Theories of Hospital Inflation: Some Empirical Evidence." *Journal of Human Resources* 8: 181-201.

Enthoven, A. C., and Noll, R. G. 1977. "Regulatory and Nonregulatory Strategies for Controlling Health Care Costs." Stanford Graduate School of Business, Stanford, Calif.

Feldstein, M. S. 1971a. *The Rising Cost of Hospital Care.* Washington, D.C.: Information Resources Press.

_____. 1971b. "Hospital Cost Inflation: A Study of Nonprofit Price Dynamics." *American Economic Review* 61: 853-72.

_____. 1971c. "A New Approach to National Health Insurance." *The Public Interest*, no. 23 (Spring), pp. 93-105.

_____. 1974. "Econometric Studies of Health Economics." In *Frontiers of Quantitative Economics*, vol. 2, ed. M. D. Intriligator and D. A. Kendrick. Amsterdam: North-Holland.

_____. 1975. "How Tax Laws Fuel Hospital Costs." *Prism*, April.

Feldstein, M. S., and Taylor, A. 1977. "The Rapid Rise in Hospital Costs." Council on Wage and Price Stability, Executive Office of the President, January.

Feldstein, P. 1966. "Research on the Demand for Health Services." *Milbank Memorial Fund Quarterly* 43: 128-65.

Fuchs, V. R. 1975. *Who Shall Live?* New York: Basic Books.

Gaus, C. R., and Hellinger, F. J. 1976. "Results of Prospective Reimbursement Systems in the United States."*Topics in Health Care Financing*. Germantown, Md.: Aspen Systems.

Gibson, R. M., and Mueller, M. S. 1977. "National Health Expenditures, Fiscal Year 1976." *"Social Security Bulletin*, April, pp.3-8.

Hellinger, F. 1976, "The Effect of Certificate-of-Need Legislation on Hospital Investment." *Inquiry* 13: 187-93.

――――. 1976. "Prospective Reimbursement through Budget Review: New Jersey, Rhode Island, and Western Pennsylvania." *Inquiry* 13: 309-20.

Joseph, H. 1971. "Empirical Research on the Demand for Health Care." *Inquiry* 8: 61-71.

Klarman, H. E. 1970. "Increases in the Cost of Physician and Hospital Services." *Inquiry* 7:22-36.

――――. 1977. "The Financing of Health Care." *Daedalus,* Winter.

Newhouse, J. P., and Phelps, C. E. 1974. "Price and Income Elasticities for Medical Care Services." In *The Economics of Health and Medical Care,* International Economic Association, ed. M. Perlman. London: Macmillan. New York: John Wiley.

Noll, R. G. 1975. "The Consequences of Public Utility Regulation of Hospitals." In *Controls on Health Care.* Washington, D.C.: Institute of Medicine, National Academy of Sciences.

Rosenthal, G. 1970. "Price Elasticity of Demand for Short-Term General Hospital Services." In *Empirical Studies in Health Economics,* ed. H. E. Klarman. Baltimore: Johns Hopkins Press.

Salkever, D. S., and Bice, T. W. 1976, "The Impact of Certificate-of-Need Controls on Hospital Investment." *Milbank Memorial Fund Quarterly: Health and Society* 54 (Spring) 185-214.

U.S. Department of Health, Education, and Welfare, Social Security Administration, Office of Research and Statistics. 1975. *Health Care Expenditures, Prices, and Costs: A Background Book.* DHEW Publication no. (SSA) 75-11909.

Yett, D. E.; Drabek, L.; Intriligator, M. D.; and Kimbell, L. J. 1970. "The Development of a Microsimulation Model of Health Manpower Supply and Demand." In *Proceedings and Report of Conference on a Health Manpower Simulation Model,* vol. 1. Washington, D.C.: Division of Manpower Intelligence; Bureau of Health Manpower Education; Department of Health, Education, and Welfare.

――――. 1975. "A Microeconometric Model of the Health Care System in the United States." *Annals of Economic and Social Measurement* 4: 407-33.

{9}

The Critical Issues in U.S. Energy Policy

ROBERT S. PINDYCK

Energy policy has turned out to be one of the more divisive issues facing this country. For a long time now, we have been unable to plan and implement a coherent and rational energy policy, and have instead adhered to old and misguided policies and programs, failing to recognize their implications for energy markets. The best example of such outdated programs is the system of price controls on oil and natural gas, which has resulted in a growing gap between our consumption and our production of energy. By now we have experienced serious and regular shortages, and have become increasingly dependent on imported oil. A growing fraction of our growing level of imported oil is coming from the Arab countries, and as a result, we have never been more vulnerable to an oil embargo than we are today. Yet we have done little to protect ourselves against an embargo. We have a program to store crude oil reserves for standby use, but its implementation is proceeding very slowly, and the planned stockpile is inadequate in size. And we have legislated no other standby program that could be used to ameliorate the effects of an embargo.

In April 1977, the Carter administration proposed an energy program that would have gone at least part way towards helping us close the growing gap between our consumption and production of energy. The proposed crude oil equalization tax, for example, in replacing our existing system of crude oil price controls and entitlements, would have helped to raise the prices of oil paid by consumers closer to their world levels, thereby reducing consumption. Similarly, the proposed tax on industrial use of natural gas would have greatly reduced the increasing wastage of that fuel and helped to reduce further natural gas shortages. The administration's proposals, however, ran into considerable opposition in Congress, and the result has been that we are now not much closer to a coherent energy policy than we were in 1977.

The congressional opposition that arose in response to the administration's original proposals is symptomatic of the considerable division that exists over the desired objectives of energy policy. At the same time, it shows the failure to face up to some basic issues involved in energy policy.

There has been a deep and persistent conflict in the objectives of national energy policy: on the one hand we have had the proclaimed goal of self-sufficiency and reduced imports, but on the other hand we have attempted to protect consumers from increases in energy prices. For a long time the goal of low energy prices has dominated our energy policy, with the result that we have become much more dependent on imported energy. In effect, we have attempted to use energy policy as a means of reaching distributional goals. (This has been an important political fact of life that has applied not only to energy policy, but to other policies and programs as well.) This is not surprising, since politicians often lose votes when they attempt to raise the price of anything. It has been unfortunate, however, not only because of its distorting effects on energy markets, but also because, as we shall see, it does not even manage to achieve its distributional goals. Distributional goals can be much better met through distributional instruments, such as taxes and transfer payments.

Today we face four critical issues in energy policy. First, we must recognize that the growth in oil imports and the natural gas shortages of the past decade have resulted from policies that have maintained a low price of energy in the United States—some 25–30 percent lower than the world price—and that a continuation of such policies will result in an ever-growing dependence on imported energy. Second, we must learn that low-priced energy is not the same as cheap energy, that energy has become expensive, and that one way or another consumers will pay more for it—either directly through higher prices, or indirectly through the higher taxes needed to subsidize imports and to subsidize high-cost alternatives to conventional energy sources. Third, we should stop confusing price controls with conservation objectives, and recognize that controls can result in *overconservation* of domestic energy resources, so that measured over any period of time, consumers experience a net welfare loss. Finally, we must recognize that we are becoming increasingly vulnerable to an oil embargo, and that the pain that we suffer during an embargo will depend considerably on our preparedness, and on the government's response to the embargo itself. Let us examine these issues in turn, and then consider their implications for a national energy policy.

The Conflict over Low Prices and Self-Sufficiency

In another article, Robert Hall and I pointed out that increased energy imports have largely been the result of policies designed to keep the price of energy low (Hall and Pindyck 1977). Energy consumption in the United States during 1977, in barrels of oil-equivalents, was about 39

million barrels per day (mbd), of which 31 mbd were filled by domestically produced oil, natural gas, and coal, and the remaining 8 mbd imported. A rough "consensus" estimate of the price elasticity of energy
demand in the United States is −0.25.[1] Based on a number of econometric studies, a reasonable estimate for the price elasticity of supply is
0.2.[2] In the few years up to and including 1977, U.S. energy prices were
held at about 30 percent below world prices, and the result was an increase in consumption to some 8 percent (or 3 mbd) above what it would
have been. Thus 5 mbd of the 8 mbd of imports for 1977 were the result
of low prices.

How have we managed to keep U.S. energy prices well below their free
market levels? The more important policies include the price controls-
entitlements program for crude oil that was instituted during the energy
crisis of 1974 and our long-standing system of price controls on natural
gas wellhead prices. The crude oil price controls-entitlement program
has basically worked by taxing the domestic production of oil and using
the proceeds of the tax to subsidize imports. Under the provisions of the
program, the government sets an average price that domestic producers
may receive (around $8.00 per barrel in 1977, and about $9.50 by the
end of 1978). In order to refine domestic crude oil, however, producers
must purchase an "entitlement" at a cost (in 1977) of approximately
$2.00 per barrel, and this is the tax on domestic production. On the
other hand, refiners who import crude oil at the world price of about
$13.00 per barrel receive entitlements worth about $3.00 per barrel,
which is how imports are subsidized. In 1977, the cost of oil to refiners
was the same $10.00 per barrel either way.

It is ironic that the crude oil price controls-entitlements program has
had the effect of putting the U.S. government in the business of subsidizing oil imports, most of which come from OPEC—the cartel that
increased oil prices in the first place. Nevertheless, as long as the domestic price of oil is controlled and imports fill the gap between consumption and domestic production, a subsidy for these imports is a logical necessity. Furthermore, low domestic prices for oil mean that imports
can only grow; and as they do, greater strains will be placed on the tax
and subsidy program. The dollar volume of the subsidy will grow as the
base for the tax shrinks, so that revenue from the federal budget will be
needed to continue the program unless the domestic price of oil is allowed
to rise.

It is therefore fortunate that in early 1979 President Carter decided to
eliminate this program completely, thereby allowing domestic oil prices to
move to their free market level. As a result, domestic producers of crude
oil will, by 1981, begin receiving the world price (about 60 percent above
what they received in 1977), and we can expect that after three or four
years this will increase the domestic supply of oil by about 12 percent

(1 mbd). The cost of oil to refiners will rise by about 30 percent, and these higher costs will be passed on to consumers, thereby reducing the demand for oil. Of course, the final cost to consumers of oil products will rise by much less than 30 percent, since a major component of the retail price of oil products is in marketing and distributing costs. Thus, retail gasoline prices, for example, will increase by about 7 or 8¢ per gallon—about 10 or 12 percent.

The second major policy that has kept the price of energy low has been the long-standing regulation of natural gas field markets by the Federal Power Commission (FPC). The FPC has for many years held the wellhead price of gas far below the world market level. These price controls subsidized the consumption of natural gas by those who could obtain it (so that since 1970, demand has grown at an average annual rate of 5.3 percent) and removed the incentive for producers to explore for and extract natural gas (so that production ceased growing in 1970, and began declining in 1972). The result was a shortage of gas, which began in 1971, when some industrial consumers found their noninterruptible (firm) contracts being interrupted; continued growing through the early 1970s, as it became impossible to have gas lines installed in new homes built in many regions of the country and as more industrial consumers found their supplies curtailed; and became particularly serious during the winter of 1977. By the FPC's own reckoning, the 1976–77 shortage resulted in nationwide curtailments that ran to 23 percent of "firm" requirements, additional unemployment of about 1 million people during January, and over $4 billion of lost GNP. In addition, persistent shortages of natural gas have contributed about 2 mbd to our oil imports, as consumers unable to obtain gas shifted their demand to oil or electricity.

After many years without success, efforts to deregulate natural gas finally culminated in the Natural Gas Act of 1978. This act calls for gradual increases in the new contract wellhead prices of "new" natural gas, with all new contract prices approaching the free market level by 1985. Unfortunately, the act calls for separate regulations to be applied to each of some twenty categories of gas, and will thereby impose a costly regulatory morass on the industry. Nevertheless, it will finally move us in the direction of deregulation, and will help to eliminate the natural gas shortages that we have experienced in the past.

Why did we adhere to these low-price policies as long as we did, given that they are responsible for the problems of shortages and growing imports? Policymakers are not ignorant of the simple economics of supply and demand. Instead, there has been a strong desire to prevent consumer prices from rising, and to block the windfall gains that would have otherwise accrued to producers when world energy prices rose dramatically in 1973–74. Energy policy has thus been guided largely by *distributional* objectives—mainly the objectives of preventing a redistribution of income from energy consumers to energy producers. These distributional objectives are of extreme importance to the American public (which is why the energy taxes proposed by the administration in 1977 were received so coldly by the Congress). Unfortunately, however, energy policy is the wrong way to achieve distributional goals, which can be better achieved using such distributional policy instruments as taxes and transfer payments. As we shall see, policies designed to maintain low energy prices not only result in shortages, growing imports, and poorly functioning energy markets, but they do not even provide cheap energy!

Why Low-Priced Energy Is Not Cheap Energy

Our country's energy policy indeed succeeded in maintaining a low price of energy in the United States. There is, however, a concomitant cost to this policy that must ultimately be paid one way or another by American consumers. One example of this cost is the subsidy needed to maintain low domestic crude oil prices while filling the gap between consumption and production with more expensive imports. As mentioned just before, the source of this subsidy so far has been what is in effect a tax on domestic producers of oil, but as imports become a larger fraction of consumption, general tax revenues will also be needed.

There are other examples of how recent energy policies impose a cost on U.S. consumers. We began to deal partially with natural gas shortages by entering into long-term contracts to import liquefied natural gas (LNG). But just as tickets to a Broadway show are sold by scalpers at unreasonably high prices when the box office prices have been set too low, LNG represents an unreasonably costly alternative to domestic natural gas that could be purchased at lower prices under deregulation. It is interesting to note that recent contracts signed with Algeria and Indonesia (members of OPEC) call for a wholesale price (after regasification in the United States) of $4.00 to $5.00 per thousand cubic feet—about double the average world market price for energy, equivalent to oil at $24.00 to $30.00 per barrel, and about double the price of natural gas that would prevail under deregulation. These high prices will, of course, be averaged into consumers' gas bills. Thus, consumers are saved from high prices through regulation, only to have to face still higher prices for LNG imports.

As shortages and dependence on foreign imports grow, taxpayers will be asked to finance the difference between the high cost of producing energy in the United States and the low price that consumers are asked to pay. For years the government has subsidized nuclear-generated electrical power, yet even today the future of such uses of atomic energy is seriously under question. Recent policy is moving further in the direction of subsidizing production: the Energy Research and Development Administration (ERDA) began financing domestic energy projects which were feasible only if a permanent guarantee from the taxpayers was given that the output can be sold for considerably more than the current world price. Indeed, there is a danger today of deep government involvement in economically inefficient energy forms such as gasified coal and shale oil: the Department of Energy is, in fact, now planning massive subsidies for these nonconventional energy sources. So far, private industry has been unwilling to involve itself because these energy sources are too expensive and are likely to remain so for some time in the future. Cost estimates are continually revised upward every year, and it is not surprising that private firms are unwilling to commercialize these forms of energy without government assistance: they simply make no economic sense. But rather than subsidize costly new energy sources, it is preferable to purchase oil from OPEC at world market prices. Offering government guarantees or subsidies to the developers of new energy forms simply requires the nation to pay much more for energy than is necessary. And asking Americans to pay for the cost of energy through higher taxes rather than through prices results in a much greater level of energy consumption; individuals can avoid high energy prices by limiting their consumption, but they have no choice regarding the taxes they must pay.

The point here is a simple one. Whatever the price set by American policy, energy is no longer a cheap commodity. One way or another—directly through higher prices or indirectly through higher taxes—Americans will pay more for it.

Energy Policy and Conservation

Proponents of natural gas or oil price regulations have occasionally argued that price controls are desirable because, by discouraging current production, more of our energy resources are conserved for the future. (Some of these people have also claimed that higher prices have no impact on production!) This argument is highly misleading, and it is one that confuses many people. Let us examine the issue of conservation in some detail, and try to clarify its implications for energy policy.

We do not really know how much oil and gas there is under the ground in the United States, and obviously, as prices rise, estimates of "potential" reserves will grow. But suppose our current estimates of potential and proved reserves were accurate and represented a fixed resource base. How fast should we use this finite, exhaustible resource? The conservation-minded might feel that we should use the resource slowly, saving most of it for the future. But then the question is, *how* slowly should we use the resource? Should we use none of it at all over the next ten years, and save all of it for the future? Clearly it is not sufficient simply to say that we should "conserve," whatever that means. The real question is, What rate of resource exploitation is optimal from the point of view of society? This may seem like a very difficult question, but thanks in part to the seminal work of Harold Hotelling some forty-five years ago as well as to a good deal of more recent work on the economics of exhaustible resources, we do have at least the beginning of an answer to it.[3]

We know, for example, that if the industry that produces the resource is *competitive*, if extraction costs are constant, and if each producer extracts the resource at a rate that will maximize his stream of discounted profits (taking into account, of course, the depletion of the resource base over time), then the market mechanism will ensure that the *rent* for the resource—i.e., its price net of extraction costs—will rise at the rate of discount. Furthermore, if the resource were managed by a central planning agency whose objective was to maximize society's discounted stream of utility resulting from the consumption of the resource, the optimal policy would also be to extract the resource at such a rate that price net of extraction costs rises with the rate of discount. In other words, if producers are indeed competitive, the rate of resource exploitation resulting in the free market is equal to the socially optimal rate of exploitation.

At this point, you might believe that producers in the oil and gas industries are not really competitive, so that there is no reason to expect them to exploit the resource at the socially optimal rate. Leaving aside the issue of whether or not oil and gas producers are competitive, let us consider the implications regarding conservation if they are *not* competitive. If these equity-maximizing producers do have some degree of monopoly power, they will indeed exploit the resource base at a rate other than the socially optimal one. In fact, by increasing current prices, they will exploit the resource base *too slowly*, i.e., they will be *overly conservationist*. This fact is very important to keep in mind. If one believes that oil and gas producers have monopoly power, one cannot at the same time argue that they must be regulated so that we better conserve our natural resources. If one believes that the industry behaves as a relatively competitive one, then one should also recognize that the market-generated rate of resource exploitation will be much closer to the socially optimal one than a rate resulting from price controls.

Recognizing Our Vulnerability to an Embargo

We must now face the fact that there is at least a reasonable likelihood that we may experience another oil embargo sometime during the next several years. Another Arab-Israeli war would probably be accompanied by an oil embargo by the Arab members of OPEC, and even if another war does not break out, the failure of diplomatic efforts to at least partly resolve existing tensions could result in an embargo. Furthermore, as exemplified by the recent turmoil in Iran, political instability in one or two of the key oil-exporting countries could lead to what is in effect an embargo, even if the Arab-Israeli conflict is resolved.

Unfortunately, the likelihood of another embargo is not well appreciated by most citizens nor, it appears, by those involved in the design, legislation, and implementation of energy policy. We have a program to store crude oil reserves for standby use, but its implementation is proceeding very slowly, and the planned stockpile may be of inadequate size. This program calls for storing oil in underwater salt domes off the Gulf Coast. The total stockpile would be one billion barrels of oil, which could provide us with 6 mbd for six months. This stockpile (were it available now, which it is not) would certainly be adequate if an embargo were to occur today, or even in the next two or three years. But given our rapidly growing dependence on Arab oil, it is not clear that it would be adequate were an embargo to occur in, say, 1981, when we might well be importing 8 mbd from the Arab members of OPEC and another 5 or 6 mbd from other OPEC and non-OPEC countries. Furthermore, according to this program, we would reach the one billion barrel stockpile only in 1984. In 1981 the planned stockpile would be only a half-billion barrels, and so far, stockpile development is lagging far behind what is planned.

In addition, we have legislated no other standby programs that could be used to ameliorate the effects of an embargo. There are no plans for *regional* stockpiles of oil, coal, or natural gas that in the short run could protect those parts of the country which, because of transportation costs or lack of access to pipelines and other supply sources, would be hardest hit by an embargo. We have no programs of tax or other incentives that could quickly be called into effect during an embargo to limit the low-priority use of gasoline and other oil products. And we have no program whereby regulated sectors dependent on oil, such as trucking, railroads, airlines, and electric utilities, could raise their rates quickly to pass through higher taxes on oil, so that their customers would limit the use of energy-intensive services. Programs such as these should be made a high priority. We must recognize how our vulnerability to an embargo is growing, so that we may adopt new policies that will correct what could become an intolerable situation.

We must also better understand just what is likely to occur as a result of another embargo—and as a result of government response to an embargo. For many people, the thought of an embargo conjures up images of long lines at gasoline stations. In fact, the gasoline lines during the 1973–74 embargo were a result of a combination of government-imposed price controls and supply allocations. While temporary supply disruptions might occur, the major *direct* impact of an embargo will be on oil (and other energy) prices. Indirect effects, such as longer-term supply disruptions and economic recession, will depend largely on how the government responds to the direct effects. We must therefore be prepared now to respond rationally to the next embargo.

We must recognize, for example, that unless supply and demand are balanced during an embargo, supply "allocation" can do nothing to avert shortages. In the 1973-74 embargo, the federal government relied on only a single tool to deal with the embargo—the gigantic bureaucracy called the Federal Energy Administration. The FEA tried to be responsible for the movement of every barrel of oil in the United States. Even though the FEA did nothing to increase supply and very little to decrease demand, it attempted to "allocate" oil to users so that everything would come out even. But allocation without balancing supply and demand was impossible and the result was gasoline shortages.

Since an oil embargo will result in significantly higher oil prices, it will certainly have an inflationary impact on the economy. This inflationary impact will be of short duration, but it will be unavoidable; and, as opposed to the long-term demand-oriented inflation that we usually face, there is little that can be done with monetary and fiscal policy to counteract it. Therefore, should an embargo occur, we should respond to it with an *expansionary* monetary and fiscal policy. The extra stimulus from monetary and fiscal policy will be needed to counteract the adverse effects of an embargo on unemployment and GNP. If the economy is kept on an even keel with a limited rate of inflation, perhaps we will not find ourselves in a position where we are fighting inflation at the same time an embargo occurs. Then we will be in a position to tolerate the modest burst of inflation that will inevitably accompany an embargo.

Because exactly the wrong steps were taken by the government during the 1973-74 embargo, there was a greater strain on the country than was necessary. For example, the embargo was not met with an expansionary monetary and fiscal policy. Instead, a tax increase was proposed while the effects of the embargo were still being felt, and a contractionary monetary policy was imposed during and just after the embargo. This helped cause the most severe recession since World War II. In addition, the government did nothing to increase domestic supplies during the embargo. Government reserves were not brought into production, nothing was ever done about state restrictions on production, and efforts to reduce oil consumption were limited to the 55 mph speed limit. As prices rose, little was done to help the poor, and the lack of assistance was a major obstacle to a constructive response to the embargo.[4]

What Can Be Done?

We will never have a rational and comprehensive energy policy until we accept the "facts of life" about energy. Once we recognize that the era of cheap energy is over, no matter what price we artificially impose, we might begin to ask consumers to pay the full cost of energy directly, rather than indirectly through taxes and subsidies. This will provide a real incentive to conserve, thereby reducing demand. (The consumer who pays part of his energy through his taxes has little incentive to conserve.) It will also provide the needed incentive for producers to increase supplies, so that the growth of imports may be halted.

It is encouraging that we are now moving towards the deregulation of oil and natural gas markets—in stages so as to minimize any inflationary impact and to allow demand to respond over time (remember that demand and supply elasticities are larger in the long-term than in the short term). Higher fuel prices will result, of course, and will place a burden on low-income families, and distributional measures will be needed to alleviate this burden. Short of a negative income tax, the simplest measure would be to expand our current food stamp program to include fuel or that portion of a family's rent allocated to fuel and gasoline purchases. Expanding the food stamp program so as to shield the bottom 20 percent of the income distribution from any increases in fuel costs would cost the taxpayers about $2 or $3 billion per year— just a fraction of the budget of the Department of Energy, and certainly much less than the cost of subsidizing the energy consumption of all consumers.

Finally, it is important to prepare now to counteract any future oil embargos. Since dependence on imports raises an issue of national security, an antiembargo program is essential to prevent OPEC, and in particular its Arab members, from influencing the international policy of the United States. The most important antiembargo measure is a standby domestic source of oil, but standby programs for limiting oil consumption in the event of an embargo are also needed, as is the determination to respond to any embargo with an expansionary macro-economic policy.

At the time, we can only be cautiously optimistic. Energy policy is beginning to move in the right direction, but the public, and many of its elected representatives, still believe that low-priced energy is equivalent to cheap energy. It would be unfortunate indeed if we failed to come to grips with the key issues in energy policy. Our eventual accommodation to the high cost of energy will then be all the more difficult.

Notes

1. Surveys of demand elasticity estimates are presented in Pindyck 1977*a*, 1977*b*, and 1979.
2. For one such study (of the natural gas industry), see MacAvoy and Pindyck 1975*a*,

1975*b*. The study found supply elasticities around 0.3–0.4. Here I use a more conservative estimate of 0.2.

3. See Hotelling 1931. For a further discussion of the economics of exhaustible resource exploitation, see Solow 1974.

4. For a further discussion of OPEC and America's import dependence problem, see Pindyck 1978.

References

Darmstadter, J., Dunkerly, J., and Alterman, J. 1977. *How Industrial Societies Use Energy.* Baltimore: Johns Hopkins Univ. Press.

Hall, R. E., and Pindyck, R. S. 1977. "The Conflicting Goals of National Energy Policy." *The Public Interest,* no. 47 (Spring)

Hotelling, H. 1931. "The Economics of Exhaustible Resources." *Journal of Political Economy* 39 (April): 137–175.

MacAvoy, P. W., and Pindyck, R. S. 1975*a*. *The Economics of the Natural Gas Shortage (1960–1980).* Amsterdam: North-Holland.

———. 1975*b*. *Price Controls and the Natural Gas Shortage.* Washington, D.C.: American Enterprise Institute.

Pindyck, R. S. 1977*a*. "Interfuel Substitution and the Industrial Demand for Energy: An International Comparison." MIT Energy Laboratory Working Paper EL 77-026WP, August.

———. 1977*b*. "International Comparisons of the Residential Demand for Energy." MIT Energy Laboratory Working Paper EL 77-027WP, August.

———. 1977*c*. "Prices and Shortages: Policy Options for the Natural Gas Industry," In *Options for U.S. Energy Policy.* San Francisco: Institute for Contemporary Studies.

———. 1978. "OPEC's Threat to the West," *Foreign Policy.* no. 30, (Spring), pp. 36–52.

———. 1979. *The Structure of World Energy Demand.* Cambridge: MIT Press.

Solow, R. M. 1974. "The Economic Resources or the Resources of Economics." *American Economic Review* 64 (May): 1–14.

{ 10 }

Technology, Population, and the Agro-Industrial Complex: A Global View

RICHARD H. DAY

Technological Change in Economic Thought

Among Adam Smith's many important contributions to economic thought was his doctrine that extension of the market makes possible the division of labor. According to this doctrine, growth in output makes different kinds of production techniques economical, techniques which raise the productivity of labor, and thereby the wealth of nations. Malthus observed in his *Principles of Economics* that the subsistence wage, which must ultimately come to pass because of population growth and the law of diminishing returns, could be indefinitely postponed by the development and application of new techniques. Later in the nineteenth century, both Marx and Mill gave considerable attention to various aspects of technological change, while early in our own century, Schumpeter, whose innovating entrepreneur was the catalyst for economic development, gave technological change a central role in his system of thought.

In our own time we know from the work of such able scholars as Ed Mansfield that the study of technological change is alive and well. That work is giving us a better and better insight into the conditions of invention, innovation, and diffusion, especially at the level of the individual business firm. Unfortunately, however, the broader implications of technology have received too little attention from contemporary economists (though of course they have not been ignored by popular pundits such as, for example, Alan Toffler in his *Future Stock*). Indeed,

This paper, while presenting a new synthesis and overall point of view, incorporates extensive portions of three earlier works listed in the references, namely, Day 1967, 1968, and 1976. My thanks to the publishers of those works for their cooperation.

during much of the past quarter century economic theorists have been overly concerned with the balanced growth of model economies (i.e., mathematical equations) with "neutrally" changing technologies. More practical, policy-oriented fiscal and monetary economists have focused on considerations of a macroeconomic nature: total employment, average price levels, aggregate productivity, and aggregate growth. Even though many of the greatest economists, as we have just reminded ourselves, have given major attention to technology and social change, we seem to have been and to be now relatively heedless of it in our teaching, in our research, and in our advice to policymakers.

In the meantime, however, technology has not been constant nor has it led to neutral changes in productivity along balanced growth paths. If anything, invention, innovation, and diffusion of new products, new inputs, new production, marketing, and decisionmaking methods are proceeding at a faster pace than ever. They are leading now, as they have in the past, to overlapping, imbalanced waves of development, to counterpoints of growth and decline as old modes of production and consumption are abandoned in favor of more competitive alternatives and as established mores give way to new patterns of living.

These facts are sometimes recognized by politicians and general commentators, but often too late to plan effective action to alleviate their social effects. The recent onset of the energy crisis underscores this fact. It seems to have been recognized long after it was in the making; little seems to have been done to prepare for it; few agree on its importance, or, conceding its importance, few agree on what to do about it.

What I want to do in this chapter is to share some reflections on technological change and economic development, its past role in shaping human evolution, its current role in modifying the conditions of modern life, its future role in limiting or expanding human activity. Let us begin with the very broadest brush to obtain a picture of technology's significance.

The Great Ages of Humankind

Throughout the entire history of our species, economic development has proceeded through four more or less distinct epochs: (1) the food-collecting stage preceding the development of the bladed tool about 50,000 B.C.; (2) the age of the hunting band, which gave way to civilization around 10,000 years ago, when plants and animals were domesticated; (3) the agriculture-urban age, involving the organized production of food and artifacts and a settling of people into farms or farming villages and cities; and (4) the scientific-industrial revolution of the past several centuries, characterized by a radical increase in agricultural and industrial output by the use of machines, mechanical power, and scientific methods of cultivation, husbandry, and fabrication.

Each of these epochs has involved an increase in food production and in population. Current estimates of population during these epochs is shown in Figure 10.1. Prior to the domestication of plants and animals, human population grew so slowly that if it had continued to grow as it has for millenia, it would have reached a total in our own time of a mere 4 or 5 million. With the establishment of agriculture, however, a new epoch of population growth ensued. Given man's dependence on animal power and his own labor—a dependence that continued throughout the Renaissance—the population during this age of agriculture and urbanization grew to about 140 million. Had this age continued and not

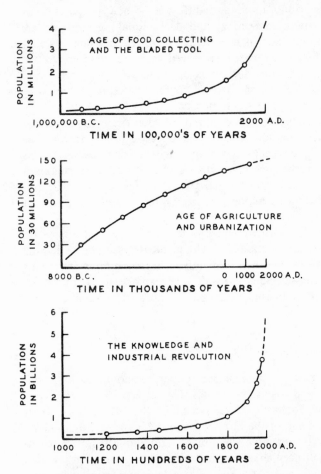

Figure 10.1. Population growth: the great epochs of man. Adapted from Deevey 1960. Copyright © 1960 by Scientific American, Inc. All rights reserved.

spread to the Western hemisphere, population would not have surpassed 150 million or so by now. This is nonetheless a thirty-fold or forty-fold increase in human numbers compared to the age of hunting and fishing. During the fifteenth and sixteenth centuries, agriculture and city life spread to the New World. At the same time, the foundations for the industrial revolution were laid in Europe. As it unfolded, population growth experienced a marked acceleration, in part because of the extension of the urban-agricultural system to the new lands, in part because of the massive increase in agricultural productivity made possible by the industrial revolution.

Malthus, writing early in the nineteenth century, estimated that the world population was about one billion and that it was doubling about once every quarter century. Although he overestimated the actual growth rate, which at that time was closer to a doubling every half century, the Malthusian figure has nearly been reached in our own time. Indeed, recent figures stagger the mind: the world population is approaching a total of 4 billion at a rate of some 5,000 net additions per hour! Note carefully the differences in scale in the three diagrams shown in Figure 10.1. The population curve shown for the age of agriculture and urbanization would take up just a little more than the width of the dot on the horizontal axis used in plotting population for the preceding age of food collecting and the bladed tool. The curve for the knowledge and industrial revolution occupies less than one tenth of the time span covered in the preceding epoch.

The awesome nature of the interaction of technology and population can perhaps best be put into perspective by shifting from the archeological and historical time scales of Figure 10.1 to the cosmic time scale of astronomers such as Jastrow or Meadows. In the last decades these scientists have, through the most exacting kind of observation and calculation, arrived at a theory of stellar evolution that tells us, among other things, that our own solar system came into being about 4.5 billion years ago and that it has about an equal time before it perishes. That theory is not our concern, but if we measure population from this astronomical perspective—from the beginning of the earth to the projected end of life on earth as we know it—we obtain the diagram shown in Figure 10.2. The long, slow, steady ascent of man from straggling bands of humanoids through all the great civilizations which have risen and declined—indeed, the evolution of man and all the great epochs of his history and prehistory—are mere details disguised within the thickness of a line!

Medieval Agriculture and the Industrial Revolution

Underlying the human explosion in the lifetime of the earth is a

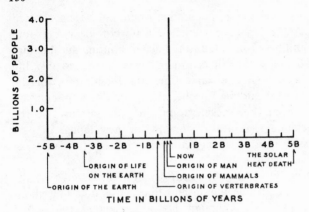

Figure 10.2. Human explosion in the life of the earth. Reproduced from
Day 1976, p. 265.

progression of technological inventions and diffusions, occurring inter-
mittently, to be sure, but at an accelerating pace. In the medieval
period, for example, the perfection of the heavy plow, the horse collar,
the three-field rotation system, and a variety of related inventions made
possible the substitution of the heavy war horse for the ox and the
expansion of a more efficient agriculture to the northern European
plains. Lynn White summarized the broader significance of this development as follows:

It was on those plains that the distinctive features both of the late medieval and
of the modern worlds developed. The increased returns from the labor of the
northern peasant raised his standard of living and consequently his ability to buy
manufactured goods. It provided surplus food, which, from the tenth century on,
permitted rapid urbanization. In the new cities there arose a class of skilled
artisans and merchants, the burghers, who speedily got control of their communities and created a novel and characteristic way of life, democratic capitalism. And in this new environment germinated the dominate feature of the
modern world: power technology. (White 1962, p. 78)

Development of the modern capitalistic factory system required
numerous technological innovations, and occurred over a long period of
time. Most historians, I believe, agree that it accelerated noticeably in
the decade preceding and following the American Revolution, the same
period in which Adam Smith wrote and published his most celebrated
work. This acceleration was caused partly by the perfection and rapid
diffusion of the "spinning jenny" and other inventions which made
possible the mechanized production of cloth. First sold by Hargreaves in
1768, spinning jennies increased rapidly, so that after only twenty years,
there were 20,000 of these machines, each able to do the work of at least
six to eight spinners (Mantoux 1962, p. 218). This meant a net reduction

of at least 100,000–140,000 cottage workers, *nearly 20 percent of England's population at that time*!

The exact social consequences are still disputed. The yeoman farmer had already begun to decline in importance because of the enclosure movement, the adoption of advanced farming practices, and the shift from grain farming to sheep grazing. But by 1765, the freeholder was still an important class, and some writers agree that it was only in the twenty years following this date that his extinction as a major social class in England came to pass (Mantoux 1962, pp. 136–85; Toynbee 1962, pp. 30–39). Since spinning was a source of off-farm income that helped the rural freeholder to survive, Toynbee's conclusion that "the yeomen began to disappear when the spinning wheel was silenced" must be basically correct. Of the 160,000–180,000 freeholders, the combined forces of improved agriculture, enclosure, and the mechanization of spinning must have eliminated a great portion.

The Industrialization of Agriculture

Indirect effects of the industrial revolution spread all the way to the New World, where cotton production in the Deep South developed in response to the expansion of textile production in Europe and New England. More than a century and a half later the cotton thinners, weeders, and pickers of this "cotton belt" were, in turn, to fall victim to rapid investment in new technique. Beginning gradually in the late 1930s, the adoption of labor-saving, yield-increasing technology increased rapidly through the late forties and early fifties. In some cases, the diffusion of a new technique grew by more than 100 percent per annum. Greatly lowered physical labor coefficients of new techniques created relatively profitable investment opportunities, since capital-intensive, low-variable cost methods could be substituted for labor-intensive, high-variable cost methods of production.

The magnitude of the change in technology in southern U.S. agriculture can perhaps be grasped best by considering the unskilled labor required by each of four technological stages.

Stage 1 Sharecropper unit. Mule-powered cultivation, handpicking of cotton and corn.

Stage 2 Partial mechanization of preharvest operations on the operator's share of the plantation. Tractor-powered land preparation; mule-powered cultivation; handpicking of cotton and corn; small-scale combines for harvesting soybeans, oats; three-man hay balers for hay crops.

Stage 3 Complete mechanization of preharvest operations except some handweeding of cotton and corn. Handpicking of cotton;

complete mechanization of corn; self-propelled combines for oats and soybeans; one-man hay balers for hay crops.

Stage 4 Complete mechanization. Introduction of rice; a very small amount of handweeding of cotton.

The seasonal distribution of labor required by each of these stages is shown in Figure 10.3. One can readily see how labor costs were drastically reduced from one stage to another and in a quite uneven manner.

The consequence of the diffusion process initiated by those developments was a radical change in the institutional structure of southern agriculture, and had a dramatic impact on urban life in both the South and North. Thousands of sharecroppers and small farmers left the farm. Southern agriculture shifted from a plantation-sharecropping organization to large-scale family and commercial farming much like that found in other major farming areas in the United States. The periphery of shanties enclosing rural villages grew at an increased rate, while southern and northern cities found their slums swelling with sharecroppers and their descendents.

A similar process of technological diffusion and human emigration was also at work in other parts of the United States. From 1940 to 1960, the index of man-hours of farm work dropped from 191 to 92 for the United States as a whole, and in the Delta states of Alabama, Louisiana, and Mississippi, from 247 to 93. On the other hand, output per man-hour in the production of cotton alone increased more than three-fold, from an index of 36 to one of 127.

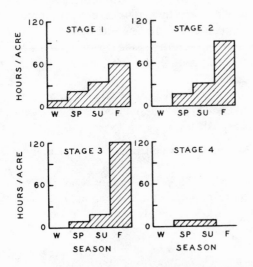

Figure 10.3. Seasonal distribution of unskilled labor demand in cotton production by stage of technology. Reproduced from Day 1967, p. 440.

In all, 17 million farmers (more than twice the present population of Sweden) left American farms between 1940 and 1960. In Mississippi alone, almost one million people left agriculture. In the ten counties of the Mississippi Delta, the rural farm population dropped by more than half in only the ten years between 1950 and 1960. By contrast, agricultural economists gave their attention to problems of agricultural surpluses. They urged policies that would move resources out of agriculture even faster. As we know now, they *were* moving out and at a rate about 100 times as fast (in absolute terms) as in the period of the yeoman's demise 175 years earlier.

Many of the farmers were not prepared for life in the cities. The cities, in turn, were completely unprepared to receive them, especially the blacks. The wind had been sown. Americans were soon to reap the whirlwind. In 1964, journalists coined the phrase "the long hot summer." In that year, thousands of blacks, many of whom must have come from farms or been descended from displaced agricultural workers, marched through the streets of Birmingham. That, as we all know now, was only the beginning. The racial violence of these times, however, has tended to obscure the underlying economic problems aggravated by a mass emigration of people probably unprecedented in history. When we add to the population increase of 47 million the displaced farm population, we find a total inflow of 64 million people into the nonfarm areas of our country in only a twenty-year span. That number is more than one third of the U.S. population in 1960, and roughly equal to the entire current population of West Germany!

This chain of events began with invention; continued with the farmer's effort to increase his profits by investing in the new products, inputs, and production methods; moved through production and resource adjustments; and ended with migration. It is easy for macroeconomic measures of economic activity to disguise such revolutionary, microeconomic movements. During this period of feverish agricultural and urban change, most economists regarded the United States as having grown rather sluggishly!

Two decades ago, when I began research on this topic, the process just described was well underway in Europe. The tractor was rapidly displacing the horse and the ox, production patterns were shifting in composition and location, and average farm size was rapidly increasing. In some parts of the continent the mass migration was already well under way. By now, European agriculture has been almost wholly industrialized, and what were once essentially farming countries, like Sweden and Italy, are now essentially urban cultures. During the time of transition many European economists, like their American counterparts, were occupied with a concern for a slowdown in aggregate growth. The most recent cases of agricultural industrialization have occurred in the Third World, in parts of Asia, Africa, and South America. The case I am most familiar with is that of the Indian Punjab, where Inderjit Singh and I conducted a study somewhat along the lines of my earlier investigation of the rural American South. The process of transition, while well-established, was in its early stages. But signs of growth and development were evident: a sprinkling of motor-powered tubewells replacing the ox- or camel-powered Persian wheel, occasional tractors, new hybrids, widespread use of commercial fertilizer, and so forth. On the basis of our projections made at the time (the empirical work was completed about 1970), this region should very soon be joining the ranks of developed agricultures—that is, if new forces unanticipated by us then, but seeming now to form credible threats, do not intervene.

The Agro-Industrial Complex

The emerging threat to continued increases in industrial production, agricultural productivity, and human numbers can be understood by considering the structure of industrial agriculture. I shall call this structure the *agro-industrial complex*. Figures 10.4 and 10.5 show the trends which have generated this new complex. The trend in the production of crude oil, shown in Figure 10.4, is somewhat dated. Since this graph was drawn, production in the United States has declined; and in the world as a whole growth in petroleum output has tapered off, presumably prior to an absolute decline as readily accessible supplies are exhausted.

Associated with the trend in crude oil production are other major industrial and agricultural developments, some of which we have already discussed. A few of these are summarized in Figure 10.5. These include increases in the production of tractors and trucks using internal combustion engines and in the production of fertilizer, much of which is derived from natural gas and petroleum feedstocks. The first trend has

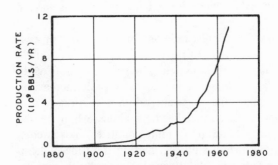

Figure 10.4. World production of crude oil. From Hubbert 1969, p. 162.
Reproduced with permission of the National Academy of Sciences, Washington, D.C., and the author.

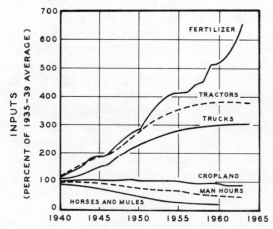

Figure 10.5. Changed technology of U.S. agriculture. From Pratt
1965. Copyright © 1965 by Scientific American, Inc. All rights reserved.

made possible—as we have seen—the substitution of mechanical power
for animal power, the great reduction in manpower requirements for
producing food, and the migration of people from rural to urban set-
tings. This trend, together with that for the production of fertilizer,
shows how products manufactured in various industrial sectors, which
in turn draw on resources from outside agriculture, are substituted for
farm-produced inputs and rural labor. Note that the tractorization of
farming in the United States took a mere two decades. It displaced a
primary source of power on which agriculture had been dependent for
several centuries. We have emphasized how a similar process has already
been completed or is underway in many other parts of the world.

The corollary expansion in world food production enabled per capita
food consumption to increase slightly for a time even in the face of a
rapidly rising world population. The increase was temporary, however;
and in spite of it the world as a whole *has barely more than is needed
for good nutrition*. Industrialization and the growth in agricultural output notwithstanding, at least half of the world's population even now
lies in calorie-deficient areas or on the edge of starvation even when
there are no unusual droughts. The ridicule heaped on Malthus from
the late nineteenth century to our own time in the context of the world
dynamics and limits to growth controversy must surely turn to at least
grudging admiration at his prescience.

What we have, then, is an intimate link between industry, agriculture,
and population. The interdependence is even more intricate than indicated, however, for natural gas—whose trend is basically like that of
petroleum, and from which ammonia compounds are synthesized for the
manufacture of fertilizer—is also a major input for heating, power gen-

156   *Richard H. Day*

eration, plastics, and synthetic rubber. Recent developments have not only increased agriculture's dependence on the nonagricultural economy but have placed it in the position of competing for resources used for entirely different purposes. Exhaustion of these resources is therefore both a threat to affluence for those few of us in the world who have it, and a threat to basic subsistence levels.

While industrialization has done little to raise the average global standard of living measured in calories, it has caused a greatly accelerated trend in the urbanization of the world's population. McC. Adams (1968) tells us that urbanization closely followed the introduction of agriculture and that changes in agricultural productivity were directly related to the size and sophistication of cities. As noted above, traditional agriculture alone made possible a thirty-fold to forty-fold increase in population. We also know, through the work of Lynn White (1962), that the development of horse mechanization, the three-field rotation system, and the introduction of the potato had a great deal to do with the rise of the city in Northern Europe. This laid the foundation for the extension of the Renaissance to England, France, and Germany, which in turn paved the way for the industrial revolution and the growth which followed. Even if we measure urbanization by counting only those cities with populations of over 100,000, its trend, summarized in Figure 10.6, is pronounced.

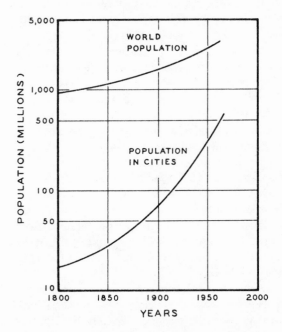

Figure 10.6. Rapid urbanization of the world's population. From Davis 1965. Copyright © 1965 by Scientific American, Inc. All rights reserved.

Evidently, a rapidly increasing proportion of the world's poor and under-nourished are located in highly concentrated urban environments. Certainly, the dependence of the city on agriculture should be clear; *although agriculture may decline in political importance, the inverted pyramid of people in cities who depend on it grows larger and larger.* As a corollary of the recent industrialization of agriculture, this inverted pyramid of people—which I again emphasize is growing at an explosive rate—is also dependent on a stock of petroleum and natural gas supplies that is shrinking at an equally rapid rate.

A major by-product of the interaction of technology and economic development has yet to be mentioned. It is the production and accumulation of pollution. Pollution has always been a major problem for man. On the one hand, we are reminded that much improvement has taken place just within the past century in developing waste disposal systems—an improvement that may have had as much influence on declining death rates as medical advances. On the other hand, sources of pollution entirely overlooked before have now been discovered. The effect of pesticides and mercury on animal life was dramatized by Rachel Carlson. The potential feedback on humans of which she warned has now been experienced prominently in several parts of the world. Greatly complicating the picture is the fact that some new "advanced" technologies, with great potential for reducing shortages, add to rather than subtract from the problem. For example, nuclear wastes, which are by-products of nuclear reactors, are growing at a rapid rate, and their effective control could pose problems millenia hence.

Two additional trends in environmental pollution are thought to be related to real and potential economic threats. These are the accumulated quantities of carbon dioxide and particulate matter in the air. The former, whose trend is shown in Figure 10.7, is thought to cause a general heating up of the atmosphere. A possible consequence (discussed by Plass in 1959) is a recession of the polar ice cap and flooding of major coastal cities throughout the world. The accumulation of particulate matter—the second trend—is thought by some, including Revelle (1974), to cause a cooling off of the atmosphere and thus a possible return of ice age conditions in the temperate zones and extensive drought in subtropical regions. Evidence that the latter trend is presently winning out over the former trend appears to be growing. While highly controversial, these hypotheses must be taken seriously, and the possible implications for world agriculture and industry must be studied.

Let me summarize the discussion so far. The interaction of technology and economy have led to explosive global trends in population, production, resource utilization, urbanization, agricultural industrialization, pollution, and climatic change. Can the kind of technological advance that underlies these trends provide panaceas in the future for accumulat-

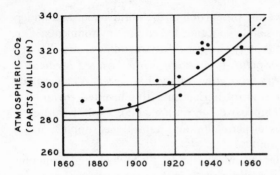

Figure 10.7. Carbon dioxide pollution. From Plass 1959. Copyright © 1959 by Scientific American, Inc. All rights reserved.

ing economic ills? The magnitude of the problem is greater than ever before, and the rate of technological discovery can scarcely be guaranteed to come in time, especially without consummate effort now and in the coming years. Great civilizations have declined and disappeared before. The extent to which these seemingly remote events were due to problems like those we now face is unknown, but such a possibility cannot be dismissed. In any case, it is surely not impossible, and may be likely that we face a protracted period of changing economic, social, and political structures throughout the world, occurring as rapidly as any that have gone before, as accommodation is made—for better or for worse— to the trends in global development briefly outlined in these remarks.

Let us reflect, then, on the problems of adaptation we now face.

Problems of Adaptation

The first concern of living systems is homeostasis: the maintenance of critical variables within the boundaries that define continued survival. Man, in his economic activity, can be no exception. Yet man, like other species, may fail. Individuals who fail to adapt effectively to changing circumstances die or live unpleasant lives. The same is true of populations or of entire species. The behavioral problems faced by an individual are complicated not only by the interdependencies among his kind but also by the accumulated effects, transmitted through the environment, of his predecessors' past activities. For example, overpopulation leading to overgrazing may destroy the environment of a ruminant species to such an extent that effective adaptation is eventually foreclosed, as has actually occurred in the Sahel, a living example of Hardin's tragedy of the commons (Hardin 1968). Human beings, however, are armed with an instrument that vastly extends the ability to cope with an impoverished inheritance. It is the synthetic faculty of mind that enables people to discover and to invent new activities that expand the inventory of resources that can be exploited.

Some students of ecology argue that the behavior of many animal species serves to limit population, so that an optimum relationship is maintained between the population and the resources that sustain it. The average product per individual is at a maximum. In this way the chance of maintaining homeostasis is maximized. Wynne-Edwards (1962) asserts that the cultural patterns of primitive human groups evolved in this way, but the effect of civilization and its rapid cultural evolution broke down the primitive barriers that limited population growth and resulted in runaway human expansion. If that is so, then runaway expansion has been sustained by runaway economic growth. During the course of this explosive development, specific resources in specific localities have been exhausted. The resulting scarcities probably contributed to a temporary abatement of economic expansion or even to the demise or decline of the resource-dependent populations. But inventive activity has, in effect, created new resources to replace those used up, and the process of expansion has been renewed, often in the hands of a new, formerly less fortunately endowed group. Consequently, homeostasis for the species as a whole has been maintained, not through the control of numbers as in more primitive beings, but through the evolution of technology. Humanity is, in short, dependent on inventive genius and on the socioeconomic infrastructures within which inventive activity flourishes.

Until recently, the conception of economic growth provided by orthodox theory was quite different. Resource exhaustion and the corresponding great waves or epochs of economic activity were not accommodated within its borders. Instead, balanced, intertemporal, efficient growth of capital stocks, accumulating in harmony with an exponentially growing population, sustained by perfectly competitive prices, and maximizing a utility function defined over an infinite horizon, was the picture most often presented in the rigorous theories of growth. These theories may, in fact, effectively describe economic growth in societies well-endowed with resources, for there appears to be a pervasive tendency for societies to grow and exploit resources as fast as possible. When, however, resource exhaustion is close enough to affect perception, a more general model is required, one that includes the foresight of resource exhaustion, the control of population, and limitations on affluence.

A model based on discounting future values but incorporating exhaustible resources will generate trajectories which have the initial appearance of exponential growth at a maximal rate. But they must eventually pass into minimal exponential decay. The path as a whole looks much like the typical bell-shaped exploitation curve for a single resource. Inventive activity and its effect on production interrupts this bell-shaped history and leads either to prolonged or accelerated exponential growth, or to economic waves of growing or diminishing amplitude.

If discounting of the future does dominate strategic choices, it is clear that man's most intensely rational modes of adaptation—dynamic programming and optimal control methods—bias choices in the direction of the living generation. The only way our strategic choices can be prevented from impoverishing unborn generations is through inventive activity. That alone makes possible indefinite or renewed expansion.

If people also discount the past, they will be happy with what they get. That is, the destruction of past ways of life as old technology gives way to new is looked upon by most people not with regret but with satisfaction. If, however, technological advance should diminish so much that contraction eventually sets in, the benign feelings of the living generation for the past may give way to bitter regret. Previous growth, looked upon as optimal by their predecessors, will be thought of as nonoptimal, or pessimal, just as an unfortunate heir may regret the plundering of his inheritance by profligate parents or relatives. So it seems that the optimizing man may be deceived in believing that what he does now is in the best interest of future generations. To put the matter another way, what we call optimal growth may better be called deceptively optimal growth.

The beauty of the market mechanism, at least in theory, is that it appears to support optimal growth without centralized direction. It is argued that the market brings about a state of economic efficiency with no social control behind it. Consequently, when inefficiencies arise, or resources appear to be exploited too fast, the orthodox economic remedy is to create markets with the appropriate mechanisms to cause externalities to be internalized and social efficiency restored, again without direct social control.

If, however, there is a tendency for private purpose to follow deceptively optimal adaptation, it may be necessary to overlay private purpose and the market system with institutions through which a public purpose is formed that will regulate present economic activity in the interest of generations yet unborn. Technological inventiveness may be sponsored. At the same time, exploitation of existing resources may be restrained and population expansion discouraged. These institutions must be insulated from the rationality of the typical economic man who, when guiding his action by deceptively optimal strategies, will oppose public controls as irrational or suboptimal.

That public purpose can be established within a society dedicated to individual freedom is demonstrated in our own country. Great domains of grasslands, forests, and minerals have been placed under public control. The constant pressures to release them from the public domain and to allow their exploitation for present enterprise illustrate the inevitable tension between future-oriented, public purposes, and private, deceptively optimal strategies.

The resolution of this inherent conflict by the establishment of socialism is no guarantee that future-oriented strategies will be pursued. Indeed, most centralized planning models incorporate time preferences in just the way Bohm-Bawerk said characterized impatience and Ramsey said characterized immorality in man. Evidently, a socialist state, like the capitalist one, must develop special institutions whose primary function is to protect the future from the present.

The problems of global development no longer appear to be local. In former times the exhaustion of forests may have led to the decline of maritime civilizations. But later, those who were able to employ appropriate technology for the exploitation of coal and iron could send great navies to every corner of the earth. Great powers have come and gone; the flow of economic activity has waxed and waned. Nonetheless, until now, the general trend of population and economic development has been ever-accelerating expansion.

Now the great economic powers draw on the global supply of resources. The interdependencies among nations have led to the rapid, worldwide diffusion of technology, crowding out primitive peoples who fail to adapt and establishing industry and industrialized agriculture everywhere. Accompanying these trends is the growing dependence on and competition for rapidly diminishing resources. The developed nations, having exhausted their own supplies, begin to urge the conservation of supplies belonging to others. Those others, throwing off the constraining customs of traditional culture, appear to be assuming the values of deceptive optimality that govern the developed countries.

Can the world, in this uneven state of advancement, with its conflict of local interests, evolve a world purpose to stand as guardian of the world's future in the face of national autonomy and the desire for national expansion? Can nations reorganize themselves to recognize and effectively pursue this world purpose of long-run well-being for the species as a whole without massively destructive conflict that would destroy all semblance of well-being in the short run? These are the fundamental problems of what we may call whole-earth economics.

If these problems are to be solved, the way people really adapt and the way economies really work must be better understood. It could be, as I have suggested, that modes of behavior presently pursued are not optimal but deceptively optimal and maladaptive. If that is the case, we must find it out in a convincing enough fashion to motivate a successful search for new strategies more suited to benefit our descendants. Then, if the great inventiveness of the mind does not fail us in our century of greatest need, our species will prevail, if not forever, then for a very long time.

References

Bryson, R. 1974. "World Climate and World Food Systems, III: The Lessons of Climatic History," IES Report 27. Madison: Univ. of Wisconsin, November.

Carlson, R. 1962. *Silent Spring*. Greenwich, Conn.: Fawcett.

Cipolla, C. 1975. *Economic History of World Population*. New York: Penguin Paperback.

Davis, K. 1965. "The Urbanization of the Human Population." *Scientific American*, September. Reprinted in *Man and the Ecosphere*, ed. P. Ehrlich, J. Holdren, and R. Holm. San Francisco: W. H. Freeman, 1971.

Day, R. H. 1967. The Economics of Technological Change and the Demise of the Sharecropper." *American Economic Review*, May.

_____. 1968. "Investment in New Technology and Social Change." Paper presented at XX Internationale Wirtschaftstagung, Donau-Europaisches Institut, Vienna, 10 June 1968. Published in German as "Investitionen in die neue Technologie und der Soziale Wandel." In *Problems der Konjunkturvenflachung*. Vienna: Jupiter 1968.

_____. 1976. "Global Trends, World Models, and Human Adaptation." In *General Systems Theorizing: An Assessment and Prospects for the Future*. Proceedings of the 1976 Annual North American Meetings, The Society for General Systems Research, Washington, D.C.

Day, R. H., and Singh, I. 1977. *Economic Development as an Adaptive Process: The Green Revolution in the Indian Punjab*. Cambridge: At the University Press.

Deevy, E. S., Jr. 1960. "The Human Population." *Scientific American*, September. Reprinted in *Man and the Ecosphere*, ed. P. Ehrlich, J. Holdren, and R. Holm. San Francisco: W. H. Freeman, 1971.

Hardin, G. 1968. "The Tragedy of the Commons." *Science* 162: 1243–48.

Hubbert, M. 1969. "Energy Resources." In National Academy of Sciences, *Resources and Man*. San Francisco: W. H. Freeman.

Jastrow, R. 1967. *Red Giants and White Dwarfs: Man's Descent from the Stars*. Chicago: New American Library.

Malthus, T. R. 1963. *An Essay on the Principles of Population* (1817). Homewood, Ill.: Richard D. Irwin.

_____. 1820. *Principles of Political Economy*. In *The Works and Correspondence of David Ricardo*. Vol. 2. *Notes on Malthus' "Principles of Political Economy."* ed. P. Srafa. Cambridge: At the University Press, 1957.

Mantoux, P. 1962. *The Industrial Revolution in the Eighteenth Century* (1928). Trans. Marjorie Vernon. New York: Harper.

McC. Adams, R. 1968. "The Natural History of Urbanism." In *The Fitness of Man's Environment*. New York: Smithsonian Institution.

Meadows, A. J. 1967. *Stellar Evolution*. London: Pergamon.

Plass, G. N. 1959. "Carbon Dioxide and Climate." *Scientific American*, July. Reprinted in *Man and the Ecosphere*, ed. P. Ehrlich, J. Holdren, and R. Holm. San Francisco: W. H. Freeman.

Pratt, C. 1965. "Chemical Fertilizers." *Scientific American*, June. Reprinted in *Man and the Ecosphere*, ed. P. Ehrlich, J. Holdren, and R. Holm. San Francisco: W. H. Freeman.

Revelle, R. 1974. "Food and Population." *Scientific American*, September, pp. 161–70.

Sampedro, J. 1967. *Decisive Forces in World Economics*. Trans. S. E. Nodder. New York: McGraw-Hill.

Toynbee, A. 1962. *The Industrial Revolution* (1884). Boston: Beacon.

White, L., Jr. 1962. *Medieval Technology and Social Change*. Oxford: Oxford Univ. Press.

Wynne-Edwards, V.C. 1962. *Animal Dispersion in Relation to Social Behavior*. New York: Hafner.

{ 11 }

Productivity Performance of the United States: Issues and Problems

NAKE M. KAMRANY AND DAVID M. CHEREB

Introduction

In this chapter, the relationship between productivity, technology, and economic growth is explored. Professor Robert Solow of M.I.T., in his pioneering study on United States economic growth, attributed 87.5 percent of the growth of the U.S. economy to what he termed the "residual"—the difference between increments of growth in total output and that amount which is attributed to the contributions of labor and capital.[1] Technology is thought to be the main contributor to this residual. Another study[2] has reported that technological progress from 1949 to 1968 accounted for 40 percent of the real income in private (nonfarm) output, as shown in Figure 11.1. This amounts to about 20 percent more output than might otherwise have been achieved with the same quality of labor and capital. Thus, according to the study, as a result of technology, a cumulative output of $8.2 trillion (as opposed to $6.9 trillion) was delivered, for a net gain of $1.3 trillion. The net gain represents a growth in the technology factor of 1.7 percent per year during the 1949–68 period. By 1968, the compounding growth of technology amounted to 37 percent of the total output. The study concludes that, on the average, each dollar spent on research and development (R and D) returned slightly over seven dollars in technologically induced economic gains following expenditures over the eighteen-year period. The discounted rate of return for such an investment was thought to be 33 percent per annum.[3] It is rather difficult to quantify precisely the impact of R and D on economic growth, or its rate of return. Nevertheless, if the conclusions of these studies are valid, it follows that expenditures in R and D and in resulting technologies in general appear to be a very good national investment.

The role of technology in the economy has been strongly debated

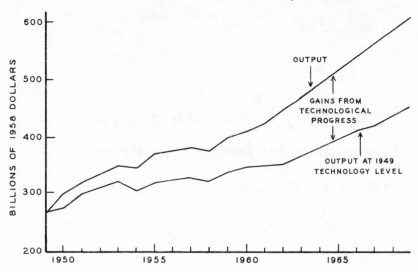

Figure 11.1. Output and gains resulting from technological progress, 1949–
1968. From "Economic Impact of Stimulated Technological Activity,"
Summary Volume, Midwest Research Institute, November 1971.

both inside and outside of economics. The controversy within the profession, however, is primarily definitional and methodological. Controversy over the impact of technology upon economic growth does not
concern its effect upon economic growth per se, but the way in which
this impact is measured, its magnitude, and various attributes assigned
to the quantity and quality of the various factor inputs, such as capital
and labor. Table 11.1 shows the range of estimates that have been made.
The differences in these estimates derive from the method of calculation,
definitions of factor inputs, and whether technology is assumed to be
exogenous or endogenous. The differences are technical ones and do not
question the crucial role of technology in economic growth. There is a
broad agreement among economists that technology significantly contributes to economic growth.

Recently, the emergence of stagflation (simultaneous inflation and
unemployment), the unfavorable balance of merchandise trade, and the
poor performance of the economy have drawn the attention of the
policymakers to the issue of the United States' *productivity performance*
and its relations to the rate of growth of technology. In the discussion
that follows, we have empirically analyzed the relevant recent data (time
series and cross-section comparison) concerning U.S. productivity, technology, and economic growth. Our analysis indicates that (*a*) productivity
growth in the United States has been declining since the midsixties,
(*b*) this declining trend of productivity growth is a long-term decline
and is not to be discounted as seasonal or cyclical, and (*c*) a major

Table 11.1. Various Estimates of the Share of Technology in Growth

Author	Dates Covered	Share of Technology in Growth
Robert M. Solow	1909-1949	87.5%
Midwest Research Institute	1949-1968	40%
John Kendrick	1948-1966	over 90%
Edward Denison	1929-1957	32%
Jorgensen and Griliches	—	4%
R. R. Nelson	—	inadequate means of measurement

Sources: Robert M. Solow, "Technical Change and the Aggregate Production Function," *Review of Economics and Statistics* 39 (August 1957): 312-20; "Economic Impact of Stimulated Technological Activity," *Summary Volume,* Midwest Research Institute, 1971; John Kendrick, *Postwar Productivity Trends in the United States, 1948-1969* (New York: National Bureau of Economic Research, 1973); Edward F. Denison, "The Sources of Economic Growth in the United States and the Alternatives before Us," Committee for Economic Development, Supplementary Paper no. 13, New York, 1962; idem, *Accounting for United States Economic Growth, 1929-1969* (Washington D.C.: The Brookings Institute, 1974); D. W. Jorgenson and Z. Griliches, "The Exploration of Productivity Change," *Review of Economic Studies,* vol. 34; R. R. Nelson, *Effects of Research and Development on the Economy,* p-2787, The Rand Corporation, Santa Monica, Calif., 1963; idem, *The Efficient Achievement of Rapid Technological Progress: A Major New Problem in Public Finance,* p-3286, December 1965; idem, *Full Employment Policy and Economic Growth,* p-3072-3, February 1966; idem, *Technological Advance, Economic Growth, and Public Policy,* p-2835, December 1963; *The Rate and Direction of Inventive Activity* (Princeton, for the National Bureau of Economic Research, 1962).

underlying reason for the declining rate of U.S. productivity is the decline in investment for generating technologies through investment in R and D, education, capital goods, and other technology-related factors.

This long-term downtrend in U.S. productivity was pointed out by Professor William D. Nordhaus of Yale University (now a member of the Council of Economic Advisors), who gives the following percentages of annual growth per man-hour for the periods indicated:[4]

1948-55	3.11%
1956-65	2.51%
1965-71	1.88%

Nordhaus describes a secular (long-run) rather than cyclical downtrend in productivity as follows:

A careful examination of the postwar experience reveals a slowdown in productivity growth in recent years over and above that which could be explained by cyclical conditions alone. For the entire economy, the average annual rate of productivity growth cyclically corrected fell from 3.20 percent in 1948-55 to 2.54 percent in 1955-65, and then to 2.03 percent in 1965-71. Disaggregating to twelve broad industry groups serves to explain most of the deceleration simply in terms of change in the composition of demand and unchanging rates of productivity growth in individual industries. More precisely, the estimated aggregated productivity growth with unchanging individual industrial productivity growth was 3.13 percent, 2.53 percent, and 2.23 percent, respectively, for the three periods.

A further dissection of the cause of the slowdown indicates that it was due mainly to differences in productivity levels among industries, rather than to different rates of growth or productivity among industries. In this regard, the contributions of agriculture and FIRE were especially important, while durable manufacturing and government also retarded growth. Projections of future patterns of demand indicate that the productivity growth rate for the 1970's should proceed at a rate slightly lower than predicted for the last few years. Specifically, if demand follows historical patterns and if productivity changes in individual industries remain at their postwar averages, the rate of productivity growth per man hour should be about 2.1 percent annually, as compared with 2.6 percent annually for the entire 1948-71 period. [5]

Nordhaus's main reasons for the productivity slowdown are that (1) there is an accelerating shift toward industries with low productivity levels (durable manufacturing is one of them); (2) this shift is likely to continue through 1980, resulting in a further decline in productivity growth if left alone, and in a reduction in the growth of potential output; and (3) higher utilization rates of existing plant and equipment will not produce major productivity gains.

George Perry attributes the recent slowdown to shifts in employment composition; currently, the shift is toward women and the young, whose wage and productivity rates are low. As this demographic shift slows down, an increased rate of productivity will resume. [6] But this conclusion has not been proven since Perry's publication in 1971. Moreover, the decline in productivity rates over the last few years (since Perry's publication) has been in industries (such as durable manufacturing) which do not have high percentages of women or of the young as employees.

Over the decade 1967-77 the average productivity growth for the United States was 1.6 percent, almost half the rate of the 1959-67 period (3.6 percent). Edward Denison, of the Brookings Institute, has pointed out that the noncyclical reasons for the decline in the rate of productivity growth are rooted in a decrease in the rate of investment in (1) education, (2) capital stock, and (3) R and D technology. He also lists a reduction in the quality of the labor force, structural changes, resource allocations, economies of scale and labor force age-sex composition as contributing factors in the slowdown. [7] In the next section, recent U.S. investment data in these four areas are examined and compared with productivity performance. It will be shown that investment in these areas is much higher among the United States' competitors, such as Japan, the U.S.S.R., and Western Europe. The results are obvious.

While the United States experienced the highest growth rate among the industrial nations during 1870-1950, its relative performance was below average for the 1950-65 period, and it had the lowest growth rate during 1965-71 (see Table 11.2). Table 11.3 illustrates the lower U.S. R and D investment and employment of professional manpower compared with other industrial nations. Table 11.4 shows the long-term decline in U.S. annual expenditures for R and D and employment in R and D. The rate of this decline was much higher in the government sector than in the private sector. Japan's rate of productivity has been *three* times higher than that of the United States.

Table 11.2. Average Rate of Growth in GNP per Employed Civilian (Percentage per Year)

Country	1870-1950	1950-1965	1965-1971
U.S.	2.4	2.5	1.3
France	1.7	4.6	4.9
West Germany	1.6	4.8	4.3
Belgium	1.6	3.0	3.7
Netherlands	1.1	3.7	4.7
Italy	1.5	5.5	5.7
United Kingdom	1.6	2.2	2.5
Unweighted average for six European countries	1.5	4.0	4.3
U.S.S.R.	1.7*	4.2	4.3
Japan	1.4*	6.8	9.6

Source: Michael Boretsky, "Trends in U.S. Technology: A Political Economist's View," *American Scientist,* January-February 1975, Table 2. Reprinted courtesy of the publisher.
*Growth in per capita GNP.

Table 11.3. R and D Expenditures and Employment of Professional Manpower, 1967

Country	R&D Expenditures (av. 1963-67): Ratio to U.S. per $ worth of GNP	Employment of Professional Manpower (1967): Ratio to U.S. per $ worth of GNP
U.S.	1.00	1.00
France	1.35	1.37
West Germany	1.44	1.61
Belgium	0.69	1.00
Netherlands	1.82	2.42
Italy	0.50	0.79
Common Market	1.22	1.38
United Kingdom	1.69	2.17
Canada	0.64	0.88
Japan	1.21	2.86
Western Europe	1.14	1.34
Western Europe, Canada, and Japan	1.12	1.56

Source: Boretsky, "Trends in U.S. Technology," Table 1. Reprinted courtesy of the publisher.

Table 11.4. Average Annual Growth Rates in U.S. R and D Effort, 1953-1971 (Percentages)

Years	Total Industrial R&D Effort		Federal Government R&D Effort*		Private Sector R&D Effort	
	Expenditures	Employment	Expenditures	Employment	Expenditures	Employment
1953-57	21.0	15.7	32.5	25.5	11.5	9.4
1957-63	8.6	5.9	9.2	6.3	7.7	5.6
1953-63	13.3	9.7	18.0	13.7	9.2	7.0
1963-69	6.4	2.4	2.6	−0.8	9.3	9.1
1969-71	0.0	−3.0	−5.5	−10.1	3.0	1.4

Source: Boretsky, "Trends in U.S. Technology," Table 1. Reprinted courtesy of the publisher.

*Largely Department of Defense and NASA.

The effects of lower productivity rates on inflation (price index) are evident. The 1974 double-digit inflation of 11 percent corresponded to a 2.9 percent productivity decline, both unprecedented in the post–World War II period. Likewise, the data in the succeeding sections demonstrate that industries with high rates of productivity growth (high technology industries) have experienced major increases in employment.

There are a number of reasons for the recent and projected decline in the rate of productivity and in the gross national product (GNP), including

(a) a slower growth of the labor force;

(b) a shift in the demographic composition of the labor force;

(c) a shift in the ratio of nonproductive to productive population;

(d) a slowdown in the rate of increase in the stock of plant and equipment due to the 1974–75 recession;

(e) increased expenditures required for pollution control and environmental conditions;

(f) higher costs of energy and raw materials;

(g) a shift toward industries with low productivity levels;

(h) a decline in the rate of technological enhancement as measured in R and D expenditures for economic growth; and

(i) some movement towards a less materialistic life style.

New technology originates in both the private and public sectors and is mainly a function of R and D expenditures. Public sector expenditures in technology have been primarily in large systems directly related to the National Aeronautics and Space Administration (NASA) and to national security. Nevertheless, as shown in Table 11.4, R and D expenditures have gone down in both the public and private sectors since 1963, although the rate of decline was more pronounced in the public sector.

It should also be noted that two thirds of the private-sector investment in technological innovation is directed at product innovation (i.e., model changes), rather than at process innovation (i.e., production methods or new assembly equipment), although the economic effects of process technologies may be much greater upon growth in output, employment, exports, and social rate of return than product innovation.

In summary, the following points can be made concerning U.S. productivity and technology:

1. U.S. prosperity at home and influence abroad is rooted in the national productivity rate.
2. Productivity is a function of the rate of technological advance.
3. Since the midsixties, the rate of U.S. productivity has slowed down.
4. A major reason for the slowdown in U.S. productivity is the decline of public and private investment in technology as measured by R and D expenditures.

These trends point to an unfavorable U.S. position compared to its past performance or its potential performance, or compared to other industrialized nations. Moreover, a closer look at productivity growth shows that the high technology industries have had strong productivity growth and a very favorable balance of trade. For example, the aerospace industry, one of the high technology industries, has had above-average productivity growth and has had a very large favorable trade balance for the entire post-World War II period.

Empirical Analysis

Recent Trends: Output, Income, and Productivity. The average U.S. productivity growth rate from 1959 to 1977 was 2.4 percent (see Table 11.5), and as can be seen in Figure 11.2, there has been a great deal of variability in the growth rate. The 1960s were years of relatively smooth, high productivity growth. The decade of the 1970s, on the other hand, has been very volatile, and the average growth has been much lower. For the 1959-67 period, the average productivity growth was 3.6 percent, while for the more recent 1967-75 period it was only 1.6 percent per year.

Productivity increases are the major cause of growth in real income over time, as illustrated in Figures 11.3 and 11.4. For the 1959-77 period, real disposable per capita income increased 59 percent (an average annual rate of 2.6 percent per year). The 1970s has not been a period of strong growth in per capita real income because of recessions and the lower-than-average rate of productivity growth. Of course, the

Table 11.5. U.S. Productivity Data (Private Business Sector)

Year	Output Per Hour		Unit Labor Costs	
	1967 = 100	% Δ	1967 = 100	% Δ
1959	76.8	3.6	89.1	1.0
1960	78.1	1.6	91.4	2.6
1961	80.6	3.3	92.1	0.7
1962	84.4	4.6	92.1	0.1
1963	87.7	4.0	92.0	−0.1
1964	91.3	4.1	93.2	1.3
1965	94.7	3.7	93.4	0.2
1966	97.8	3.2	96.8	3.7
1967	100.0	2.3	100.0	3.3
1968	103.3	3.3	104.1	4.1
1969	103.7	0.3	111.0	6.6
1970	104.5	0.7	118.1	6.4
1971	107.8	3.2	121.9	3.2
1972	111.0	2.9	125.2	2.7
1973	113.1	1.9	132.9	6.2
1974	109.9	−2.8	149.5	12.5
1975	111.8	1.8	161.1	7.7
1976	116.5	4.2	168.7	4.7
1977	119.3	2.4	179.0	6.1

Source: Data from *Economic Report of the President,* 1978.

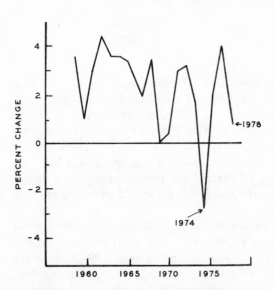

Figure 11.2. Output per house for nonfarm private business. Data from *Economic Report of the President,* 1977

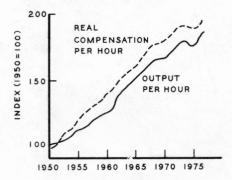

Figure 11.3. Income and productivity, 1950-1975. Data from U.S. Department of Labor, *Monthly Labor Reviews*

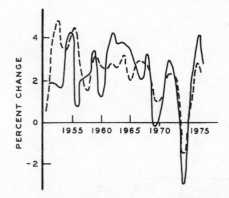

Figure 11.4. Income and productivity rates of change, 1950-1975. Data from U.S. Department of Labor, *Monthly Labor Reviews*

two recessions in the 1970s (1970-71 and 1974-75) were the major cyclical reasons for the poor performance in productivity changes in recent years. There have, however, been other noncyclical reasons why the U.S. productivity growth rate has slowed, as discussed below.

We have seen that productivity growth is important for real income growth. But, productivity is also an integral part of the rest of the economy. In the last several years, we have had rapid rates of general price increases (inflation). One measure of inflation, the consumer price index (CPI), is graphed in Figure 11.5. Although inflation has been with us for virtually the entire post-World War II period, recently we have had double-digit levels of inflation (11 percent in 1974), and it is no coincidence that these higher rates of inflation have been associated with lower rates of productivity and higher unit labor costs (another measure of inflation). This can be seen by comparing Figures 11.5 and 11.6. When productivity is high, inflation is mitigated. In 1974, when

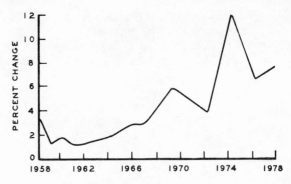

Figure 11.5. Consumer price index, 1958-1977. Data from *Economic Report of the President*, 1978

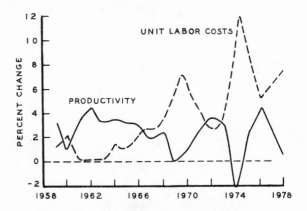

Figure 11.6. Productivity and unit labor costs, 1958-1977. Data from *Economic Report of the President*, 1978

inflation hit double-digit levels for the first peacetime period in our history, productivity change was a − 2.9 percent, the steepest decline in the post–World War II period. One way to fight inflation is to have high productivity growth. In general,

> % change in output price = % change in input costs − % change in productivity.

Productivity is also related to profit rates and the unemployment rate. Figure 11.7 shows that during the 1960s, when productivity growth was relatively stable, profit rates were high and unemployment was low. The major reason behind this situation was strong growth in the gross national product. But the strong GNP growth was aided by strong and steady positive changes in productivity.

Sources of Productivity and Growth. The United States has had a long story of increases in output per labor hour. The late nineteenth and ventieth centuries are unique in history for their rapid progress in the andard of living. What are the reasons for this growth? The main iputs into production are labor, capital, materials, and technology. Then value added is used as the measure of output (as in the GNP oncept), the inputs are labor, capital, and technology, with material subtracted from the value of output, since it is generally only a pass through cost. As shown in Figure 11.8, four major inputs into production have contributed to the growth of productivity. These four factors are the major reasons for productivity growth.

Education. Education has increased the quality of the labor force and has accounted for almost 14 percent of the growth of productivity. In 1959, the median school years completed by the civilian labor force was 12.0 years. In 1976, it was 12.6 years. The largest increase in educational attainment has been by nonwhites—an increase of 3.5 years.

Capital Stock. Another major source of productivity growth has come from increases in the capital stock. The United States has one of the highest levels of capital per worker in the world. The growth of the capital stock has contributed 26.4 percent to the growth of productivity. More capital per worker means that each worker has more powerful tools and equipment with which to work. The introduction and widespread use of computers is an example of the benefits of capital equipment in increasing labor productivity.

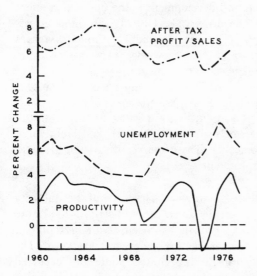

Figure 11.7. Effects of productivity on other variables, 1960–1977. Data from *Economic Report of the President,* 1978, and Data Resources, Inc.

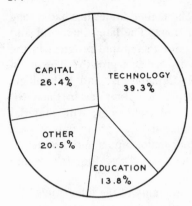

Figure 11.8. Sources of labor productivity growth, 1948–1969. Data from Edward F. Denison, *Accounting for United States Economic Growth, 1929–1969* (Washington, D.C.: Brookings Institution, 1974).

Technology/Research and Development. The major source of productivity growth as estimated by Edward Denison is "advances in knowledge and not elsewhere classified." This is the residual after accounting for all changes in input which seem to have an effect on output. In Figure 11.8 this is labeled technology. The modern business environment is best characterized by an attitude of change. To facilitate change, business must innovate. Countries, industries, and companies must continually seek new and better ways to produce new and existing products in order to survive over time. Research and development is the major ingredient in advancing the frontiers of knowledge. The United States now invests about $40 billion per year in this area. R and D stimulates future innovations and provides the industrial knowledge necessary to build new, improved capital equipment.

Other. The category we have labeled "other," which accounts for 20.5 percent of the growth in output per hour, is made up of several factors. These are improved resource allocation, i.e., a movement away from the farms (9.9 percent), economies of scale (13.9 percent), and labor force age-sex composition (−3.3 percent). These sources of growth are also important for future gains in productivity.

Reasons for the Productivity Slowdown. The rate of productivity growth has slowed down dramatically since the mid-sixties. As Figure 11.9 shows, the recent period of growth has been about *half* that of the earlier period. What are the reasons for the recent slowdown? The slowdown in the productivity rate in the United States has occurred for several reasons, discussed in the ensuing paragraphs.

Recession. The major reason for the change in the growth of productivity has been two recessions (1970–71, 1974–75) within a four-year

Table 11.6. Labor Force Composition Changes

	1957	1967	1976
Mean age (yrs.) of labor force	40.1	38.9	37.7
Female participation rate	36.9%	41.1%	47.4%

Table 11.7. Education Growth

	1957	1962	1967	1972	1977
Median years of education	10.9	12.1	12.3	12.5	12.6
Five-year average growth		0.8%	0.34%	0.32%	0.16%

period. But even when corrected for cyclical variations, there remains a statistically significant reduction in the average rate of productivity growth.

Quality of the Labor Force. The growth in the quality of the labor force has slowed because of a large increase in young, inexperienced workers, and also because of the influx of women in the labor force. Neither of these changes is detrimental in a social sense, but they have decreased productivity changes. As shown in Table 11.6, the mean age of the labor force has declined, and the female participation growth rate has increased.

Educational Growth. The educational growth rate of our labor force has slowed. The growth in the median years of education in the future will be at much slower rates than in the past, according to the U.S. Labor Department. The median education level increases for the 1957–77 period are shown in Table 11.7.

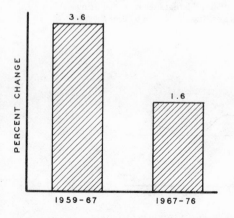

Figure 11.9. Average annual growth in productivity (data for private, nonfarm business sector). Data from U.S. Department of Labor

Sectorial Shift. Agriculture is one of the highest sectors in productivity gains. The value of agricultural output relative to the other sectors is decreasing, however. Thus, it contributes less to the total productivity rate. Another sector that has been increasing in weight is the service sector. Our society is increasingly becoming a service society, and while this is a result of our high standard of living, it contributes to a decrease in productivity changes, because the service sector is a lower-than-average productivity growth rate sector.

Investment in Capital Goods. In the past, the United States invested heavily in future productive capacities, for example, in capital goods (plant and equipment). In 1966, fixed capital investment was 14.7 percent of the gross national product. Recently there has been a slight decline in capital investment. This decline has been accompanied by a large increase in the labor force, resulting in a slowdown in the growth of capital per worker. To maintain gains in labor productivity, capital investment is required. Figures 11.10 and 11.11 illustrate the growth of capital per worker and the recent slowdown in that growth.

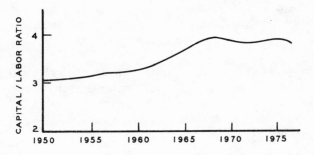

Figure 11.10. Capital-labor ratio, 1950–1975 (data for manufacturing sector). Redrawn from Data Resources, Inc., *U.S. Long-Term Review,* 1978

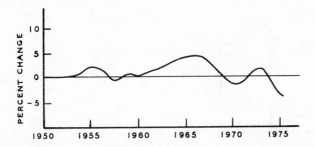

Figure 11.11. Growth of capital-labor ratio, 1950–1975 (data for manufacturing sector). Redrawn from Data Resources, Inc., *U.S. Long-Term Review,* 1978

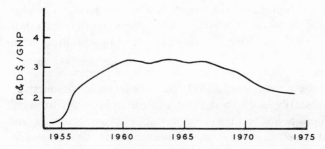

Figure 11.12. U.S. research and development intensity, 1955-1975. Data from National Science Foundation

Research and Development. Another reason the United States is suffering from sluggish productivity changes is a reduction in our research and development intensity. The major reason for the decline is reduction in the relative contribution by the federal government. Technological change is the major factor for improving the efficiency of production over the long run. The applied new technology allows us to conserve our scarce resources and maintain growth in the standard of living. U.S. research and development expenditures, as a percentage of the gross national product, have decreased almost 50 percent since the early sixties (from 3 percent to approximately 2 percent of the GNP—see Figure 11.12).

Increased Pollution Abatement Cost. The 1970s was a decade of transition in dealing with the environment. While concern for pollution predates 1970, it has only been since then that significant sums of money have been spent for this purpose. These expenditures divert funds away from other investments that would add directly to measured productive capacity. Even though the environment is enhanced (or at least prevented from further decay), our economic measurement system registers the expenditures as nonproductive.

Increased Government Regulations. The extensive Occupational Safety and Health Administration (OSHA) regulations and similar regulations are another example of nonproductive interference in the production process. While safety is enhanced, this does not show up directly in additional output—but the cost to industry is direct. Thus, input costs go up while economically measured output does not.

Employment Effects of Productivity and Technology

Technological inventions and innovations that result in productivity gains are viewed by some as ways to reduce the work force and to substitute machines for people. In agriculture, technological advance has indeed reduced employment. In manufacturing, the record is mixed. It should be noted, however, that historically, during periods of rapid technological innovations, overall employment opportunities have expanded.

Two recent studies, one by the National Science Foundation and the other by Data Resources, Inc. (DRI), show that rapid productivity gains do not necessarily lead to a reduction in the work force. In many cases just the opposite has occurred—employment has increased. Figure 11.13 shows that the effect is ambiguous. Let us examine the relationship among the growth of output, productivity, and employment. Rapid productivity gains reduce pressure to increase prices and help make the product more competitive. This price advantage may cause demand to increase and thus create opportunities for *more* employment, not less. Some specific examples of the mixed effect of productivity changes on employment are illustrated in Figure 11.14.

An even stronger relationship emerges when industries are grouped according to their research and development intensity. In the DRI study these are called high technology, mixed technology, and low technology industries, according to the ratio of R and D to sales for that industry. Figures 11.15 and 11.16 show that the high technology industries have had, on the average, higher productivity gains *and* higher-than-average employment gains. The basic reason for this is the strong growth in output by these high technology industries. For high technology industries where high productivity growth has not led to rapid output growth,

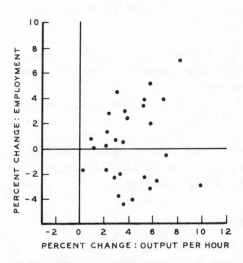

Figure 11.13. Relationship between employment and output. Each dot represents a different industry.

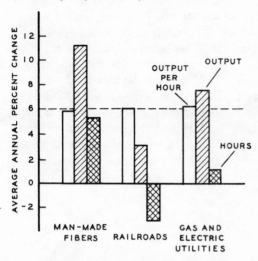

Figure 11.14. Relationship between productivity and employment in
different industries, 1960-1971. Redrawn from U.S. Department of Labor,
Monthly Labor Review, 1978

employment gains are small or even negative. The railroad industry is
an example of this behavior.

International Comparison

Productivity Gains in Other Countries. Table 11.8 compares U.S.
productivity performance with seven of its major trading partners during
the period 1960-75. Japan's rate has been three times higher than that
of the United States, and during this period, U.S. performance, with
respect to overall annual rate of change in output, was the lowest among
the group. We have already mentioned the factors which contribute to
productivity growth and the negative influence of recent changes in the
United States. Over the last twenty years the United States has lost
some of its comparative advantage. We will now examine these same
factors (education, capital growth, etc.) from an international point of
view.

The strong relation between investment in capital goods and productivity growth is illustrated in Figure 11.17. Thus, the nations which
improve their productivity the most are those which invest most heavily
in future productive capacity. A related factor is capital growth per
worker. As shown in Figure 11.18, the United States invested less in
future productive capital, as a percentage of GNP, than any other major
industrial nation.

If we look at our export intensity, shown in Figure 11.19, we see that the United States has become increasingly involved in international trade. The ratio of exports to GNP has almost doubled since 1960 (from 5 percent to 9 percent). In a comparative sense the U.S. ratio is still relatively low (Canada's ratio is 27 percent, Japan's is 13 percent). But it is likely that, barring a major trade war, we will continue to become more heavily involved in international trade. We produce many goods desired by other nations, and vice-versa. Because of different inflation rates, productivity rates, and different resource distributions, we can expect that over time some of our industries will lose ground to foreign competitors and some will gain. Because of floating exchange

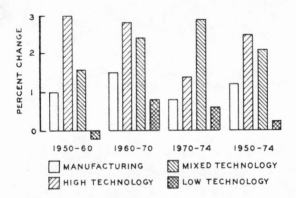

Figure 11.15. Average annual growth of employment, 1950-1974. Redrawn from Data Resources, Inc., *U.S. Long-Term Review,* Summer 1977.

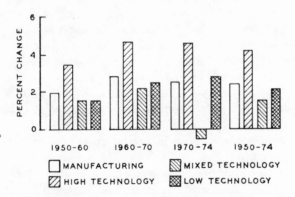

Figure 11.16. Average annual growth of output per employee (in real terms), 1950-1974. Redrawn from Data Resources, Inc., *U.S. Long-Term Review,* Summer 1977.

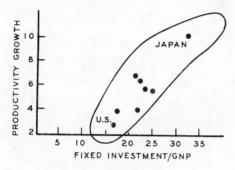

Figure 11.17. Productivity growth and fixed investments for eight countries. Data from U.S. Department of Commerce, *International Economic Indicators,* 1960–75.

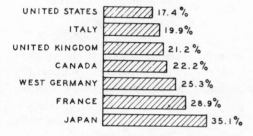

Figure 11.18. Fixed capital formation as a percentage of GNP in seven industrialized nations, 1970–1975. Redrawn from *International Economic Report of the President,* 1977

rates we can also expect, in the long run, that any overall trade imbalances between nations will be mitigated.

By looking at our trade balance (Figure 11.20) we see that large surpluses are not now as frequent as in the past. An excess of imports to exports is now more likely than a surplus. In 1977, the United States had a record trade deficit of $31 billion. The quadrupling of oil prices since 1972 and the increased dependency on foreign oil are the largest

Table 11.8. Average Change in Output per Man-Hour in Manufacturing (Percentages)

	1960–75		1960–75
United States	2.7	West Germany	5.7
United Kingdom	3.8	Italy	6.2
Canada	4.0	Sweden	6.6
France	5.6	Japan	9.7

Source: Council on International Economic Policy, 1977.

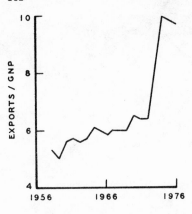

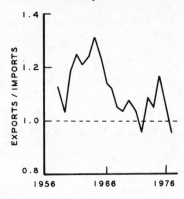

Figure 11.19. Exports as a percentage of GNP, 1956–1976. Data from *International Economic Report of the President*, 1977

Figure 11.20. U.S. Trade balance, 1956–1976. Data from *International Economic Report of the President*, 1977

causes of our recent problems; however, long before 1973, we were losing our international competitiveness. Our lower rate of productivity growth vis-a-vis that of other nations is a fundamental reason for this decline.

It has been mentioned by some that the maturity of our economy and the already high level of our capital-labor ratio are such that the marginal efficiency of capital is low. If this should be the case, at current interest rates it would not be profitable to invest heavily in new plant and equipment. Yet several other countries have capital-labor ratios which are in the same range as that of the United States, but they invest at higher rates and have higher productivity rates.

Research and Development. Since World War II, the use of organized research and development has become widespread in industry, and government suppo.. has substantially increased. In the 1960s, R and D expenditures were approximately 3.0 percent of GNP, while now we invest about 2.0 percent. This reduction is significant and is even more dramatic when we look at the behavior of several other nations. Figure 11.21 shows that while the United States is reducing its commitment to R and D, Russia, Japan, and West Germany are all increasing their commitment. Because of the time lag involved, it takes two to seven years before the effects of new R and D spending are felt in the marketplace. These trends have existed for almost a decade; some of our recent poor international trade performance may be directly traceable to the differential movements in the R and D growth rates of the recent past.

The downward trend in R and D investment in the United States may be stabilizing at 1.9–2.1 percent of the GNP invested in R and D. Many economists feel that this is too low. The methodology and the empirical evidence for determining the proper R and D intensity is a topic of current research. But even if we were to increase the intensity of R and D now, it would take several years before any impact on productivity growth and international trade would be felt. As a result of the trends in the last two decades, the United States no longer has the highest standard of living in the world (Figure 11.22). If the lower U.S. growth rate persists (as many predict), many of the major industrialized nations will surpass the United States in per capita income

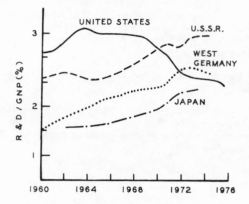

Figure 11.21. Research and development intensity in four industrialized nations, 1960–1974. Data from T. A. Vanderslice, General Electric Company, 1976

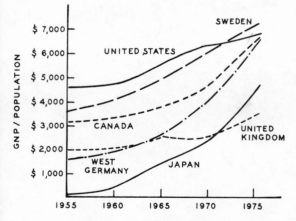

Figure 11.22. Output per person in six industrialized nations (1974 US$). Data from *International Economic Report of the President,* 1977, and *International Financial Statistics,* December 1977.

by 1990. The data signify the rates of change, or trend rate over time. As shown in Figure 11.22, in 1955, the U.S. output per person was significantly higher than the rest of the countries. This gap has been substantially closed over the last twenty years as the rates of change in the per capita GNP of other nations have been higher than that of the United States. As can be seen, Sweden crossed the U.S. line in the early seventies. One may extrapolate these trend lines to estimate when the remaining nations will catch up with and surpass the United States.

Notes

1. Robert M. Solow, "Technical Change and the Aggregate Production Function," *Review of Economics and Statistics* 39 (August 1957): 312-20.
2. "Economic Impact of Stimulated Technological Activity," *Summary Volume,* Midwest Research Institute, November 1971.
3. Ibid.
4. W. D. Nordhaus, "The Recent Productivity Slowdown," *Brookings Papers on Economic Activity,* no. 3 (1970).
5. Ibid., pp. 528-29.
6. George L. Perry, "Labor Force Structure, Potential Output, and Productivity," *Brookings Papers on Economic Activity,* 3 (1971).
7. Edward F. Denison, *Accounting for United States Economic Growth, 1929-1969* (Washington, D.C.: Brookings Institution, 1974).

{ 12 }

Major Issues Concerning U.S. Technology Policy

EDWIN MANSFIELD

Introduction

During the past fifteen years, there has been a continual ferment over U.S. technology policy. Some issues have persisted over this entire period; because of inadequate knowledge or strong disagreements, they have remained unresolved. Other issues have faded from the scene as conditions changed or as solutions were found, while still other issues have come on stage. Given the enormous variety and complexity of the issues concerning U.S. technology policy, it is impossible to provide a comprehensive, balanced, and coherent overview in a brief space. All that can be done is to discuss a few central questions which have occupied the attention of economists and policymakers in recent years. I make no pretense to treat these issues in any real depth; all I can reasonably expect to do is introduce you to each of them, with the hope that perhaps you will be stimulated to delve deeper in your subsequent reading and discussions.

Specifically, I shall discuss the following six questions concerning U.S. technology policy. First, how can we as a nation go about assessing the social impact of new technologies? Second, in the important area of pharmaceuticals what has been the effect of government regulation on the rate of technological change? Third, to what extent is it true that innovation is now the province of only the largest firms and that considerable monopoly power is a prerequisite for rapid technological change? Fourth, are we as a nation underinvesting in civilian technology? Fifth, should our government attempt to block the transfer of our advanced technology to other non-Communist countries? Sixth, what are the pros and cons of transferring our technology to the Soviet Union? Needless to say, I shall not attempt to resolve each of these very complex questions. Even if far more information were available concerning each of them, such a resolution would have to be based on value judgments, not on economic (or other) evidence alone. What I hope to do is to provide a reasonably coherent sketch of the factors involved and the arguments on each side, and, where appropriate, some indication of my own opinions.

The Role of Technology in the American Economy

At the outset, we must define technological change. Technological change consists of advances in knowledge concerning the industrial and agricultural arts. Such advances result in new and improved products and processes, as well as new techniques of organization and management.[1]

To understand the issues discussed below, it is essential to recognize the important roles played by technological change in the American economy. First, technological change is one of the most significant factors responsible for economic growth. (By *economic growth* we mean the growth of output per capita.) A seminal study carried out twenty years ago by Robert Solow concluded that about 90 percent of the long-term increase in output per capita in the United States was attributable to technological change, increased educational levels, and other factors not directly associated with increases in the quantity of labor and capital.[2] A more recent, and more exhaustive, study by Edward Denison concludes that the "advance of knowledge" contributed about 40 percent of the total increase in national income per person employed during 1929–57.[3] Although these studies are useful, their results are rough. Because of the complex interactions among the various factors that affect the economic development of a country, it is difficult to estimate from historical statistics the precise effect of a nation's rate of technological change on its rate of economic growth. Yet the results of these and other studies leave little doubt that the effects of technological change on economic growth have been very substantial.

Second, technological change has played a very important role in our nation's defense policies, which in turn have affected major portions of our economy. Realizing that any nation that falls significantly behind in military technology will be at the mercy of a more progressive foe, the great powers have spent enormous amounts on military research and development, precipitating several revolutions in technology in the past forty years. Most important have been the successful development and improvement of fission and fusion bombs, although significant achievements have also occurred in delivery vehicles, guidance techniques, radar, and other areas. In 1976, the federal government spent almost $11 billion on defense research and development (R and D) and almost $3 billion on space R and D; together, defense and space R and D accounted for almost 60 percent of the federal government's R and D expenditures. This percentage has decreased in recent years; for example, in 1969, about 80 percent, rather than 60 percent, of the federal government's R and D expenditures were for defense and space work.[4] But the largest single component of federal R and D is still defense R and D.

Third, technological change can affect the unemployment rate, as well as the content and nature of jobs. During the early 1960s, there was a prominent debate over the extent to which the high unemployment rates that prevailed then were due to changes in techniques. Some economists laid the blame for these high unemployment rates at least partly at the door of automation; others believed that they were due largely to an inadequacy of demand for goods and services. The problem of labor displacement due to technological change is not as prominent now as it was in the early 1960s, but it has by no means vanished. Policymakers are still obliged to cope, as best they can, with the changes in the composition and distribution of the labor force induced by technological (and other) changes. Collective bargaining is concerned continually with the problem of permitting changes in techniques while protecting worker security.

Fourth, technological change is a key element in the competitive struggle among firms. The extent and quality of a firm's R and D program can make it an industry leader, or head it toward bankruptcy. To cite but one example, duPont's position in the American chemical industry has certainly been due, in part at least, to its skill as an innovator. Among its major innovations were nylon, acrylic fibers, acetal resins, and neoprene. Technological change can transform an industry. For example, the electronics industry, both here and abroad, was changed dramatically by technological developments during the past twenty-five years.[5] Recognizing the importance of technological change, firms spend about $17 billion of their own money on R and D. During the early 1960s, their expenditures increased at a rapid rate, but during the late 1960s and early 1970s they increased much more slowly. In part, this slowdown in the rate of increase may have been due to a leveling off, or reduction, in the perceived profitability of industrial R and D.[6]

Technology Assessment

The first question concerning U.S. technology policy that we consider is, How should we, as a nation, go about assessing the impact of new technology? During the late 1960s, economists like E. J. Mishan argued that the adoption of new technology had resulted in "the appalling traffic congestion in our towns, cities, and suburbs, ... the erosion of the countryside, the 'uglification' of coastal towns, ... and a wide heritage of natural beauty being wantonly destroyed."[7] As public awareness of environmental problems grew in the 1960s, more and more emphasis was placed on the costs associated with technological change in the civilian economy. For example, ecologists like Barry Commoner pointed out that the application of modern technology had resulted in considerable air and water pollution.[8] Gradually, technological changes that had once been heralded as modern miracles were viewed with more and more suspicion. Eventually, some were banned, as evidence mounted that their unexpected side effects could cause damage and even death.

In the late 1960s, policymakers became increasingly interested in technology assessment, which is the process whereby an attempt is made to appraise the technical, political, economic, and social influences arising from science and technology. In 1969, the National Academy of Engineering concluded that "technology forecasts on a broad range of subjects are feasible and can be expected to be useful to the decision-making processes of the Congress, when prepared by properly constituted, independent, *ad hoc* task forces with adequate staff support and time. ... It is useful to classify technology assessments as initiated (*a*) by an existing social problem or (*b*) by the potential of a new technology. ... Technology assessments can help alert the nation to future benefits and to future problems and can thus provide the public support necessary for national programs designed to secure the benefits and to avoid those problems."[9]

In 1969, the National Academy of Sciences also issued a report endorsing the idea that the government should engage in technological assessment. The report pointed to the fact that many technologies are adopted on the basis of narrow criteria which ignore externalities: "With few exceptions, the central question asked of a technology is what it would do (or is doing) to the economic or institutional interests of those who are deciding whether or how to exploit it." In the words of the report, "no mechanism exists to trigger ... studies [of the effects of new technologies] in a systematic way at early stages in the process of development and diffusion; to explore means of deciding whether a given set of events does indeed represent an 'early stage' in a significant technological trend; to examine the terms of reference of the methodologies of such studies as are being undertaken; or to inject the results of such studies systematically into the decision-making process itself."[10]

The Office of Technology Assessment (OTA) was created by the Technology Assessment Act of 1972 to help the Congress anticipate, and plan for, the consequences of the uses of technology. OTA began operations in January 1974. OTA's assessment activities have progressed in seven principal areas: energy, food, health, materials, research and development policies and priorities, oceans, and transportation. It is not my purpose to try to evaluate OTA's activities; instead, I want to focus on the basic questions that confront society in this area. These questions were stated very well by the National Academy of Sciences:

How can we in the United States best begin the awesomely difficult task of altering present evaluative and decisionmaking processes so that private and public choices bearing on the ways in which technologies develop and fit into society will reflect a greater sensitivity to the total systems effects of such choices on the human environment? How can we best increase the likelihood that such decisions (domestically and, in the end, globally) will be informed by more complete understanding of their secondary and tertiary consequences, and will be made on the basis of criteria that take such consequences into account in a timelier and more systematic way? [11]

Clearly, these are some of the most fundamental questions regarding technology that face our nation. Unfortunately, however, these questions are as difficult to answer as they are important. For one thing, it is notoriously difficult to forecast the future development and impact of a new technology. The techniques used by technological forecasters generally seem crude, even by the standards of the social and management sciences. For another thing, new technologies affect various parts of the population and the economy in different ways, and it is difficult to weigh the interests of the various groups involved. Although some critics fear that technology assessment may result in the delay or frustration of much-needed technological changes, it seems clear that when the adoption of new technologies is potentially hazardous, some attempt must be made to assess the risks to society at large. For example, although there is considerable controversy over the adequacy of some recent assessments of the risks from nuclear power, assessments of this sort certainly should be made. But this does not answer the question of how they should be made, or who should make them: all it says is that some mechanism must be established to investigate and report the nature and extent of the externalities.

Government Regulation of New Drugs

In recent years, there has been a notable amount of controversy over the effects of government regulation on technological change. One area where this controversy has been particularly shrill has been the pharmaceutical industry. [12] During the past forty years, a wide variety of important new drugs have been developed to ease pain and extend life. Among the most heralded have been penicillin, streptomycin, the polio vaccine, tranquilizers, and oral contraceptives. The Food and Drug

Administration (FDA) is charged with the regulatory responsibility of determining whether a new drug should be marketed in the United States. Obviously, the public should be protected from the sale of flagrantly unsafe or harmful pharmaceutical products. Before 1962, the FDA was required to determine whether or not a new drug was unsafe, but not whether it was effective in its intended use. In 1962, the law was changed. No longer was safety the sole consideration; now the FDA had to be shown that a new drug was also effective.

Recently, there has been a considerable amount of controversy among economists as to whether or not this 1962 change in the law was beneficial. According to Sam Peltzman of the University of Chicago, it has been a bad thing. Because it is more costly and time-consuming to prove the efficacy, as well as the safety, of a new drug, the cost of developing and bringing to market a new drug has increased, the result being that fewer new drugs have been marketed. Peltzman calculates that the reduced flow of new drugs (due to the change in the law) has cost consumers about $300 million. Included in this figure is the amount that consumers would have been willing to pay for the new drugs that would have been marketed under the old regulations, but that were not marketed under the new ones.[13]

Not all economists, however, find Peltzman's calculation persuasive. According to T. McGuire, R. Nelson, and T. Spavins of Yale University, "Peltzman's analysis provides no real evidence on which one can rest a judgment of this sort."[14] The Food and Drug Administration has also tried to rebut many of Peltzman's charges. For example, the director of FDA's Bureau of Drugs claimed that most of the decrease in the flow of new drugs "is accounted for by the marked decline in marketing of [drugs] ... considered by experts to be incompatible with the practice of sound therapeutics."[15]

Controversy here is likely to continue, since the facts are hard to get and those that can be gotten are difficult to interpret. Economics certainly has a role to play in resolving this controversy, as witness the contributions of Peltzman and others. But the findings of economists must be tied to research efforts of pharmacologists and other scientists. Most recent studies by economists seem to suggest that the increased stringency in FDA's premarket approval regulations has contributed to a decline in the number of new drugs available in the U.S. market. It is very difficult, however, to isolate the effects of regulation from other factors; and existing evidence is by no means conclusive.

Antitrust Policy and Innovation

While technology assessment and government regulation have often focused on preventing the improper adoption of new technology, this does not mean that technology's benefits—as well as its possible costs and risks—have not been recognized. In considerable measure, public policy is geared to the promotion of technological change. Thus, policymakers are interested in whether or not our antitrust laws tend to reduce the rate of technological change. Is it true, as John Kenneth Galbraith and Joseph Schumpeter have claimed, that innovation is now the province of very big firms? Is considerable monopoly power, as measured by high market concentration, conducive to a rapid rate of technological change? In recent years, economists have begun to study these questions in a systematic way. Although we are far from having complete or definitive answers, quite a few generalizations seem warranted, based on the evidence gathered to date.

The first point that must be made is that the role of the small firm is important at the stage of invention and the initial, relatively inexpensive stages of R and D. Based on the findings of many studies, it is clear that small firms and independent inventors play a large—perhaps a disproportionately large—role in conceiving important new ideas and major inventions. Moreover, although the development of these ideas often requires more resources and different kinds of management skills than some of these small firms have, the investment required for development and innovation is seldom so great or so risky that only the largest firms in the industry can do the developing or the innovating. Indeed, my own studies of the drug, petroleum, steel, and coal industries show that, in all of these industries, the firms that carried out the largest number of innovations—relative to their size—were not the biggest firms, at least in the time periods I studied.[16]

The available evidence suggests, too, that the biggest firms generally do not spend more on R and D, relative to their size, than somewhat smaller firms. There seems to be a threshold effect. A firm has to be a certain size to spend much on R and D, as defined by the National Science Foundation. But beyond a certain point, increases in size no longer bring any disproportionate rise in R and D expenditures. This seems to be true in all industries studied, with the exception of chemicals. Of course, the threshold varies from industry to industry; but according to F. M. Scherer, increases in firm size beyond an employment level of about 5,000 employees are generally not accompanied by a more than proportional increase in innovation inputs or outputs. Thus, the evidence does not seem to indicate that giant firms devote more resources, relative to their size, to inventive and innovative activities than do their somewhat smaller competitors. Moreover, there is some evidence that, per dollar of R and D, the biggest firms get less inventive and innovative output than smaller firms.

Of course, firm size and market structure are two different things. A big firm need not be a monopolist or anything close to it. From the point of view of antitrust policy, it is particularly important to explore the relationship between the extent of concentration in an industry and the industry's rate of technological change. Far too little work has been carried out in this area to support firm or confident conclusions. But certain patterns are beginning to emerge. In general, most studies of the relationship between industrial concentration and the rate of technological change seem to conclude that a slight amount of concentration may promote more rapid invention and innovation. Very fragmented, splintered industries, like construction, do not seem to be able to promote a rapid rate of technological advance. But beyond a moderate amount of concentration, further increases in concentration do not seem to be associated with more rapid rates of technological advance. In part, this may be due to less competitive pressure and fewer independent loci for decisionmaking.

Finally, three additional points should be noted. First, there is a great deal of evidence that new firms and firms entering new markets play a very important role in the promotion of technological change. Existing firms can be surprisingly blind to the potentialities of new ideas. Second, economists generally agree that the ideal market structure for stimulating technological change is one where there is a mixture of firm sizes. Complementarities and interdependencies exist among larger and smaller firms. Third, cases sometimes arise where industries are composed of such small firms, or markets are so fragmented, that technological change is hampered. Firms cannot afford to do much R and D, and they may find it difficult to use new techniques. The risks involved in innovation are too great for any single firm. In such cases, it may be good public policy to supplement the R and D supported by the private sector. Of course, a good example of this is agriculture, an area in which the government has supported a great deal of R and D for many years.[17]

Are We Underinvesting in Civilian Technology?

While some observers fear that technological change may result in large, and often unforeseen, social costs, others are concerned that, from a purely economic viewpoint, we as a nation may be underinvesting in civilian technology. Because it is often difficult for firms to appropriate the benefits that society receives from new technology, there may be a tendency for too few resources to be devoted to new technology. Also, because R and D is a relatively risky activity, there may be a tendency for firms to invest too little in it, given that many firms tend to be averse to risk and that there are limited and imperfect ways to shift risk. Nevertheless, these factors may be offset, partially or fully, by other factors, such as oligopolistic emphasis on nonprice competition or existing government intervention.

To shed light on whether there is an underinvestment in R and D in particular areas of the private sector, economists have tried to estimate the social rates of return from past investments in new civilian technology. The results, both for agriculture and manufacturing, almost invariably indicate that the average and marginal social rates of return from such investments have been very high. There are a variety of important problems and limitations inherent in each of these studies, and they are very frail reeds on which to base policy conclusions. Nonetheless, it is remarkable that so many independent studies based on so many types of data result in so consistent a set of conclusions.

Despite the weakness and incompleteness of the existing evidence, most economists who have studied the question seem to feel, on the basis of this evidence, that some underinvestment of this sort probably exists, and there has been some discussion of the measures the government might take to reduce the shortfall.[18] Unfortunately, each of the principal measures suggested to date—government grants and contracts to industry and universities to increase our investment in civilian technology, increased use of government laboratories for such purposes, and tax credits for R and D—have important drawbacks. In particular, with regard to grants and contracts (as with any selective mechanism), one runs into the problem that the social benefits and costs of increases in various kinds of R and D are very hard to forecast. With regard to the increased use of government laboratories, there are problems in having R and D conducted by organizations that are not in close touch with the marketing and production of the product. Tax credits would reward firms for doing R and D that they would have done anyway, would not help firms with no profits, and would encourage firms to redefine R and D to include as much as possible. Some of these problems might be solved by a tax credit for increases in R and D, but many problems remain.

At present it is difficult, if not impossible, to specify what combination of these and other measures would be most effective in compensating for whatever underinvestment there is in civilian technology. There seems, however, to be considerable agreement on the following five points (1) if such a program is deemed worthwhile, it should be neither large-scale nor organized on a crash basis; (2) it should not focus on helping sick industries merely because they are sick, (3) it should not involve the government to any significant extent in the latter stages of development work; (4) a proper coupling between technology and the market should be maintained; (5) the advantages of pluralism and decentralized decisionmaking should be recognized.[19]

International Technology Transfer

Thus far, we have been concerned with issues in U.S. technology policy that are related primarily to domestic rather than international matters. In recent years, policymakers have devoted considerable attention to international questions. To understand these issues, we must recognize that the available evidence suggests that, for a long time, U.S. technology has tended to lead that of other industrialized countries. For example, during the late nineteenth century, it appears that total factor productivity was higher in the United States than in Europe, that the United States had a strong export position in technically progressive industries, and that Europeans tended to imitate American techniques. In the 1960's, Europeans expressed considerable worry over the technology gap. They claimed that superior know-how from scientific and technical achievements in the United States had permitted American companies to obtain large shares of European markets in fields like aircraft, space equipment, computers, and other electronic products.

During the 1970's, American observers have expressed increasing concern that this technological lead is being reduced. Several types of evidence have been put forth in this connection. First, the 1975 annual report of the National Science Board contains a study suggesting that the percentage of major innovations originating in the United States fell substantially from 1953 to 1967, and has remained relatively constant since 1968. Second, the percentage gain in productivity during 1960–74 was smaller in the United States than in France, West Germany, Japan, or the United Kingdom. Indeed, the percentage gain in productivity in Japan was over four times that of the United States during this period. Third, while R and D expenditures have been decreasing as a percentage of gross national product in the United States since 1964, they have been increasing in other countries, such as Japan, West Germany, and the Soviet Union. Of course, all of this evidence is far from unambiguous, but nonetheless it has evoked widespread concern.[20]

Some groups have suggested that we try to interfere with the international transfer of technology in order to prevent our advanced technology from seeping out to competitors in other countries. For example, the AFL-CIO proposed in 1971 that "the President [be given] clear authority to regulate, supervise, and curb licensing and patent agreements on the basis of Congressionally determined standards."[21] In general, economists seem to be uncomfortable with such proposals to interfere with the international diffusion of technology. They point out that it would be very difficult to stem the diffusion of technology, and that even if it could be done, it would invite retaliation. After all, there are mutual benefits from international specialization with regard to technology, and technology flows both out of and into the United States.

Moreover—a point that is often ignored—if U.S. firms could not transfer and utilize their technology abroad, they might not carry out as much research and development, with the result that our technological position might be weakened. My own studies indicate that, although there may be some tendency for firms to emphasize domestic markets, this tendency is not so strong that public policy can assume that decreased opportunities for international technology transfer would have little or no effect on U.S. R and D expenditures. On the contrary, although such measures would not result in enormous cuts in percentage terms, they apparently would prompt a perceptible and significant reduction in our R and D expenditures, which might tend to weaken our own technological position.

Some observers have also argued that the government should support and stimulate R and D in industries where our technological lead seems to be narrowing. In the long run, the international competitiveness of particular American industries most certainly will depend on our policies with respect to science and technology, but one cannot conclude from this that government support for civilian technology should be focused on industries that are having increased difficulties in meeting foreign competition. Whether or not more R and D should be supported or encouraged in a particular industry depends on the extent of the social payoff there from additional R and D, not on whether or not our technological lead there seems to be shrinking.[22]

East-West Technology Transfer

Up to this point, I have been stressing mainly the transfer of technology to non-Communist countries. Another major issue concerns the extent to which the United States should permit the transfer of advanced technology to major Communist countries like the Soviet Union.[23] During the early 1970's, the United States, as part of its policy of détente with the Soviet Union, began to increase the extent of technological cooperation; an important step in this direction was the May 1972 U.S.-U.S.S.R. Summit Agreement on Cooperation in the Fields of Science and Technology. This agreement set up a joint commission, the aim of which was to promote technological transfer between the U.S. and U.S.S.R., and to do cooperative research and development in areas such as the application of computers to management, energy, and chemical catalysis.

This was an important step in U.S.-U.S.S.R. relations. But it was by no means the first time that the Russians have imported Western technology. On the contrary, in the 1890's, there was a massive infusion of Western technology (and capital) into basic Russian industries, like steel. Again in the late 1920s and early 1930s, there was a very significant import of Western technology concerning electrical equipment, machine tools, and other types of equipment. And in the 1950s, there was an absorption of processes to produce fertilizers and synthetic fibers. Now, as in these previous periods, the U.S.S.R. seems to be intent on importing technology of various kinds, with particular emphasis on areas like computer technology and integrated circuits.

Despite its large investment in R and D and its high level of scientific accomplishment in many areas, the Soviet Union continues to lag behind the West in these and many other aspects of civilian technology. The Soviets have encountered important difficulties in getting new technology out of the laboratory and into widespread application, owing, in part at least, to the rather sharp separation of R and D from production, which has tended to reduce the economic relevance of R and D and to thwart the transfer of technology. In addition, the incentive system facing Soviet managers seems to have discouraged innovation, as well as the transfer of many kinds of technology.

The advantages to the United States of increased U.S.-U.S.S.R. technology transfer are generally regarded to be of three broad types. First, it is hoped that technological cooperation will result in improvements in political and diplomatic relations between the East and West. Second, it is hoped that increased technological cooperation will result in the West's gaining access to technology developed in the Soviet Union and Eastern Europe. Third, it is hoped that increased technological cooperation will result in increased U.S. exports to the Soviet Union and Eastern Europe.

On the other hand, many policy analysts and economists have warned that the United States should be cautious in this area. For one thing, it is feared that increased technology transfer will result in an enhancement of Soviet military capabilities. Second, it is feared that increased technological cooperation will result in increased competition with the Soviets in economic areas. Third, it is feared that the economic benefits to the West may not live up to the optimistic expectations that have sometimes been publicized.

To the Soviet Union, American technology is a means of raising the Soviet economic growth rate. Soviet gross national product grew at an average annual rate of 6.4 percent in 1950-58, 5.3 percent in 1958-67, and 3.7 percent in 1967-73. Confronted by this decline in the rate of growth of GNP (and in the rate of growth of productivity), the Soviet leaders seem to be intent on obtaining advanced technology from the West to reverse this trend, which they view with some concern. Without question, technology transfer from the West can help the Soviets in this regard. What is less obvious is whether the Soviets will be able, in the foreseeable future, to remove or offset the institutional barriers which seem to have prevented them from achieving a high rate of innovation (and rapid diffusion of innovation) outside the military and space fields.

Conclusions

It should be evident from the foregoing discussion that the issues concerning technology policy are of vital importance to this and future generations, that they require much more research, and that they entail much more than economics alone. It is no exaggeration to say that the safety of portions of our population may depend on whether or not some adequate means of technology assessment can be found, that our rate of economic growth may depend, in part at least, on whether we are under-investing in civilian technology, and that our economic and political relations with the rest of the world are bound up with our policies toward international technology transfer. It is clear as well that government regulatory and antitrust policies can have an appreciable effect on the rate and direction of technological change.

Unfortunately, many of these issues are as difficult as they are important, and the available information is far less than is needed by policy-makers. Progress is being made toward a better understanding of these issues, and economics is making a significant contribution to this progress. But advances in this area tend to be slow and uneven. Despite the progress made in the past ten or fifteen years in our understanding of the economics of technological change, it is likely that these questions, perhaps altered slightly in form, will absorb economists for many years to come. But if the rate of advance in the future is as great as in the recent past, we should be much better able to resolve many of these issues in the next decade or two.

Notes

1. For further discussion, see E. Mansfield, *The Economics of Technological Change* (New York: Norton, 1968).
2. R. Solow, "Technical Change and the Aggregate Production Function," *Review of Economics and Statistics,* August 1957.
3. E. Denison, *The Sources of Economic Growth in the United States* (New York: Committee for Economic Development, 1962).
4. National Science Board, *Science Indicators, 1976* (Washington, D.C.: National Science Foundation, 1977).
5. J. Tilton, *International Diffusion of Technology: The Case of Semiconductors* (Washington, D.C.: Brookings Institution, 1971).
6. See E. Mansfield, J. Rapoport, A. Romeo, E. Villani, S. Wagner, and F. Husic, *The Production and Application of New Industrial Technology* (New York: Norton, 1977).
7. E. Mishan, *Technology and Growth* (New York: Praeger, 1969).
8. B. Commoner, "The Environmental Costs of Economic Growth," in *Economics of the Environment,* ed. R. Dorfman and N. Dorfman, 2nd ed. (New York: Norton, 1977).
9. National Academy of Engineering, Committee on Public Engineering Policy, *A Study of Technology Assessment,* U.S., House of Representatives, Committee on Science and Astronautics, July 1969.
10. National Academy of Sciences, *Technology: Processes of Assessment and Choice,* U.S., House of Representatives, Committee on Science and Astronautics, July 1969.
11. Ibid.
12. This section is based on E. Mansfield, *Economics: Principles, Problems, Decisions,* 2nd ed. (New York: Norton, 1977), p. 574.
13. See S. Peltzman, *Regulation of Pharmaceutical Innovation* (Washington, D.C.: American Enterprise Institute, 1976).
14. T. McGuire, R. Nelson, and T. Spavins, "An Evaluation of Consumer Protection

Legislation: The 1962 Drug Amendment—A Comment," *Journal of Political Economy*, May 1975.

15. See H. Grabowski, *Drug Regulation and Innovation* (Washington, D.C.: American Enterprise Institute, 1976).

16. E. Mansfield, *Industrial Research and Technological Innovation* (New York: Norton, for the Cowles Foundation for Research in Economics at Yale University, 1968); and E. Mansfield, J. Rapoport, J. Schnee, S. Wagner, and M. Hamburger, *Research and Innovation in the Modern Corporation* (New York: Norton, 1971).

17. For references to many of the relevant studies, see E. Mansfield, "Federal Support of R and D Activities in the Private Sector," in *Priorities and Efficiency in Federal Research and Development*, Joint Economic Committee of Congress, 1976.

18. For example, see the papers by George Eads, John Kendrick, M. Nadiri, Nestor Terleckyj, and myself presented at the National Science Foundation's Colloquium on Research and Development and Productivity, 9 November 1977.

19. This section is based in part on my paper "Returns from Industrial Innovation, International Technology Transfer, and Overseas Research and Development," which was presented on 21 May 1977 at the NSF Symposium on the Relationship between R and D and the Returns from Technological Innovation, and will be published by the National Science Foundation.

20. For a much lengthier discussion of this evidence, see E. Mansfield, "Economic Growth or Stagnation: The Role of Technology," presented as part of the 1977–78 Key Issues Lecture Series at New York University and published in *Economic Growth or Stagnation*, ed. J. Backman (Indianapolis: Bobbs Merrill, 1978).

21. See the testimony by A. Biemiller before the Subcommittee on Science, Research, and Development of the House of Representatives, 28 July 1971.

22. See my testimony in *Federal Research and Development Expenditures and the National Economy*, U.S., House of Representatives, Hearings before the Committee on Science and Technology, 28 April 1976; and E. Mansfield, R. Romeo, and S. Wagner, "Foreign Trade and U.S. Research and Development," *Review of Economics and Statistics*, February 1979.

23. This section is based partly on my "East-West Technological Cooperation and Competition," *NATO Review*, August, 1975. This material also appears in my book *Economics: Principles, Problems, Decisions* (see n. 12, above).

{ 13 }

Stages in Soviet Economic Development: A Sixty-Year Record

JOHN P. HARDT

Overview

Soviet economic development may be divided into three periods over the sixty years of Soviet power from 1917 to 1977, as follows: 1917-28—the transitional period from the political revolution of 1917 to the economic revolution of the first Five-Year Plan in 1928; 1928-55—the Stalinist period of the first Five-Year Plan periods; and 1955-77—the current, post-Stalinist period.

The first period (1917-28) was largely a time of economic recovery, establishment of political power, and a predevelopment "industrialization debate" for determining the Party policy and doctrine to be followed in the subsequent period. The economic prescriptions of the rivals to succeed V. I. Lenin—Nikolai Bukharin, Leon Trotsky, and Joseph Stalin, who participated in the industrialization debates of the 1920s—provided the alternative policy prescriptions for determining subsequent economic development plans. After the resolution of the political power struggle in the initial period, subsequent economic plans were guided by the clearly defined Stalinist economic objective of establishing a heavy-industrial, defense production, economic power base in as short a time as physically possible. Although silenced by Stalin's victory, the alternative viewpoints presented and discussed at the time by Stalin's rivals have had recurring importance in the Stalinist and post-Stalinist periods in the Soviet Union as well as among the various socialist countries in Eastern Europe and in the People's Republic of China. This has been especially true of the ideological and economic development views of Nikolai Bukharin.

An earlier version of this paper, discussing the fifty-year record, appeared in Vladimir G. Treml, ed., *The Development of the Soviet Economy: Plan and Performance* (New York: Praeger, 1968). Portions of the earlier article are used with permission.

The Stalinist period (1928–55) was characterized by a single-minded objective of overcoming economic backwardness by transforming a rural economy into an industrial-urban, militarily strong state. The development means employed required a mobilization of the entire society in support of the objectives of the single leader, Joseph Stalin, in building this strong heavy-industrial base and military capability for Soviet Russia comparable to that of the advanced Western nations.

The specific objectives of the Stalinist model for development were the following:

1. Priority allocation of resources to satisfy military program needs, designed to at least equal the preparedness of other nations;
2. Maximal output of heavy-industrial products, such as coal, electric power, steel, and machinery, with preference to physical quantities rather than to technological change;
3. Provision of minimum consumer goods to ensure effective manpower utilization.

In evaluating Stalin's objective of overcoming economic backwardness, we must think of economic rationality primarily in the sense of internal consistency. Thus, our focus of concern in the Stalinist period is not primarily on the excesses of the Stalinist system in collectivizing agriculture and limiting foreign trade, but on evaluating the fulfillment of economic goals chosen by Stalin.

In the post-Stalin period (1955–77), with the Stalinist industrial base attained, the more difficult general objective became that of transforming an industrial society into a modern, technologically dynamic economy capable of meeting the multiple needs of a global power. The diversity of goals required for economic modernization was reinforced by the relative weakness of the post-Stalin leadership resulting from the end of unitary control by the Stalinist personality dominating the Party and state. The much more powerful economy and global political power brought about by Stalin's successes provided both an opportunity for significant economic development and myriad problems in attaining the multiple, often competitive goals.

With a new general objective and with a different pattern of political constraints and advantages, the post-Stalinist model contained the following revised specific objectives:

1. Allocation to military programs, although still first priority, was constrained by policy choices among military and civilian programs and an introduction of an economic accounting system for military programs;
2. Optimal choices were made among a wide range of industrial,

agricultural, and material production goals with special attention to technological change;
3. Output of consumer goods became a priority concern. Agriculture and light industry were given special attention in allocation
   of investment and manpower.

Although the control instruments of the Stalinist institutional system
(the collective farm system, the incentive wage payment system, the
foreign trade monopoly) were retained, the market shift to material
incentives and the acceptance of an important degree of foreign economic
interrelations changed the quality of those institutions.

There are some similarities between the two development periods—
the Stalinist and the post-Stalinist—and the economic doctrines of
development processes of some earlier Western economic epochs. The
Stalinist period may be likened to some aspects of mercantilism in
Tudor England and certain characteristics of the Physiocratic school
doctrine in Bourbon, France; the current, post-Stalinist period has some
similarities to the beginning of libertarianism in eighteenth-century
English politics and the epoch of the classical economics of Adam Smith
and David Ricardo. These historical parallels with certain aspects of
Western development, however, are at best interesting frames of ref-
erence. The development of the economy in the various stages in Soviet
Russia bears far more affinity to prescriptions of Marx, Engels, and
Lenin and the traditions of Russian economic history than it does to
Western doctrine and patterns of economic development. Even as the
Soviet Union today faces its myriad problems in attaining a position
of economic superpower, its doctrines, policies and institutions remain
socialist and Eastern. Any tendency for the current development to
converge with other patterns is more likely to revive deemphasized
Marxist-Leninist prescriptions and Eastern patterns of the theoretical
or empirical past than to converge with Western patterns of development.

Still, the views developed in the Stalinist period may be compared
with those of eighteenth-century English mercantilists and French
Physiocrats, in that the same unity of effective groups with analogous
goals of national aggrandizement, which led to the type of economic
theory supported by the mercantilists and Physiocrats in the eighteenth
century in England and in France, may have obtained for the Soviet
Union in 1928. Just as the diversity of groups that arose in libertarian
England gave rise to the emergence of classical economics, so the growing
diversity of social groups in the post-Stalin era—pluralism within the
elite—may have led to a regeneration of the economic science in post-
Stalin Soviet Russia.

How then today, after the first six decades of Soviet power, does the
performance of the Soviet-planned economy measure up to its promise

or to the expectations of its architects? Have the ideological precepts of Marx, Engels, and Lenin, which influenced both the political revolution in 1917 and the economic revolution in 1928, given way to a new pragmatism arising from the need for efficient administration of a modern Soviet state and economy? Has Soviet success under Stalin in overcoming historical Russian economic backwardness been offset by failure to develop the efficient allocation and administration system necessary to cope with the increasing demands of modern society? How did the strategy and performance of the Stalinist era condition the subsequent development in the post-Stalin period? Have the measured economic successes of Stalinism left as legacies major problems and constraints that impede the changes necessary for the post-Stalin system to meet its new goals?

Perhaps the ultimate question is, Can or will the Soviet leadership, faced by prospects of unacceptable retardation of economic growth and quality problems, move beyond the current modification of the Stalinist system to basic changes in the pillars of that system: *in resource allocation policy,* a redressing of the unbalanced preference of "guns" over "butter"; *in economic organization,* a withdrawal of the direct Party involvement in economic administration and a development of a system simulating Western market-type efficiency; *in foreign economic relations,* a significant shift from economic isolation or autarchy to interdependence? An affirmative answer would mean a return to the concept of Marxist-Leninism of Stalin's main ideological rival, Nikolai Bukharin, and a move to Western industrial resource priorities and management mechanics. Leninist market socialism might be the next, the fourth, stage of Soviet development.

The First Stage: From Political to Economic Revolution, 1917–1928

The Bolshevik leadership under V. I. Lenin was capable of taking power in 1917, and of proceeding to destroy the institutions of the old regime. But it was not capable, in the short run, of establishing new institutions and proceeding toward attaining its economic development goals. An overriding goal for all Bolsheviks was that of overcoming economic backwardness by industrialization of Soviet Russia.[1] Important as this consensus was, the ability to move toward its attainment had to await the firm establishment of Soviet political power and the recovery of the economy from the ravages of World War I and the Civil War. When the War Communism period was brought to an end by the Kronstadt Revolt of Soviet sailors near Leningrad, the economy had fallen to a point so low—one-fifth of the 1913 level—that it was barely reasonable to consider it an operating economy.[2] The Kronstadt rebellion was viewed by some as a serious threat to the Soviet leadership's retention of political power. This threat to the life of the Bolshevik state may have crystalized the important ideological discussions that ensued, influencing subsequent economic policy. The ideological challenges appeared to be resolved on the side of Party control: worker and professional participation in management ("one man" over "collegial" and "red" over "expert"), egalitarian versus progressive piece-rate system (the "rule of poverty" versus the "bourgeois right"); reduction versus retention of control mechanisms (the "withering away of the state" debate). These debates and others were all resolved on the side of Stalin's control version of Lenin's principle of democratic centralism and were institutionalized by the Stalinist system. All of these precepts find current expression in development and policy debates throughout the socialist economies, although their recent surfacing has been largely in Eastern Europe and in the People's Republic of China.[3] They can be assumed to be actively present in the Soviet Union beneath the surface.

The Soviet revolution of 1917 preceded the economic revolution of the first Five-Year Plan by a full decade. During the preindustrialization period, the contradictions surrounding the promises of the revolution did not have to be opened to question. The Leninist prescription for revolution called for the destruction of the czarist administrative apparatus and its replacement by a new administration directed by the Communist Party.[4] At the time, no contradiction was perceived between this approach and the Marx-Engels precepts of an egalitarian relationship between the state and the individual, with primary emphasis on the proletariat—the workers and the peasants—and of the withering away of the authoritarian state once the purposes of the dictatorship were established. As it later became clear in the Stalinist era, democratic centralism and dictatorial control of the state by the Party are not compatible with these concepts. During the revolution and the period of War Communism, however, this incompatibility was not yet manifest, a circumstance duly reflected in the spirit of the 1919 Party Program.[5]

According to the Leninist concept of democratic centralism, a small core of professional revolutionaries should decide for the masses when changes should take place and how they should be consummated. The conscious will of this elite—that is, the Party—was thus to express the will of the masses. The spontaneous expression of the majority was regarded as antithetical to the Leninist view. During the period of War Communism, the contrasting views of Lenin and of Marx and Engels could be stated together in official policy, as they were in the 1919 Party Program, without the contradictions being apparent.

Marx provided very little specific guidance for the development of the Soviet economy. As aptly put by E. H. Carr,

What Marx bequeathed to posterity was, therefore, not an economic prospectus of socialism but an economic analysis of capitalism; his economic tools were those appropriate to the capitalist system. "Political economy," with its familiar categories of value, price, and profit, was something that belonged essentially to capitalism and would be superseded with it. ...

But the economic policies of the transition period through which the revolution must pass in the struggle to create the socialist order had to be worked out empirically by the workers who had made the revolution.[6]

Certain notions of Marx and Engels nevertheless were incorporated into the revolutionary lexicon: egalitarianism; mass support and participation, particularly by the proletariat; and a dialectic process of change oriented towards reducing the coercive instruments of state power. The apparent contradictions raised by the adoption of these ideas were not clarified in the statements of Soviet leaders. Again, in E. H. Carr's view, Lenin himself was not entirely clear, or perhaps candid, about the rationale for War Communism:

But Lenin was not wholly consistent in his diagnosis of the driving forces behind war communism. In one of the two speeches which introduced NEP to the Tenth Party Congress he ascribed war communism to "dreamers" who supposed that it would be possible in three years to transform the "economic base" of the Soviet order; in the other he described war communism as "dictated not by economic, but by military needs, considerations and conditions."[7]

With the advent of the New Economic Policy (NEP) in 1921, the need to begin to establish a new state apparatus brought the two ideological faces of the Bolshevik revolution into conflict.[8] By 1920, the problems of administering the economy were coming to take precedence over the task of seizing and holding power.[9] The lines of a Soviet-planned economy were already being drawn at the Tenth Party Congress in December 1920, when Lenin personally initiated the comprehensive plan put forward by GOELRO (State Commission for the Electrification of Russia).[10] The Party, led by Lenin, was beginning to turn to the development of the state and its economy. Lenin chose to emphasize the heavy-industrial sectors characterized by electric power—the so-called commanding heights of the economy. Still, he was not, at that point, able or required by the economic conditions in a war-ravaged country to choose a course of total economic development. He decided to concentrate efforts on development of key, controlled sectors. For the rest—the uncontrolled economy—he opted for recovery, thus postponing the more basic choice of a plan for the entire economy. The period of NEP was, in Lenin's view, an explicit ideological and political retreat from the promises of the revolution and War Communism. In the view of a leading Party ideologist, Nikolai Bukharin, however, it was a transition or a step forward.[11]

Forced to turn to administration in the period 1920–22, Lenin appeared to uphold contradictory views. Some Marxian humanism was evident in his adoption of the so-called rule of poverty, and some egalitarianism was present in the principle of wage payments and work assignments. Each cook, in his words, was to be capable of governing the state.[12] The growing contradiction between these egalitarian notions and Lenin's own idea of Party dominance planning had not yet been resolved when Lenin became incapacitated in 1922. After Lenin's death in 1924, Stalin gave unequivocal support to the view of the centralized dominant Party rules abandoning the more humane pluralistic prescriptions of Marx and Engels. It can only be inferred that Lenin, had he lived after 1924, would have followed the same path.

The confrontation between these conflicting views came later, in the wage policy debate of 1926 and in the abandonment of egalitarian wage policy in 1931. These events formed the theoretical underpinning for the eventual adoption of the highly progressive, differentiated, piece-rate wage plan and the Stakhanovite system. An atypical quotation from Karl Marx's "Critique of Gotha Programme" established the Stalinist rationalization for this abandonment of Marxian egalitarianism.[13] The slogan, "Each according to his contribution," rather than "Each according to his need," was the basis for abrogating egalitarian policy.[14] Similarly, the proletarian nature of the Soviet state came to be changed. The promise of a Soviet labor policy based on Marxian views was progressively minimized.[15]

Though there was a retreat from control by workers in industry with the introduction of "the bourgeois specialists," the influence of the latter was countered by the participation of trade unions and Party members in management—the so-called triangle. This modified proletarian influence, tempered by the needs of economic recovery, gave way to state control with the establishment of one-man rule and to control by the Red Directors with the initiation of the Five-Year Plan.[16]

Subsequently, Stalin began to move away from the concept of "the withering away of the state"[17] during the Five-Year Plan period. Many Bolsheviks had held the view that control institutions would gradually disappear as the state moved towards socialism and eventually towards communism. The subsequent progressive development of coercive institutions of state economic planning clearly reflects the departure from Engels's view of the appropriate historical process.

By 1926–28, a recovery had taken place in Soviet factories and on its farms; basically, 1913 levels of production had been regained. The Soviet economy had got back to its economic takeoff point.[18] Then, a decision could be made—indeed, in the view of the post-Lenin leadership, a decision apparently *had* to be made—on the overall course of economic development. From the time of Lenin's death in 1924 until 1926, there was a debate among Soviet leaders on economic development, the so-called industrialization debate.[19] Its resolution in 1926, in favor of the group led by Stalin, signalled the commitment of the Soviet Union to rapid industrial development. This decision, translated into the first Five-Year Plan in 1928 (not in 1917), constituted the economic revolution in the Soviet Union.

The Second Stage: Stalinist Economic Development, 1928-1955

Resolution of the industrialization debate coincided with the establishment of Joseph Stalin as the leader of the Party and the acceptance of his "centrist" position on economic development.

The Stalinist pattern of economic development grew out of the end of the economic policy discussions. With the initiation of the First Five-Year Plan, the policy differences were formally resolved. Ostensibly, Stalin's view had prevailed over that of the Left, personified by Leon Trotsky, and that of the Right, personified by Nikolai Bukharin, though, in fact, Stalin accepted most of the premises and policy proposals advanced earlier by elements of the Left.[20]

In the period 1924-28, the post-Lenin leaders theoretically faced problems similar to those perceived by their czarist predecessors in 1913: establishment of an industrial-defense base consonant with other ingredients of national power, including population, natural resources, and physical size; creation and expansion of the urban-rural infrastructure of a modern society; and improvement of levels of consumption consonant with the economic capabilities of a great power in the modern world. Stalin and his opposition approached these problems with very different views on priorities, timing, and means of attainment.[21]

The Left, led by Leon Trotsky, took the view, still evident as late as 1931 in the German policy of Karl Radek, that economic development in Soviet Russia could be linked to an industrially advanced economy in a communist Germany.[22] This led to continuation of revolution outside the Soviet Union, a policy that easily accommodated the Marxist idea of industrial development's failing to occur in rural Russia. In his debates with the Trotskyite Left, Stalin took the view that socialism in one country, the dominance of domestic considerations over foreign affairs, was preferable to permanent revolution. His view was presumably influenced by the succession of failures to bring about revolution not only in Germany but also in Hungary and China.[23]

The Right, led by Bukharin, offered another view. Bukharin recommended the economic option of balanced growth: gradual development of a heavy-industrial base and defense industry concomitant with improvement of the infrastructure of an urban and rural society and with increased consumption. This conflicted with Stalin's support for concentrating investment in the industrial-defense establishment at the expense of nonpriority sectors such as transportation, housing, and consumption. The Right, in effect, argued for a continuation of NEP, which it viewed as transition rather than retreat. Bukharin's views seem appropriate for a pluralistic, albeit elitist, society attempting simultaneously to meet the multiple needs of the expanding power base in a developing great state, the infrastructure of a modern society, and consumption improvements for the average citizen. But post-Lenin Russia was not a pluralistic society. There was, at best, factionalism within the small Party elite in the post-Lenin succession period, 1924–28, with competition for control of the dictatorial Party. In contrast, the Party's view of the imperative needs of the state was for rapid transformation from an agriculturally based, weak national power to an industrially-based, strong great power. [24]

At the time, the imperative, in the Party's view, was to enhance Soviet national power rapidly; judged by this criterion, both Trotsky's and Bukharin's solutions were inadequate. The continuing failures of the revolution abroad—which, if they had been successes, might have complemented Soviet power—weakened Trotsky's case for permanent revolution; pragmatically, there was little promise of early revolutionary success elsewhere. Bukharin's solution, because it envisioned a gradual approach, failed by definition to meet urgent time requirements. Stalin's countersolution, which based economic power on developing a domestic base at the expense of other objectives and doing it rapidly, appeared to be the proper solution because of the political imperatives facing the leadership at the time. [25]

Indeed, Stalin's political primacy and his political views of the necessity of economic development colored the adopted policy and the developed solutions. As judged by the speeches Stalin gave and by the policies which followed, his conception of economic development has been compared to a military campaign with him a field commander facing specific objects with limited means. Economic analysis was thus moved away from any degree of sophistication and measurement among alternatives. In this sense the development of consistent patterns for the Stalinist development and the articulation of a Stalinist blueprint for economic development is left largely to an historical assessment by Western observers. Some would not accept the economic development under Stalin as an end in itself but as one of several means for firmly establishing political power. In this, however, we accept the view that the dominant position of Stalin, particularly as established at the 1934 Party Congress, permitted him to move along those lines of economic development which he found necessary, rather than the view that his economic policy was a means of further establishing his political dominance.

The Stalinist decision to direct maximum resources to heavy industry in the shortest possible time was embodied in the first Five-Year Plan.

It required deemphasis of other economic ends and deferral of many longer-range programs. Levels of consumption were depressed, since resources for light industry and agriculture were concentrated on increasing production of energy and metals and on expanding machine-building.[26] Heavy-industry increments were then used primarily to meet military needs and additional investment requirements in the same preferred industries.

This approach was effective in providing substantial industrial growth, but it posed some basic questions:

(1) How could sufficient food be obtained from the countryside to feed an expanding urban-industrial population without producing consumer goods incentives for the peasants? The answer was to replace the market mechanism, which limited the cities' food supplies in the 1920s, with state control over the distribution of the harvest and over prices. State control of grain procured at low prices was the essential feature of the collectivized system of agriculture.[27] Soviet agricultural policy was influenced by the procurement difficulties during NEP, referred to as the "Scissors Crisis."[28] In 1923, largely because prices of goods purchased by the peasants increased as their supply decreased, coincident with a fall in grain prices, deliveries by the peasants to the cities fell, and bread shortage crises developed in the cities.

(2) How could incentives be provided—even for urban-industrial workers in heavy industry—with a deemphasis on the production of consumer goods? The response to this problem was the progressive, piece-rate system, which, by unequal distribution of limited real income, was thought to compensate for disincentives in a stable or declining income per capita. Moreover, the wage policy was supplemented by punitive economic laws and by extensive inspection and control systems for both workers and managers.[29] This policy was further supported by a labor draft that led to an unprecedented shift of manpower from agriculture to industry.[30]

(3) How could scarce resources for export be controlled to provide a maximum contribution from imports towards the fulfillment of economic plans? The state trading monopoly was the instrument put to work here, and the policy was primarily that of selectively and minimally importing to meet bottleneck needs in industrialization.[31]

(4) How could the transition from controlling the key sectors to planning the entire economy be effected with limited data and economic intelligence? The method of balanced estimates offered a crude but effective method of planning, in physical terms, for meeting the requirements of a limited number of critical sectors. The aim, quite simply, was to increase the physical output of key industrial products—for example, steel, electrical energy, and coal—as rapidly as possible. This short-run goal was met remarkably well.[32]

Though it may be argued that the Stalinist pattern was necessary, given the political priorities of the Soviet Party leadership for rapid improvement of the economic basis of state power, some programs cannot be defended by this simple consistency in the form in which they were adopted. The Stalinist policies of collectivization of agriculture, direct control of labor and differential wage policy, state control of foreign trade, and balanced-estimates planning of physical output were, in the main, consistent and possibly necessary, but the degree of control and coercion was, in many cases, excessive. In general, the control of all aspects of Soviet life, including the arts, and the extreme coercion employed during the purge period after 1936 were surely counterproductive.

The pace of collectivization during the first Five-Year Plan and the degree of self-sufficiency developed in foreign trade are specific examples of excess. To be sure, after 1928 the Soviet leadership had considerable basis for concern over the problem of adequately feeding the cities, since there could only be limited production of consumer goods available in the agricultural market to pay through a market mechanism for deliveries of grain from the farms. Therefore, some system of collectivized, forced deliveries at fixed prices was prescribed by the system to facilitate both rapid industrialization and maintenance of minimum diet requirements for industrial-urban dwellers. The Scissors Crisis of 1923 had brought home to all Soviet leaders the implications of agricultural procurement prices and deliveries based on plans of the state. As suggested by Jerzy Karcz, however, the analysis of the grain procurement problem that was carried out by Stalin and Professor Nemchinov on the eve of the first Five-Year Plan and that led to the aggressive collectivization program probably anticipated more severe procurement problems than were likely to occur.[33] Moreover, Stalin may not have wished the collectivization process that developed to have happened. As O. Narkiewicz notes,

Every piece of evidence suggests strongly that while Stalin (in line with most other Bolshevik leaders) believed that a certain degree of collectivization would be necessary under the five-year plan, in order to ensure a constant supply of food to the industrial centres, he had no intention, as late as the beginning of October 1929, of carrying out anything so drastic as even a 25% collectivization. ... It was the incompetence of the local administration in carrying out the grain procurements, together with the lack of technical means and transport and storage facilities, which set off the peasant revolts. Once these revolts had occurred, some way had to be found of cloaking them under the overall term of "counter-revolution." Very little ingenuity was needed to show that the peasants were rebelling against collectivization and not against grain procurements; and this was in fact done, thus confusing not only the peasants themselves, but also serious students of the situation. Stalin needed this excuse desperately, not so much to protect himself from the population, as to protect himself from both the Central Committee and the expelled opposition leaders, who had for two years been predicting just such an event.[34]

In any event, the extreme collectivization drive and the resistance in the countryside to the policies of the state may have been of the essence. The artel form of collective farm, adopted in the second Five-Year Plan, allowed for a private plot, some ownership of livestock, possession of some agricultural implements and tools, and a collective farm market to augment the income of the peasant from the sale of produce grown on his private plot. Had the artel been gradually and effectively introduced in 1928, then the extreme program that preceded Stalin's speech "Dizzy with Success," given in 1930 and aimed at eliminating the so-called kulaks or rich peasants, might have been avoided.[35] More specifically, short-term losses—almost one-third of all Soviet livestock and much of the harvest in the Ukraine during the first Five-Year Plan—might have been avoided.[36] This mistake was acknowledged, as evidenced by Stalin's speech at the time. Indeed, post-Stalin leaders criticized the similar approach taken by the Chinese in the Great Leap Forward of the late 1950s.[37]

Nevertheless, this approach may have had broader long-term effects and costs than indicated by the short-run losses in livestock and harvest. As argued by Boris Pasternak in the epilogue of *Doctor Zhivago,* once the regime had committed itself to a policy as important as commune collectivization, and once the policy had been a noteworthy failure, further political consequences were inevitable. Those who argued publicly that it was a failure and continued to resist its development had to be silenced. This, in Pasternak's view, established a war, or combat, relationship between the state and the countryside that later broadened into a basic opposition between the state and Soviet society and provided a milieu conducive to the terror and purges of the late 1930s. It is clear that economic production declined during the period of the terror, from 1937 to 1940, just when all steps were being taken to mobilize resources for maximum production.[38] Assuming, then, some relationship between commune collectivization and the terror, the full costs of the commune-style collectivization might even be thought to include the poor overall performance immediately preceding the German invasion.[39]

Autarchical foreign trade policy was a less clear excess in the Stalinist model. Self-sufficiency was an uneconomic and unnecessary application of the general logic of the Stalinist process of priority development. Indeed, the evidence suggests that before the initiation of the first Five-Year Plan, Soviet planners anticipated, planned for, and were willing to accommodate more extensive economic relations with the West than resulted. Soviet importation plans, however, fell victim to a form of "foreign trade scissors"—that is, the U.S.S.R.'s major products for export (raw materials, including grain) met with drastically declining world market prices, whereas products for importation (including skilled personnel and engineering products) maintained a rather stable position in the world market.[40] Other discriminatory foreign trade practices, growing out of nonpayment of czarist debts or political considerations, tended to preclude the consummation of a more logical or rational foreign economic policy at the time.[41] This disastrous experience during the first Five-Year Plan may have led subsequently to a hypercautious trade policy. Likewise, lingering concern over so-called capitalist encirclement may have fortified an extreme isolationist economic policy.

That Soviet leaders under Stalin chose routes of unbalanced, high-priority economic development is consistent not only with the policies of some of their czarist predecessors, such as Peter the Great, but also with certain ideas of the English mercantilists and French Physiocrats of the eighteenth century. Like the aims of these Western predecessors, Stalinist economic goals were primarily designed to enhance the power of the state. As in mercantilist England and Physiocratic France, in Stalinist Russia, the various institutional forces of the society—the military and Party apparatus, the economic and mangement apparatus, science groups, and so on—were all bent towards one view: attainment of the economic basis of a great power. This institutional unity assured the success of a single-minded planner's preference. The economic objectives of Stalinism, in the short run at least, were to postpone consideration of other major economic objectives—that is, development of the infrastructure of the society and improvement of consumption levels—in ways consonant with the expansion of the economic power of the state.

The elaboration of economic doctrine to maximize the economic basis of the state is clearly reflected in mercantilist policy in England. The capacity of such economic policy to enhance the power of the state was noted by one of the leading French Physiocrats in a plea for unity in institutional and planner's preferences: "The Sovereign authority should be one, and supreme above all individual or private enterprise. The object of sovereignty is to secure obedience, to defend every just right, on the one hand, and to secure personal security on the other. A government that is based upon the idea of balance of power is useless."[42] Similarly, Sir James Stewart, the most articulate of the English mercantilists, declared that "a statesman should develop a grand scheme of economic mobilization and frame the necessary laws and regulations to compel the citizens of the country to do those things which he as a statesman sees are conductive to national economic prosperity."[43] The central authority held control over industry and foreign commerce. Moreover, in mercantilist England, distribution and pricing of grain were controlled by public authority. A representative of the crown, known as the clerk of the market, set prices and licensed dealers in grain.[44]

The French Physiocrats differed, of course, from their own mercantilists and from the English mercantilists.[45] They did, for example,
lay down the beginnings of a liberal economic doctrine and of a more
or less systematic view of the entire economy, but these were fully developed only when Adam Smith came along and translated them into
public policy. Moreover, parallel with differences in Marxian and
Leninist views (noted above), the concept of private intent and laissez-
faire discussed by François Quesnay and developed by Adam Smith
might be related to Marxian concepts of consciousness or voluntarism,
which are relevant in the post-Stalinist discussion and antithetical to
Stalin's views of the Party and state.

Like Stalin in Soviet Russia, the Physiocrats in France had an ob-
session with maximum development of one key sector of the economy—
in their case, agriculture. This was perhaps consistent with the identity
of interests between landed aristocracy and public authority. Stalin,
of course, identified with the military-industrial base. The single-sector
focus probably limited concern to developing concepts of value and
scarcity. As in Soviet development, value became important when choices
were required. This was true in the more pluralist post-Stalin period as
well as in libertarian England.

While we cannot condone the inhumanity of the Stalinist system, we
ought to be aware that the system may well have been the only appropriate economic vehicle for meeting the priorities and goals defined
by the Soviet leadership at the time. In this context, the efficacy of the
Stalinist pattern as a form of neomercantilism, an idea set forth in
1934 by Wesley Claire Mitchell, may be reconsidered:

> There is abundant skilled testimony in favor of the opinion that provided we can
> have a market for all the goods that we can make, with our present knowledge,
> our present labor force, and present industrial equipment, it would be possible
> for us to increase the national income by a very substantial amount above the
> best records that we have ever attained. ...
>
> Well, are these engineers right? We are a bit concerned, as we watch the
> Russian experiment, as in these last few months we have watched the efforts
> of our own government, we have been concerned with the question whether a
> planned economy really is effective. Have we drawn too hasty a conclusion from
> the downfall of mercantilism? Was Adam Smith really right when he argued that
> if everyone were left to choose the occupation which is most advantageous in
> his own eyes the wealth of the community as a whole will improve at the most
> rapid rate? If Adam Smith was right in that opinion with respect to the con-
> ditions of his time, have conditions perhaps not changed in such a fashion as
> to justify very substantial modifications in the conclusions to which economists
> for three or four generations assented with very little difficulty? We want to
> know whether business cycles with their concomitants of recurring depressions
> in which a very considerable fraction of the working classes are unemployed for
> long periods and in which a very considerable proportion of our investors lose
> part of their savings cannot be obviated by more skillful economic organization.[46]

Job security had indeed become one of the enduring claims of the comparative advantage of the Soviet system.[47] In fact, the full employment requirement may be a barrier to more efficient management in Soviet and East European enterprises.

The Third Stage: Post-Stalin Development, 1955–1977

Stalin succeeded in his major aim—overcoming economic backwardness and establishing the Soviet Union as a strong power in the world. By the middle 1950s, only the United States and the potentially economically unified Europe could claim an industrial-defense basis for power rivalry with the Soviet Union. Moreover, toward the end of the decade, Nikita Krushchev could credibly claim that overtaking and surpassing the United States in some reasonably short time period—for example, by 1970—was a realistic possibility. Before Krushchev's death, however, it became clear that his formula for overtaking and surpassing, in economic terms, was not likely to succeed. The symbolism of his program, focused on the Sputnik successes and some dramatic economic changes, was found wanting as the basis of joining the economic superpower club of Western advanced industrial countries. In the post-Stalinist period, the Soviet Union could project its massive military power throughout the world and into space and have some influence on the course of all major world events. The economic and technical power of the Soviet Union, however, was limited.

Attaining both military and economic superpower status required a choice by Stalin's successors among the "guns" and "butter" type claimants: the "guns" choice, the traditional heavy-industrial military requirements, and the "butter" choice, those broader requirements for economic modernization and consumer benefits. Likewise, new demands dictated change in the economic system, in the economic control which institutions so firmly established in the Stalinist period and which were successful in bringing about the attainment of Stalin's objectives. This reformulation of the Stalinist model was required to utilize effectively the economic and technical capability that could be drawn from Western industrial economies. The need for Western technology and systems further required a change from the Stalinist economic policy of isolation to measured economic interdependence. Therefore, the critical problem of the U.S.S.R. in attaining its objective of becoming an economically and technologically advanced economic power was to change the three economic pillars on which the Stalinist system was built: first, to change the resource allocation policy; second, to change the political and economic control system for operating the economy; and third, to shift away from autarchy or economic isolation toward economic interdependence. The relatively conservative and often insecure post-Stalin leadership was faced with the formidable task of changing the foundations of the system they controlled while maintaining control of that system. Not only did these apparent requirements for change endanger the leadership's own security by eroding their system of domestic control, but it also revised priority for augmentation of the military base of power which underpinned their international system of influence. Future success also required renunciation of or change in the success formula of the past. Unlike Stalin after the industrialization debate of the 1920s, his successors have not made clear choices, but equivocated. What has resulted is a modification rather than a reform or revision of the Stalinist system.

Even before Stalin's death in 1953, changes were taking place in the Soviet body politic and its economic institutions. Since his death, changes have accelerated, especially from 1955 to date. Nevertheless, Soviet institutions do not change rapidly, nor are they flexible. Institutional stagnation is more characteristic than is change.[48]

Although by the end of the fifties the Soviet Union was overtaking and surpassing the United States not only in industrial output but also in production of meat and availability of housing, at the same time, faltering economic performance was becoming increasingly evident. The coming of the nuclear age and the space age to the Soviet Union led to spiraling resource costs.[49] Likewise, the inflexibility of the Stalinist system hampered the accommodation of the traditional coal and steel industrial base to the technology of modern industry. Without Stalin's close political control, the various economic institutions could no longer be forced to pursue unquestioningly the old Stalinist goals.

I have argued that even though there were unnecessary excesses in the Stalinist system, especially in the damaging collectivization program, the Stalinist pattern was consistent and perhaps even necessary in the political context of the times. In the current period, the rigidities of the system, limiting changes as they do, have again raised the question of the *raison d'être* of the Stalinist pattern. Is lack of flexibility an organic element of a Stalinist-type system? Or does it merely reflect the impact of Stalin's own peculiar personality? This is extending Alec Nove's question, "Was Stalin really necessary?"[50] to include the issue, "Did Stalin live too long?" As a matter of fact, it may be argued that Stalinist-type objectives do require a Stalinist-type system and a Stalinist-type personality. In this scheme, the role of Stalin as a person may be overstated.[51] Perhaps this is the answer to Wesley C. Mitchell's question as to the appropriateness of Adam Smith's theory for the Soviet Union of the first Five-Year Plan. Perhaps the single-minded pursuit of any overriding objective, including national power, necessarily imposes rigidities which are difficult to overcome. Or is the answer to the first question of consistency or necessity to be found even deeper, as suggested in the earlier discussion of the conflict between Leninist and Marxian views? Is flexibility rooted in the Leninist principle of democratic centralism? Institutions die hard even in the more loosely ordered, pluralistic societies. Would they not be much harder to eliminate or modify in a system in which practically all initiative flows from the pinnacle of power, as it did in the system ruled by Stalin?

What appears to be needed in order to bring about more efficiency are the following: (1) a macroeconomic view of the economy, relating all aspects of it in a reliable, consistent fashion with better reporting of data to provide a basis for consistent valuation of economic activities throughout the economy; (2) improved valuation of economic activities so that a price system could be employed as a basis for efficient decisionmaking among alternative needs; (3) more resource allocation for investment in longer-term payoffs, e.g., in the infrastructure of the economy and changing technology; (4) more resource allocation for consumption throughout the economy to provide incentives for increased productivity by workers and peasants.

The macroeconomic approach and the adoption of a more rational price mechanism strikes at the core of the Stalinist method of planning. Essentially, under Stalin, only the priority heavy-industrial sectors were planned, with critical industrial supply links or potential bottlenecks in the other sectors, e.g., grain procurement for the cities, importation of critical industrial goods, labor supply to industry. This was a microeconomic or partial equilibrium approach to planning. Because choices between heavy industry and other economic activities were not central to economic policy, the concept of value, as discussed in Western economics, did not directly intrude. But as more sectors rose to importance in Soviet economic policy, in conjunction with falling performance and reevaluation or expansion of priority sectors, the need for good data on the entire economy became evident. Linear economics—that is, input-output analysis and linear programming—have been given increasing attention along with the problem of data collection and manipulation.[52] Improved data and macroeconomic analytical tools can improve the economic decisions made among newly relevant economic alternatives. The value basis of choice expressed in monetary terms—i.e., the use of price mechanism—can substitute for the Stalinist reliance on physical measurements and direct methods of formulating plans and measuring performance.

Improved economic performance may result from improvement in labor productivity throughout the economy or from a reduction in the capital output ratio (i.e., from improved capital efficiency).[53] With limits on the supply of labor and capital, their efficient use has become the major concern. Labor efficiency was stimulated by administrative means in the simplified Stalinist approach. Highly differentiated income, especially in industry, with the stable or falling average real income of the Stalinist period, could no longer be relied upon for desired results in the post-Stalinist era. During the 1950s, per capita income rose, and the inequalities of income distribution narrowed.[54] The satisfaction from increasing income has not been proportionate, however. The shift from a seller's to a buyer's market has given rise to consumer choice and to rejection of low quality. Rising inventories have led to economic reforms centering on a shift from direct measures of performance such as physical production to indirect measures such as sales and profitability.[55]

The increasing capital required for increased output reflects the long-term effects of deemphasizing and postponing investment in all but the key sectors of the economy. Modernization of the industrial base and broadening of investment allocations to include transportation, housing, and agriculture are all designed to improve overall economic performance. Economic retardation is not alone the basis for the new trends toward macroeconomic analysis in Soviet planning. As in Adam Smith's time, the development of countervailing public forces in the society has given rise to concern over choices and an improved measure of value. The unity of the Stalinist Party has been shattered.

In the post-Stalin era, the military professionals, the economist-planner group, the physical scientists associated with the Academy of Sciences, the Party bureaucrats centering around the *obkoms* (regional committees of the Communist Party), and the intellectuals represented by *Novy Mir* and other Soviet journals have all gained more influence over policies by virtue of their own professional expertise.[56] They have had a common interest in securing greater delegation of power from the Party and in encouraging it to maintain a laissez-faire attitude towards the elite groups, even as each competed within its own group and with other institutional groups for the allocation of resources to strengthen its own objectives, e.g., to strengthen the defense establishment or a particular institution. The emergence of pluralism in the Soviet elite may underlie the broadening of the economic objectives of the leadership. The overall economic objective of the Soviet Union is no longer limited to mere augmentation of the industrial-defense establishment. The Soviet Union is now also concerned with improving the infrastructure of the economy, with allocating scarce resources to transportation and housing, and with paying more attention to consumer needs.

Success in overcoming the economic backwardness that limited the power of the state means that the elite groups are no longer tied together in single-minded purpose. With more power and resources, the broader needs for continued progress require different solutions. Each group has differing views and priorities. As no group has overwhelming power, decisions result from an interplay of countervailing forces or a form of consensus.

The emergence of pluralism and economic retardation may mean that it is now appropriate to consider the proposals made by Bukharin in 1926–28. Bukharin's views may have been expressed fifty years too early, but realization of his alternative of more balanced economic growth is perhaps even more difficult now than it would have been earlier. The usual problems of balanced growth are compounded by the imbalances allowed to grow to the critical point under Stalin.

Developments in transportation offer a case in point. An austerity program of three decades has limited construction of new rail lines and concentrated the movement of cargo on an outmoded rail system.[57] To be sure, a revolution in transportation was initiated with the Seven-Year Plan in 1959, which called for a shift from steam, coal-fired locomotion to diesel and electrified locomotion. This shift has been carried out at considerable expense and has probably led to substantial improvements in efficiency. Similarly, a shift from rail transport to pipelines and other means of transportation, previously exploited very intensively elsewhere, has now been heavily invested in, if at a late date, and has improved the efficiency of Soviet economic performance.[58] Yet the question can still be raised, does this short-term, though expensive, program of transport investment, compensate for the costs of long-term deemphasis on Soviet transportation? At the same time, will not the inappropriate locations of industries and the lack of specialization of Soviet industrial plants be a relatively permanent, or at least highly resistant, legacy from lack of effective transport programs, possibly resulting in many generations of inefficiencies? Likewise, investments in long-neglected urban developments, including housing, may be rather late to make planning effective in this sphere. In the attempt to meet the consumption needs of the populace, both the current and the deferred costs of neglect have become evident.

The costs of expanding production in sectors which have become important since Stalin is not just a problem of resource allocation. Such problems as inventory accumulation in consumer textiles suggest that there is a broad range of efficiency problems requiring a refurbishing of the underdeveloped segments of the economy—a bequest of the Stalinist pattern of uneven economic development. As in the case of an underdeveloped nation, the Soviet Union's investment process requires more than capital goods input. It requires, for example, a broadening of its education base and the development of an improved information-gathering and processing system. The substantial additional resources needed to achieve higher production levels in previously neglected sectors of the economy promise somewhat uncertain returns. Moreover, the ratio of new capital to incremental output is likely to be high just in the process of learning to plan and just in the course of rectifying the mistakes of neglect in sectors of deferred investments.

The mechanical solution for some of the production and investment problems in neglected sectors outside of the industrial-defense establishments often appears simple in theory: if some collective farms would just correctly apply more fertilizer, then grain yields would substantially increase; or, if certain textile plants would just use available resources more efficiently to meet the needs of Soviet citizens, then increased production would substantially ease the clothing shortage. But these sectors outside the high-priority pale became atrophied during the course of Stalinist development. More than increments of men and material are necessary to move towards a high production level and towards greater consumer satisfaction in these long-neglected, deemphasized sectors. The cumulative list of required investments is a major deferred cost of the Stalinist pattern of economic development that must now be borne. Moreover, a tight supply plan for capital, labor, and raw materials becomes even tighter with the expansion of priority sectors and the complexities of choice. No buffer sectors can easily be tapped to yield additional labor or to ensure greater production when input efficiency or other factors fall below expectation. Agriculture in particular ceases to be a reservoir of labor supply and has become a problem area for planning increased yield and factor productivity.

Perhaps an even greater cost to the Soviet state from the Stalinist type of economic development is the heritage of control involved in decision-making. Stalinist-type control can no longer be imposed to direct institutions towards a single purpose, as was true in the case of the early Five-Year Plans. The new power of institutions is largely that of constraint on change. Each of the various institutional groups in the now pluralistic power elite—the professional military, the economist-planners, the physical scientists, and the Party bureaucracy—appears to have enough strength to maintain the elements of the status quo but not enough to improve professional performance by their own criteria. Thus, the professional military may be effective in withholding resources from agriculture that are necessary for improving agricultural productivity; traditional elements in the Party may be able to frustrate economic price reforms which might, by improving overall efficiency in planning, reduce their power in economic matters; the physical scientists may be able to defend the continued enormous costs of the Soviet military space program, which is carried on at the expense of other investment programs, such as the civilian program in space.[59] Even within each of these groups, persons working for change and improvement of efficiency in overall performance have difficulty in carrying through their programs. In an era requiring rapid changes to improve economic efficiency, this institutional rigidity imposes a cost that mounts with each successive year. The unsettled leadership since Khrushchev may be a result of this process or may be a constraining factor on the resolution of it.[60]

The form of this debate is suggested by the following apparent reference by Party leader Dmitri Polyansky to other Party, and perhaps military, critics of the expensive agricultural investment and incentives program in 1966. (Ironically, though Dmitri Polyansky argued for programs which may have ameliorated the harvest disasters in 1972 and 1975, he was held responsible for those shortfalls in agricultural output. He was demoted from his Politboro position after 1972, and made Minister of Agriculture; after the poor harvest in 1975, he also lost his government job.)

What is needed to successfully implement all these measures? Above all, to insure strict fulfillment of the plans envisaged, there must be full allocation and the best possible utilization of planned capital investments and material-technical means. This has to be said because the good results of the last agricultural year have gone to the heads of some comrades. Some people are beginning to argue that collective and state farms are now able to develop with less substantial aid, that melioration plans can be cut and supplies of technical equipment and mineral fertilizers reduced. Such arguments are extremely dangerous, for they could delay implementation of the planned programme, and any attempts in that direction must be resolutely nipped in the bud.[61]

Even in military programs the apparent debate over naval programs and budgets related to Admiral Gorshkov's series of articles in *Morskoe sbornik* [Naval digest] appears to represent institutional debate on priorities and resource allocation.[62]

Spurred by the growth of new requirements, as perceived by the leadership, the pressure of attaining high performance mounts year by year. The steep rise in desired performance—indeed, required performance—and the very modest increase in actual performance lead to an ever-expanding gap, creating an increasingly unstable situation. Herein, Adam Smith's critique of the French Physiocrats appears to have a current application to the latter's modern emulators in the Soviet Union.

It is thus that every system which endeavors, either by extraordinary encouragements, to draw towards a particular species of industry a greater share of the capital of the society than what would naturally go to it; or, by extraordinary restraints, to force from a particular species of industry some share of the capital which would otherwise be employed in it; is in reality subversive of the great purpose which it means to promote. It retards, instead of accelerating, the progress of the society towards real wealth and greatness; and diminishes, instead of increasing, the real value of the annual produce of its land and labour.[63]

At the same time, the same type of institutional rigidities exhibited in the Soviet economy appears in other economies, as indicated by the *New Statesman* critique of British and U.S. government institutions:

In the U.S., Congress functions much as it did in the days of George Washington; the methods of the House of Commons have changed little, in essentials, since Disraeli first entered it; Whitehall still administers the country on principles laid down in the mid-19th century. . . .

The truth is that the government, with the best intentions in the world, is working in the dark. It lacks the detailed, industry-by-industry, factory-by-factory information on which to base selective decisions; and even if it had that information, it lacks the legislative and administrative machinery to enforce them. It is trying to operate socialist policies with a free-market civil service structure, and with a statistical machine which Gladstone himself might have found inadequate. Hence it falls back on the blunt instruments of fiscal measures, which are both socially unjust and economically inefficient.[64]

In the case of the Soviet Union, however, the stakes are higher. Whether the economic performance is improved or continues to stagnate has profound political implications. What is now being called into question is the basic Leninist concept of a nonegalitarian, dictatorial political process of economic development. With the proliferation of countervailing forces in the leadership, this concept is being increasingly challenged. It was this concept that in the short run appeared to make the Stalinist approach appropriate and consistent with Leninism. In the long run, the post-Stalin period's new requirements may call forth not only reexamination of Bukharin but a return to Marx. As E. H. Carr has aptly put it, "Marx's method was historical: all changes in the destinies and organization of mankind were part of an ever-flowing historical process. He made the assumption—the only postulate which he did not attempt to demonstrate—that modern society would in the long run always seek to organize itself in such a way as to make the most effective use of its productive resources."[65]

Toward a New State: Economic Modernization and Leninism

If economic interdependence and economic modernization continue to be the principal aim of Soviet leadership, the U.S.S.R. might, in time, join the Western industrial nations as an economic superpower. This would probably require an increased emphasis on economic modernization rather than on continued military augmentation—i.e., a change in the classic guns-or-butter choice. It would also require a change within the Marxist-Leninist framework of the institutions that guide and control the Soviet economy in order to simulate Western levels of efficiency in a market economy. Also required in expanding an efficient program of Western technology transfers would be changes in the manner imported technology is absorbed, adapted, and integrated into the Soviet economic system.

Were the Soviet Union to become an economic superpower, it might, in time, become economically competitive with Europe, Japan, and North America in the world market for industrial goods and economic power. This development might add a dimension to the traditional military basis for Soviet power in the world arena. Such basic changes, however, must be made by the Soviet leadership. Leonid Brezhnev and his colleagues are all old men with short political and physical life expectancies. The economic modernization choices involve decisions weighing more heavily benefits in future years over present benefits and weighing economic instruments over military instruments of power and influence. The traditional Stalinist leadership may be unable or unwilling to make these kinds of difficult choices, either because of its uncertainty or because of its inability to use its power for such significant changes in the system that it controls.

Assuming that the Soviet economy was still basically following the Stalinist objectives—i.e., catching up with the United States military, steadily expanding the industrial base, and meeting at least minimal consumer expectations for improved living conditions and welfare—the Central Intelligence Agency concluded a significant slowdown in economic growth was likely, and negative growth possible.

We conclude that a marked reduction in the rate of economic growth in the 1980s seems almost inevitable. At best, Soviet GNP may be able to continue growing at a rate of about 4 percent a year through 1980, declining to 3-3½ percent in the early and mid-1980s. These rates, however, assume prompt, strong action in energy policy, without which the rate of growth could decline to about 3½ percent in the near-term and to 2-2½ percent in the 1980s.

These are average figures; in some years performance could be better, but in others, worse, with *zero growth or even declines* in GDP a possibility, if oil shortages and a bad crop year coincide.[66]

Projections, certainly predictions, of economic performance in any economy are hazardous. Even with regard to our own economy, with considerably more accurate information and insight on policy changes, the record of our Council of Economic Advisors is not unblemished. To be sure, predicting variations in demand in Western industrial economics is difficult. Still, a combination of variations in supply and demand in the Soviet economy appears to pose at least equal uncertainties.

While assuming growth retardation may be inevitable within the current version or modification of the Stalinist system, the CIA report does not explore the assumption of changes in the system. Faced with the harsh consequences of the extrapolation of economic performance outlined by the CIA report, would the Soviet leaders not be willing to face basic changes in their system: a major shift in resource allocation to hold down the growth of military programs, a substantial delegation of central and Party control of the economic administration, and a significant increase in economic interdependence with the West? Are these changes unthinkable? Do developments in Eastern Europe and the People's Republic of China not indicate that a current Marxist-Leninist system need not be Stalinist? Experience outside the Soviet Union suggests that flexible Leninism is possible. The arguments of Nikolai Bukharin may now be more relevant than when they were made in the Industrialization Debate of the 1920s. Or the resolution of the contradictions of Marx and Lenin in the proper course of Soviet economic development might be reexamined to choose those discarded by Joseph Stalin.

The ultimate argument for change is that improved performance of the Soviet Union is possible by a shift in priorities away from defense claimants, by increased and effective use of foreign technology, and by efficiency-producing reforms.[67] If indeed a zero or negative growth rate is to be anticipated in poor years without change, it seems reasonable to assume that the hard choices will be faced and may be made by the leadership. If they are, the major underpinnings of the Stalinist system would be removed. The Soviet economy might then enter an economic modernization–Leninist stage of development.

Vladimir Ilich Lenin promised the Russian people peace, bread, and land in 1917. Now if Lenin's successors were to offer

(1) a redirection of the heavy defense allocations to the peaceful purposes of modernizing the economy;
(2) a significant improvment in meat, housing, and other attractive consumer goods;
(3) an improved incentive system in plant and farm which gave the citizen a stake in the outcome of his economic enterprise;

then the transitional form of Leninism seen by many of the Bolsheviks in 1917 might be recaptured. Whatever the course followed, we must assume that it is likely to be in this Marxist-Leninist, Russian tradition.

Notes

1. A. Gershenkron, "Rates of Growth in Russia," *Journal of Economic History*, Fall 1947, pp. 144-73; Henry Rosovsky, ed., *Industrialization in Two Systems: Essays in Honor of Alexander Gershenkron by a Group of His Students* (New York: Wiley, 1966).
2. Ibid.
3. Walt Whitman Rostow, *The Stages of Economic Growth: A Non-Communist Manifesto* (Cambridge: At the University Press, 1960); W. Hoffman, "Stadien und Typen der Industrialisierung," *Probleme der Welwirtschaft* (Jena), no. 54 (1931), p. 166; U.S., Congress, Joint Economic Committee, *China: A Reassessment of the Economy* (Washington, D.C.: GPO,) idem, *East European Economics Post Helsinki*, August 1977.
4. V. I. Lenin, "Chto delat?" [What is to be done?], *Sochineniya* [Works], 4th ed. (Moscow, 1950), 5: 321-23; idem, "Imperialism, kak vysshaya stadiya kapitalizma"

(Imperialism, as the highest stage of capitalism), in ibid., 22: 173–290; idem, "Gosudarstvo i revolyutsiya" [The state and revolution], in ibid., 25: 353–462; and Bertram D. Wolfe, *Marxism: One Hundred Years in the Life of a Doctrine* (New York: Dial Press, 1965).

5. Philippe J. Bernard, *Planning in the Soviet Union* (London: Pergamon, 1966).

6. E. H. Carr, *The History of Soviet Russia: The Bolshevik Revolution* (London: Macmillan, 1952), pp. 5, 9.

7. Ibid, p. 275.

8. Lenin, *Sochineniya*, vol. 32. See especially his speeches at the Tenth Party Congress (pp. 141–247) and the Tenth All-Russian Conference of the Party (pp. 377–413).

9. P. I. Lyashchenko, *History of the National Economy of Russia* (London: Macmillan, 1948).

10. Lenin, *Sochineniya*, 31: 456–500.

11. Nikolai Bukharin, *Ekonomika Perekhodnogo perioda* [The economics of transition] (Moscow, 1920).

12. Barrington Moore, *Soviet Politics: The Dilemma of Power* (Cambridge: Harvard Univ. Press, 1950), p. 175.

13. A. Bergson, *Soviet Wage Policy* (Cambridge: Harvard Univ. Press, 1946).

14. Carr, *The History of Soviet Russia*, p. 4.

15. For detailed discussion, see the study by Norton T. Dodge, "Fifty Years of Soviet Labour," in *The Development of the Soviet Economy: Plan and Performance*, ed. Vladimir G. Treml (New York: Praeger, 1968), pp. 147–80. Hereafter, this collection of essays will be cited as "Treml."

16. J. R. Azrael, *Managerial Power and Soviet Politics* (Cambridge: Harvard Univ. Press, 1966).

17. Joseph Stalin, *Marxism and Linguistics* (New York: International Publishers, 1951), p. 43.

18. Jurgen Notzold, "Agrarfrage und Industrialisierung in Russland am Vorabend des Ersten Weltkreignes," *Saeculum* (Freiburg-Munich) 12 (1966): 36–54.

19. Alexander Ehrlich, *The Soviet Industrialization Debate, 1924–1926* (Cambridge: Harvard Univ. Press, 1960).

20. Ibid.

21. V. I. Lenin, *The Development of Capitalism in Russia: The Process of the Formulation of a Home Market for Large-Scale Industry* (Moscow, 1956); Mikhail Tugan-Baranovsky, *Modern Socialism in Its Historical Development* (London: Sonnenschein, 1910); Nicholas Spulber, *The Soviet Economy: Structure, Principles, Problems* (New York: Norton, 1962); Mikhail Tugan-Baranovsky, *K luchshemu budushchemu* [Towards a better future] (St. Petersburg, 1912).

22. Max Beloff, *The Foreign Policy of Soviet Russia, 1929–1941* (London: Oxford Univ. Press, 1949).

23. E. H. Carr, *A History of Soviet Russia: Socialism in One Country* (Cambridge: Harvard Univ. Press, 1960).

24. Joseph Stalin, *Voprosy Leninizma* [Questions of Leninism], 11th ed. (Moscow, 1953), pp. 355–63.

25. Alec Nove, *Economic Rationality and Soviet Politics* (New York: Praeger, 1964).

26. Alexander Beykov, *The Development of the Soviet Economic System* (Cambridge: At the University Press, 1950); Maurice Herbert Dobb, *Soviet Economic Development since 1917* (London: International Publishers, 1948).

27. See Jerzy F. Karcz, "Soviet Agriculture: A Balance Sheet," in Treml, pp. 108–46.

28. Dobb, *Soviet Economic Development since 1917.*

29. Janet G. Chapman, *Real Wages in Soviet Russia since 1928* (Santa Monica, Calif.: The Rand Corp., 1963).

30. See Stanley H. Cohn, "The Soviet Economy: Performance and Growth," in Treml, pp. 24–54.

31. For detailed discussion, see Leon M. Herman, "The Promise of Economic Self-Sufficiency under Soviet Socialism," in Treml, pp. 213ff.

32. Hans Hirsch, *Quantity Planning and Price Planning in the Soviet Union* (Philadelphia: Univ. of Pennsylvania Press, 1961).

33. Jerzy Karcz, *Soviet Studies* (Glasgow) 18, no. 4 (1967): 399–434.

34. O. Narkiewicz, *Soviet Studies* 17, no. 7 (1966): 36–37. Also E. Zalecki.

35. Stalin, *Voprosy Leninizma*, pp. 331–36.

36. Naum Jasny, *The Socialized Agriculture of the USSR: Plans and Performance* (Stanford, Calif.: Stanford Univ. Press, 1949).

37. *Pravda*, 29 April 1964.

38. See Cohn, "The Soviet Economy."

39. *Diversity in International Communism*, ed. Alexander Dallin, with Jonathan Harris and Grey Hodnett (New York and London: Columbia Univ. Press, 1963).

40. Dobb, *Soviet Economic Development since 1917*.

41. Harold Moulton, *Russian Debts and Russian Reconstruction* (New York: McGraw-Hill, 1924).

42. François Quesnay, Maximes (Paris, 1758). The Physiocrats were in favor of a national assembly but would give it no legislative power. It was to be just a council of state concerned chiefly with public works and with the apportionment of the burden of taxation. See M. Esmein's memo on the proposed National Assembly of the Physiocrats in *Comptes rendus de l'Academie des Sciences Morales et Politiques* (Paris, 1904).

43. Wesley C. Mitchell, *Lecture Notes on Types of Economic Theory* (New York: Augustus M. Kelley, 1949), p. 51.

44. Ibid.

45. Charles Gide and Charles Rist, *A History of Economic Doctrines*, 2nd ed. (Boston: Heath, 1948).

46. Mitchell, *Lecture Notes on Types of Economic Theory*, pp. 6, 7, (italics added). These lectures were delivered at Columbia University in 1934–35.

47. P. Hanson, "Job Security," mimeographed (Birmingham University); D. Granick, *Enterprise Guidance in Eastern Europe* (Princeton: Princeton Univ. Press, 1975).

48. John P. Hardt, Dimitri M. Gallik, and Vladimir G. Treml, in *New Directions in the Soviet Economy* U.S., Congress, Joint Economic Committee, (Washington, D.C.: GPO, 1966, pp. 12–16.

49. Cohn, "The Soviet Economy."

50. Nove, *Economic Rationality and Soviet Politics*.

51. George Plekhanov, *The Role of the Individual in History* (New York: International Publishers, 1940).

52. See R. Judy and V. Treml, in *Mathematics and Computers in Soviet Planning*, ed. J. Hardt et al. (New Haven: Yale Univ. Press, 1967).

53. Cohn, "The Soviet Economy."

54. Dodge, "Fifty Years of Soviet Labour."

55. Eugene Zaleski, *Planification de la Croissance et Fluctuations economiques en U.S.S.R.* (Paris: Societe d'edition d'enseignement superieur, 1962).

56. H. Gordon Skilling and Frankyn Griffiths, *Interest Groups in Soviet Politics* (Princeton: Princeton Univ. Press, 1973).

57. H. Hunter, *Soviet Transportation Policy* (Cambridge: Harvard Univ. Press, 1957); Ernest W. Williams, Jr., *Freight Transportation in the Soviet Union* (Princeton: Princeton Univ. Press, 1962).

58. H. Hunter, *The Soviet Transport Sector* (Washington, D.C.: Brookings Institution, 1966).

59. U.S., Senate, Committee on Aeronautical and Space Sciences, "Soviet Space Programs, 1962–65; Goals and Purposes, Achievements, Plans, and International Implications," Staff Report, 89th Cong., 1966.

60. Michael Kaser, ed., *Soviet Affairs, Number Four* (Oxford: Oxford Univ. Press, 1966).

61. A Radio Moscow speech of 3 March 1967. See Polyansky speech, U.S.S.R. Regional Affairs, Moscow Domestic Service in Russian, Foreign Broadcasting Information Service.

62. Michael McGuire, ed., *Soviet Naval Policy* (New York: Praeger, 1975).

63. Adam Smith, *Wealth of Nations*, Cannan edition, 1:421; Everyman edition, 1:400–401; Modern Library edition, p. 423.

64. *New Statesman* (London), 23 September 1966, p. 1.

65. E. H. Carr, *The Bolshevik Revolution, 1917–1923* (London: Macmillan, 1952), 2:3.

66. Directorate of Intelligence, Central Intelligence Agency, *Soviet Economic Problems and Prospects,* released by the Joint Economic Committee, U.S., Congress, 8 August 1977, pp. v, ix. (italics added).

67. U.S., Congress, Joint Economic Committee, *Soviet Economy in a New Perspective* (Washington, D.C.: GPO, 1976).

{ 14 }

The Management of Surplus Productive Capacity

SUSAN STRANGE

Ships, steel, textiles—these are a few of the sectors of the world economy in which there has recently developed a marked surplus in productive capacity and in which there has been consequent earnest and often heated discussion among governments and producers over the share-out of markets and the rules, not of free trade, but of "fair" trade. Shoes, color television sets, ball bearings, furniture—the list of manufacturing sectors in which similar international negotiations have been conducted grows every year. Ahead lie new and possibly even greater problems of surplus capacity. One of the most serious has already been the subject of rather fruitless and acrimonious discussion between the European Community and Arab League countries. It is the prospect of overproduction of ethylene, the major building block of the chemical industries and one of the first by-products of petroleum that every oil-producing state aspires to make for itself. No fewer than seventy new ethylene plants are currently being planned, mostly by the oil states. All are located outside the older industrialized countries: the nations of North America and Europe, and Japan, China, and the Soviet Union. Even if these plans do not all materialize, the plans for them "foretoken either one of the biggest shifts in the international division of labour ever seen in any industry—or a lot of rusting chemical cathedrals in the desert."[1] But ships, steel, and textiles are three industrial sectors in which the record of international negotiation now stretches over the better part of a decade or more and, hence, where there should be an accumulation of evidence concerning the nature and conduct of this kind of economic diplomacy.

In this paper, I will suggest that closer examination of this accumulation of evidence from the recent past may throw some light, if we heed it carefully, on the future of international relations and on the problems of power and responsibility of industrial states. I believe that it offers us

This chapter is based on an article entitled "The Management of Surplus Capacity; or How Does Theory Stand Up to Protectionism 1970s Style?" that appeared in *International Organization* 33, no. 3 (summer 1979).

pointers on three important questions: (1) the future focus of international economic diplomacy; (2) the prospect for a new international economic order, especially for developing countries; and (3) the future role of international (or, to be more precise, intergovernmental) organizations and of the universal codes of rules associated with them in the management of the world economy.

To be as brief and clear as possible, I will first suggest the conclusions which I think might be drawn from the evidence on these three questions. I will then briefly review the recent history of negotiations in these three sectors, paying particular regard to the political factors involved. And I will finish with some conclusions on the sources of power and the perceptions of responsibility that I suggest may be deduced from the evidence and which I would argue support my initial assertions.

If the reader finds these assertions controversial (or even outrageous), I hope this paper will convince him or her that the political economy of specific sectors of the world economy is a much neglected area of international studies, one which can profit from the research efforts of historians, lawyers, sociologists, and political scientists as well as business economists. It is also one that, although it presents special difficulties because of the close interaction of domestic politics and economics with international politics and economics, deserves much closer attention than it has so far received in any of our countries.

On the first question, the future of international economic diplomacy, the negotiations which governments have conducted in these three key sectors suggest that we should now look back on international trade liberalization as past history. Since perhaps the Kennedy Round, negotiations on tariff reductions have been (for all the fanfares) an empty formality; the real diplomacy has been over the sharing-out of markets and on the manner in which quantitative restrictions are put on foreign imports.

If this is not too great an exaggeration—and I shall argue that it is a hypothesis that has to be carefully tested—it may be that looking back we shall see the liberalism of the 1950s and 1960s not as the norm of trade diplomacy but as temporary an aberration from economic nationalism as the corresponding period a hundred years ago when the Cobden-Chevalier Treaty between France and Britain heralded a few short years of trade liberalization and as the even briefer period in the mid-1920s, before the U.S. Congress passed the Hawley-Smoot Tariff Act and as world depression cut off the hopes raised at the World Economic Conference of 1927.

The second question concerns the prospects of a new (and by implication, better) international economic order. The negotiations, especially on textiles, suggest to me that developed countries are prepared to tolerate the industrialization of the developing countries only when this has a nil (or nearly nil) effect on their own industrial and employment structures. Far from there being a realistic prospect that the industrialized countries will discriminate in favor of the laggard less developed countries (LDCs), the prospect is the other way around. Quota arrangements will discriminate against them whenever they threaten to make significant inroads into major markets. Preference will be offered only to countries least able to take advantage of it. And the "opportunities" offered to the poorest and the least advantaged will be the excuse for closing doors on the rest of the Third World. Only in periods of general and rapid economic growth—assuming there will still be such periods in the future —will a break into the rich markets of the industrialized countries be possible, and even these gains will not be secure (as Japan's experience, particularly, has shown) against later revocation. Only in a few specific sectors—ships being one, fertilizers possibly another—where it may be possible for LDC producers to find willing buyers in other LDC countries and make a barter deal with them will this frustration be avoided. Just occasionally, too, particular developing countries may be able, in bilateral arrangements with either the United States, the Soviet Union, Europe, Japan, or China, to secure an expanding market share. But this will be possible only when a country possesses special bargaining power, either through its strategic or politically precarious situation or through its control over coveted scarce resources. The prospects, in short, are for more uneven development not only between the industrialized countries and the rest but among the developing countries themselves.

In such conditions, aid transfers, even if they were to be forthcoming in more generous amounts, would be ineffectual, being no substitute for market shares. The new international economic order is thus noneffective as a general "regime" applying to the whole of the undeveloped part of the world economy. And the development theories which have been generally accepted at the United Nations and within the Third World itself must now be modified. Neither the original Rostowian theory— which (very crudely put) was never that the developing countries, starting later than those of Europe and North America, would, like Japan and Australia, eventually be able to "take off," catch up, and take their share in the benefits of economic growth—nor the later Prebischian theory—which (also crudely put) advocated development via trade— would be accepted unless the LDCs had a head start to gain substantially from the transfer resources and could take effective advantage of preferential trade opportunities for the development. Whether as an assumption for policymaking or as a foundation for teaching in schools and universities, they must be abandoned and new theories substituted which take better account of the resistance put up by the industrialized countries and of the differentials in bargaining power among the aspirants to development.

On the third question, concerning the role of intergovernmental organizations and general rules or codes of conduct, negotiations in the three sectors suggest that much conventional wisdom on international organization is, in fact, unwise. Much recent writing (and teaching) operates on unconscious, or subconscious, incrementalist and neofunctionalist assumptions of continuing, uneven, but uninterrupted progress toward the development of universal world laws and of world organizations for their execution. The possibility of retrogression in international economic organization, of expanding international bureaucracy combined with increasing, not decreasing, conflict over means and rates of progress as well as over ends, is seldom seriously entertained.

But in monetary and trade matters, such a possibility surely exists, despite the smoke screen of sterile discussion on "reform." Despite the febrile activity of the International Monetary Fund, the universality of rules on international monetary relations is less now, under managed floating, than it was under the Bretton Woods regime. And in a series of other fields, the talk of "codes" and "guidelines" may also be a smoke screen concealing an increasing diversity and divergency of national practice and policies beneath formal agreement on universal principles and on general but ill-defined "rules" of behavior.

In international trade, the conventional (or neoclassical) wisdom is that the General Agreement on Tariffs and Trade (GATT), for all its aberrations, has constituted a general body of rules on commercial policy which are universally applicable. A recent study of international trade relations in the 1960s, however, reveals just how many and great these aberrations, deviations, and exceptions really were. To describe it as "process of rule adaption" is surely something of a British understatement. The authors, Professors Gerard and Victoria Curzon of the Institut des Hautes Etudes Internationales of Geneva, nevertheless concluded that in trade diplomacy, as in the regulation of traffic, "it is in everybody's interest to follow a few simple rules,"[2]—and that governments have, on the whole, recognized this.

I would submit, on the contrary, that the recent record of negotiations for the management of surplus capacity suggests that, even if governments did once believe this to be so, they no longer do. In the last two or three years almost every one of the major industrialized countries has been ready to act unilaterally in defiance of the "few simple rules" and to argue about it afterwards. Britain in April, and France in June 1977, acted unilaterally, and contrary to European Community rules, to impose quotas on textile imports. Earlier in the year, the British government offered £65 million in special aid to British shipyards, and there has been a general trend among European countries in the past year to offer soft or guaranteed loans to domestic or foreign buyers who will replenish empty order books, making a sieve out of agreements by the

Organization for Economic Cooperation and Development (OECD) setting the limits for export credit for ships. And although in July 1976 the United States argued forcefully in Geneva for an extension of the Multi-Fibre Textile Agreement (MFA), it was the first government, when these arguments were not generally accepted, to rush to renegotiate bilateral agreements modifying the MFA with Hong Kong, Taiwan, and other textile exporters in the Third World.

In short, the evidence accumulates that every major industrial country —and some minor ones—is now following a trade strategy of "Each for himself—and the devil take the hindmost." In the circumstances, the international organizations concerned with trade—primarily GATT, OECD, and the European Community—function increasingly not as the administrators or executives of multilaterally agreed "regimes," as Nye and Keohane would have us call them,[3] so much as would-be legitimizers of deviant and strictly self-serving behavior.

One fourth and final assertion of a general nature can perhaps be added. It is that the stability of the international political economy is seriously impaired by the increasing practice of bargaining over market shares both among the developed industrialized countries themselves and between them and the LDCs, collectively or individually. There are, it is true, some other important factors at work in this destabilizing process—monetary inflation; disagreement over the Law of the Sea; uncertainty over developing countries' debt repayments and credit-worthiness; the state of relations between the United States, China, and the Soviet Union; and the unsettled state of the Middle East. Between them, they are surely creating a much more unstable environment for international economic relations in the future. And this may very possibly have secondary effects on the political stability of the international system in the 1980s and 1990s.

For, whether one agrees or not with the neoclassical argument that trade liberalization gave everyone welfare gains from the more efficient allocation of resources which it made possible, there can be little doubt that while it lasted, the practice of trade liberalization, as developed since the Second World War, did at least have certain built-in stabilizing effects, creating confidence and encouraging economic development. The GATT rules for trade liberalization and the process of exchanging tariff reductions which they made possible seemed a permanent addition to the system and created confidence in a steady one-way trend. There was the ratchet device of the no-new-preference principle, the most-favored-nation principle applied to tariff cuts, and the general sense of increased risk attached to import surcharges and other "temporary" trade barriers—all of which gave a certain confidence that these barriers, once lowered, would not be lightly or massively raised again.

Market-sharing agreements seem, by contrast, much more unstable.

In making the point, I cannot do better than quote the conclusions of a Canadian economist, Professor T. K. Warley, on the results of similar agreements for the sharing of agricultural markets. This is all the more relevant since it now seems that the same political attitudes (putting welfare considerations above efficiency) which were widely adopted in industrial countries towards farmers and peasants are now being adopted towards industrial workers and manufacturing enterprises:

> International arrangements such as those described are as inherently unstable as are similar arrangements between firms in oliogopolistic industries at the national level. Recusants and fringe competitors can disrupt the arrangement. The costs and benefits of market stabilisation and price maintenance are not borne equally. Strains can develop if the participants take different views on prospective market conditions, or if they differ widely in their efficiency, balance of payments positions, or in their capacity to control production or manage stocks. The natural development of such arrangements is for them either to disintegrate or for some higher form of organisation to be sought in which objectives and rules are more clearly articulated. [4]

With these wider considerations in mind, therefore, let us briefly survey the three sets of negotiations, examining the motivations for initiating the negotiations, the issues under discussion, the factors conferring bargaining power on the parties, and the nature of the results.

Textiles

The Long-Term Textile Agreement (LTA) of 1962 was the first important multilateral arrangement regulating redistribution of market shares for manufacturers. The fact that it lasted over a decade and was then successfully renegotiated led to hopes that national policies for industrial import restriction could be made subject to universal rules and principles and to multilateral surveillance—comparable to those applied to tariff barriers—thus safeguarding the international trade system from deteriorating into a battleground for economic nationalism.

But the MFA, which was renegotiated to replace the LTA in 1974, came up for renewal again in 1976. By December 1976 the two sides were deadlocked, and have remained so. Developing countries, by and large, demanded freer access to markets, but the industrialized countries were, on the contrary, anxious to restrict access. Even before a final (and vain) attempt to reach agreement was made in Geneva in July 1976, Britain—one of the initiators of the original agreement—had resorted in April to unilateral import restrictions, and both France and Canada had invoked article 19 of GATT to put temporary checks on imports in the most sensitive categories.

At Geneva, the United States proposed to mask the underlying conflict by opening a protocol extending the MFA for another four years beyond its expiration date of December 1978; members could adhere to the protocol or not as they pleased. This failed to win approval. India, Brazil, and Egypt led other developing countries in angrily rejecting the U.S. proposal as inadequate; the European Community rejected it as overly generous, claiming that Europe had taken the brunt of the consequences of increased LDC textile exports, especially in the synthetic fiber business (polyesters, acrylics, and nylon) and in ready-made clothes like shirts and sweaters. European fiber producers had overall losses of around $1 billion in 1976, and the Textile Commission calculates that extension of the MFA as it stands would mean the loss of 1.6 million jobs for European textile workers by 1982.

By contrast, the original basis of the 1962 LTA was a coincidence of American, British, and Japanese interests in legitimizing and making multilateral the voluntary export restrictions which grew up in the later 1950s. The United States had been caught in the position of being the major market left wide open to Japanese exporters, especially of textiles. Having, for strategic reasons, pressured the Europeans into accepting Japan as a contracting party to GATT, the United States had not protected itself (as the Europeans had) by applying article 35, Nonapplication of the Agreement between particular contracting parties, to Japan. Caught between political pressures on Congress from a protectionist textile lobby and the unpleasant alternative of asking the European members of GATT to allow it yet another waiver under article 19 (in addition to the one it had just obtained for agricultural products), the United States chose to persuade the Japanese government to do its dirty work for it by agreeing, in 1957, "voluntarily" to limit textile exports. (Hong Kong, however, was less susceptible to American pressure, and Hong Kong's textile exports to the United States went from $5.8 million in 1956 to $54.8 million in 1958.)

In order to get the Europeans to buy a bigger share of this flood of Far Eastern textiles and to protect itself, the United States led the way via the Working Party on the Avoidance of Market Disruption (1959) first to the Short-term Textile Agreement and then in 1962 to the LTA. By that time Britain's interest in the agreements was just as strong—both to check the duty-free Commonwealth textiles imports, mainly from Honk Kong, India, and Pakistan, which had grown from a 4 percent to a 30 percent share of the British market in the six years before 1959, and to divert some of these sales to other European markets. (Japanese imports were kept out of Britain and France by duties maintained under article 35.) The Japanese government's interest was to keep control of business in what were obviously highly sensitive and resistant markets in its own hands and to legitimize the interindustry cartel arrangements which it preferred to "disorderly marketing," while avoiding upsetting the United States. Half of this particular loaf was a lot better than no bread. The result, as summed up by the Curzons, was a bargain in which everybody seemed to gain and no one lost, since bilateral agreements could now legitimately replace unilateral quotas.

Very briefly, the LTA legitimised bilateral agreements to restrain exports undertaken by participants. The only limitations placed on the terms of these bilateral agreements were that (*a*) the existence of market disruption should be acknowledged by both the importing and the exporting country, (*b*) that any action to restrict trade had to be justified in terms of market disruption and (*c*) that any restriction that lasted for more than a year should provide for at least five percent growth of trade per annum.[5]

The agreements had to be in respect to specific products (cotton or at least half cotton) from specific sources.

A decade later, the nature of the problem had changed. It was not Japanese textiles so much as those from developing countries, and not cotton so much as clothing and synthetic yarns and fabrics, that were invading the markets of Europe and America. (Dumping, which required not only increasing market shares but also export prices lower than domestic prices, had meanwhile been covered by the Anti-Dumping Code agreed on in 1967.)

Moreover, well-developed European markets came under increasing pressure faster than those which had started from a very small base. The tensions between the industrialized countries, therefore, were apt to increase, while the demands of LDCs for bigger market shares were, for political reasons, less muted and inhibited than were Japan's. When, in 1974, the LTA was replaced by the MFA, the LDCs had asked for a 15 percent annual increase ceiling, and accepted 6 percent only on the understanding that bilateral agreements would be phased out by 1977 and new ones permitted only under the MFA agreement, and that a textile surveillance board (TSB) should be set up to arbitrate disputes and exercise some impartial judgment on alleged disruption.

Since the mid-seventies, voluntary restraint agreements under the MFA (article 4) have been negotiated by the United States, the countries of the EEC, and other European countries, but not by Japan. The list of developing countries interested in gaining a negotiated share of the consuming markets of the First World has lengthened and includes some Latin American countries (Brazil, Colombia) and the East Europeans (Yugoslavia, Hungary, Poland, Rumania), as well as the Asian countries (Macao and Malaysia as well as Taiwan, Singapore, and Hong Kong). Some of these agreements overlap with quota arrangements made under the Generalised Special Preference (GSP) arrangements, so that some LDCs have to administer a MFA quota and then, within it, a duty-free tariff quota under the GSP. (And, as Richard Cooper has pointed out, this artificial restraint on supply from a low-cost source merely redistributes the profits either to the successful exporter or to his government without doing much for the country's development.)

The whole business of market management in textiles consequently looks a lot more complex now than it did fifteen years ago. At that time, it was basically a U.S.–Japanese–British Commonwealth problem. The United States and Japan being the only important consumer markets open to new textile exporters (except for the Soviet Union, which arranged bilaterally to take every large export of textiles from Eastern Europe, on which it now depends for between 80 and 90 percent of all its textile supplies), it was then sufficient for them to take an initiative. Their motivations were clear, and the assumption was that through international agreement, a steadily but slowly expanding place could be found for the new entrants. Dispersion of the pressure by opening up markets in other developed countries (DCs), plus some braking arrangements on the pace of change, would solve the problem.

Now, the initiative no longer lies only with the Americans and the British. Nor does it rest only with the developed countries. Since the Fourth United Nations Conference for Trade and Development (UNCTAD IV), the U.N. debate on the New International Economic Order, and the Committee for International Economic Cooperation (CIEC) discussions, the Group of 77 LDCs is also now asserting its right to demand a different kind of arrangement based on different assumptions. It wants a managed displacement of *all* DC textile industries by those of the Third World.

Instead of the rather clear and limited motives and objectives of the United States and Britain fifteen years ago, the motives and objectives (so far as they are clearly explicit at all) are now essentially conflictual. The LDCs want bigger shares faster; the DCs want to slow down the redistribution of market shares to the LDCs as a group. And within the LDCs the early birds want to keep the shares they have gained without sharing them with the Johnny-come-latelys; while within the DCs, the Europeans who have made the most room for LDC imports want the convoy principle to operate so that they can hold the line until others give up a comparable share of *their* domestic markets to the LDCs.

The ultimate objectives of international policy—the principles that should guide negotiation and agreement and bodies like the TSB—are consequently confused. The DCs are really interested in what is essentially a welfare objective, not a liberalization objective. They want to use agreement to *decelerate* change so as to relieve the political, social, and economic pressures in their societies arising from foreign competition in textiles. The LDCs are interested in using agreement to accelerate change in order to assist their economic growth. But there is disagreement between those who want to accelerate aggregate change (thus aiding the strongest semideveloped to increase their industrialization and growth) and those who want to accelerate more change in the least advantaged, most unchanged, poorest, and least-developed countries—a point of view that finds more sympathy in the United States and in some other developed countries (possibly because it promises to cause less inconvenience to them).

That there should be a difference over the objectives of international public policy is hardly surprising when there is continuing uncertainty not only within the North-South groups but even within national societies. Are old industries now to be treated as social pensioners, like peasant systems of agriculture? Some industrial policies adopted suggested they should: they are given a measure of protection, state aid to ration production and to modernize with the implied promise that they will never totally be eliminated. The Lancashire cotton industry, reduced in twenty years from 20 million spindles to 2.7 million, from 367,000 looms to 57,000, from 231,000 workers to 57,000, now expects that the irreducible bottom has been reached. But the general welfare interest of cheap T-shirts and sweaters now competes with the sectoral and regional welfare interest of the pensioner industries and their workers, just as the cheap food interest—allied to the antiinflationary interest of the states— did (and does) with the welfare of the farmers and their workers.

The confusion and multiplicity of objectives were reflected in the issues at stake when these negotiations were resumed in Geneva in July 1977. But they were often presented in rather technical form—in the disingenious form of arguments over "indicators." For instance, evidence regarding the extent of "import penetration"—such as the numbers of jobs lost (i.e., reduction of total numbers employed),[6] or the share of the home market given up in terms of volume (number of items, yards of cloth) or of value—is given in support of the proposition that the welfare of the defended industry requires a global quota in addition to bilateral quota arrangements with its chief attackers.

The globalization issue—if the principle were conceded—creates a formidable number of problems for international cooperation, agreement, and organization. First, it raises the awkward question, so far suppressed, of the relative size of global quotas accepted by the various consumer countries. Should the indicator here be population, GNP per head, or textile consumption (and in what base year including or excluding reexports), or should it be based on a program of steps towards a future goal of the irreducible industry? Japan and the East Europeans, and after them, Spain, Yugoslavia, and Portugal, would be under pressure from the front-liners like Britain, America, and, recently, West Germany to take a "fairer share."

The technical question of how to define the industry or the market, and to what extent and how it should be subdivided (into the market, e.g., for textiles and clothing,[7] shirts, gray cloth, cotton, wool, synthetics, labor-intensive products vs. capital-intensive ones), is really an argument about the equitable issue—perceived in many industrialized countries and implicitly in every agreement since the first LTA—of the acceptable rate of change. What the industrialized countries are asserting is that the strong (foreign) competitors should share the responsibility with the weak (domestic) ones for slowing down the rate of change wherever this exceeds a given pace.

A third and comparatively new (or new-old, since it also came up in agriculture in the 1930s) issue is that account should be taken of the effects of world recession. Should the pace of market-share redistribution in favor of LDCs be slowed, as COMITEXTILE, the European producers' organization, and the British textile producers have argued? (The latter protested, successfully it would seem, that a 6 percent per annum increase for LDCs may be conceded in normal times but not when demand is growing at only 2.5 percent per annum). Or, should it be speeded up, as some development economists and LDC governments urge? Obviously, the competition for market shares is fiercer as demand slackens, easier as it picks up. But how should international arrangements respond? The problem can again be presented in terms of a technical definition related to the "irreducible" domestic industry, the final fortress. But the real issue is over who carries the risk of world depression and the burden of adjusting to it. Once the fortress-industry principle is conceded, the burden shifts (so to speak) from the defenders to the attackers.

The latter, however, reject the basic assumption, contesting that when hit by oil and fertilizer prices, sagging commodity markets, and worsening deficits, the LDCs deserve, not a smaller share of the cake, but a larger one to help them survive. If the issues in textile market negotiations have grown more complex and confused, the bargaining power within them has become much more diffused. Essentially the real power rests (as it always has) with the importing countries, who in the last resort are free to give or withhold market shares as they believe their national interest demands. The existence of a one-way ratchet device in trade negotiation, as proclaimed by GATT, has been shown to be what it always was: an eye-deceiving device to aid international cooperation. It does not follow that only in the apparently unlikely circumstances of a scarcity of textiles and clothes in the world market, or in rather special and high-technology lines of production,[8] or when it is concentrated in monopoly or oligopolistic enterprises, is there a more equal balance of bargaining power between buyers and sellers.

In the absence of multilateral agreement, the prospect is for a consequent retreat into bilateral negotiations in which the Group of 77 will be unable to exercise much combined persuasion and most LDCs will be under pressure in their bilateral bargaining to offer their customers exchange benefits (orders for DC arms and other manufactures, political concessions) to compensate for concessions of domestic market shares in textiles. The United States has about thirty such pacts falling due for renegotiation; the European Community has about twenty-two. (Japan has some bilateral agreements on silk products, but these are not covered by the MFA, and it has no restrictions as yet on imported cottons or synthetics.) The Americans have offered Hong Kong a five-year agreement limiting the increase in quotas for 1978 to 1.5 percent before resuming the commitment to 6 percent a year. The European Community, if it takes the textile commission's advice, will freeze quotas for 1980, but resume the 6 percent thereafter, provided its partners accept lower differential rates for specially sensitive sectors. The commission is also suggesting that its member governments stop imposing their own unilateral import quotas out of the blue (as the French and British did) and offer LDCs more generous tariff treatment under the Generalised Special Preference arrangements. But it has already been clear that there are differences of opinion within the Brussels Commission as well as between the member countries. Policy so far has been an entirely pragmatic response to the need to do something to prevent any further fall in employment, with no long-term planning envisioned and no consultative machinery to undertake it.

Broadly speaking, therefore, it seems that the issue of textile market shares will prove increasingly divisive, both between North and South and within each group. There have been extensive efforts through international organizations to achieve agreement and cooperation, but the conflicts have not been resolved; rather, they have deepened.

Steel

Market-sharing agreements between national steel industries, with the tacit or explicit blessing of governments, have a longer history than those in almost any other manufacturing industry.[9] The interwar depression led the national associations of steel producers in Europe to set up cartel arrangements between themselves, the essence of which were voluntary export restraints and the maintenance through a period of flagging demand of a core of steel-producing capacity in each of the countries covered by the participating association. The British did not join this prewar cartel, though they reached agreement with it, and much British resistance to the whole European Community idea in the early 1950s was rooted in the belief that what the continental countries were up to with the Schuman Plan for the European Coal and Steel Community was a revival, under more direct government auspices, of the prewar steel cartel.

The conflict over steel markets still arises primarily between developed countries, as it did in the 1930s, not between developed and developing countries, as in textiles. And steel producers are generally more closely involved with governments than are textile producers. This is because steel was once *the* prime defense industry. Every state perceived the strategic necessity of having large up-to-date steel mills to turn out guns. Steel was one of the commanding heights of any great power's national economy, and the balance of power was often reckoned in terms of million tons of steel produced annually. Now it is no longer so directly strategic but it still occupies a key position in national economies because its products (like those of the oil business) are necessary for so many other large industries—ships, automobiles, consumer durables of various kinds. It is therefore a heavily weighted item in every industrialized country's wholesale price index, and the concern of governments with prices and incomes and the limitation of inflation inevitably makes the price of steel a key political issue. Another concern, as with textiles, is with the level of employment. In both industries, production often tends to be geographically concentrated, with the result that the ability of producers and unions to exert political pressure is multiplied by concentrations of voting power. In steel, the problem is felt more acutely in recessions, steel markets being much more subject to cyclical variations in demand than the markets for textiles.

The form in which the state, in developed countries, is involved with the steel producers varies much more than the degree of involvement. The postwar French steel industry, for example, stayed in rather diffuse private hands without being nationalized. But it was closely associated with government through the 1966 Steel Convention, an agreement between the government and the strong, old-established Chambre Syndicale de la Siderugie Francaise (CSSF), by which the latter agree to cooperate in state planning in return for state aid covering up to one-third the cost of modernization investments. Only recently has steel undergone the common process of state-aided concentration to create out of eighty-odd companies two national champion enterprises, Usinor-Lorraine-Escaut and Wendel-Sidelor. This corresponds more closely with the relationship between the Japanese MITI and the six major Japanese steel producers than it does with that in Germany on one side or that in Britain on the other. The Japanese MITI was described by J. E. S. Hayward as an example of "private control through finance capitalism,"[10] the banks exercising a regulatory function with the producers' trade association, and a brokerage function between the producers to ration production in times of oversupply. More recently, the German trade association has set up a larger group, Denelux, with the neighboring Benelux producers and within the very strong new Eurofer organization.

Perhaps significantly for more general international cooperation and organization, it seems to be generally agreed that in Europe neither the ECSC nor the European Community has been able to exert half as much influence as the national governments and the trade associations. A significant French veto of 1966 barred the way to the use of EEC funds, on the pattern of the FEOGA, to offer community subsidies in place of national ones to cooperative steel producers. The result in each case is that the national government takes a very direct interest in the competition for markets, at home and abroad. Conflict between states is therefore likely to have serious repercussions on political relationships between allies and to hinder development of measures and mechanisms for the management of interdependence. Steel is a good test of trilateralism.

Once again, as with textiles, the initiative for negotiations on market-sharing of steel came from the United States. But this time it proved rather more difficult to arrange within the legal framework of existing international agreements. The first agreement on voluntary export restrictions in steel was negotiated by the United States with Japan in 1968, binding the United States to put no further restrictions on Japanese imports until the end of 1973 or 1974—a provision broken by the Nixon-Connally import surcharge of 1971. More effective was the enforced revaluation of the yen in Smithsonian Agreement. The negotiations were, not surprisingly, long and difficult and were complicated by European efforts, conducted by Jacques Ferry for the producers' association, to negotiate in parallel to ensure that Japanese exports diverted from the U.S. market did not drown the European one. The third side of the triangle was closed by a U.S.-EEC-British agreement in May 1972.

The international steel situation, however, was radically changed by unilateral action of the United States in 1974–75, when the Trade Act of 1974 gave the president personal authority to impose import quotas whenever imports became a "substantial cause of serious injury" to U.S. industry and employment. The specialty steel producers (along with producers of shoes, mushrooms, cars, ferrocyanide, and other goods) quickly responded with a claim for unilateral protection on the ground of heavy unemployment in the past oil-crisis recession. But while the old practice of food and oil import quotas could be squared with GATT principles on the strength of the "grandfather clause" exempting pre-existing trade policy measures, action under the 1974 Trade Act had no such justification and was, in fact, a direct contravention of GATT's commitments. Moreover, the Trade Act sanctioned the unilateral assignment of quotas to exporting countries whenever a significant share of the market was subject to voluntary restraints. Conclusion of a U.S.-Japanese agreement in 1976, therefore, opened the way for the United States to impose quotas without consulting the Europeans. For when the United States had tried to negotiate, Sweden, for one, replied that it had not so far accepted "voluntary" restraints and still did not care to do so. To cut a long story short, the United States strategy of using its leverage on Japan to put the Europeans under pressure not only exacerbated the problems of managing the EEC steel industry; it sowed very profound dissension between Europeans and Japanese.

Moreover in this case, unlike that of textiles, it was hard to argue a welfare case on behalf of the protected United States steel industry. The unemployment in it was not due to invading imports: it was primarily the reflection of the recession coming on top of low investment and falling profitability and productivity. A recent report by Charles Bradford for the Wall Street brokers Merrill, Lynch, is clear on this point. The production of Japanese steel takes half the man-hours than that of American steel takes, and investment in only one United States medium-sized steel mill in the last fifteen years against Japanese investment in eight giant steel mills has the result that U.S. mills run at a loss, Japanese at a profit. And a powerful motive for U.S. steel producers seeking additional protection was less the level of unemployment than the capital costs they faced in conforming to environmental and pollution controls. The import quotas against Japan allowed the U.S. industry to raise prices oligopolistically by 6 percent, shifting the anti-pollution costs of the industry onto its foreign competitors and its domestic consumers. It was hardly surprising that the large and powerful United Steelworkers labor union, observing this scene, decided that they too were entitled to a share in the gravy and put in a wage claim that conflicted with government antiinflation policy.

Thus, though in its essentials the bargaining process between the major-market country seeking to cut imports, on the one side, and the major-producer country seeking to maintain a secure outlet for production, on the other, is still much the same in steel as in textiles—the latter tending to give way under threat of even more draconian restrictions being levied against it if it does not comply—the consequences do seem more far-reaching, both internally and internationally.

Internally, there is little doubt that demands from the United States —paradoxically for a country fond of proclaiming its belief in competition and its opposition to trusts and other combinations in restraint of trade —have very actively fostered the growth of cartel arrangements in its adversaries. In both Japan and Europe the producers, in order to manage their end of the constricted market, have had to intensify output regulation arrangements among themselves. Internationally, there has been a chain reaction, or vicious circle, set up, the end of which is still not in sight. One of its most recent demonstrations was the incensed Australian protest against the 25 percent reduction demanded by the EEC countries in Australian steel exports, against which Australia has threatened to retaliate by restricting uranium supplies.

In Japan the American agreement "forced creation of a 21-firm Japanese cartel to control specialty steel exports."[11] In Europe, too, the need for concerted action has given greater importance to the producers' associations. It also seems to have given new strength to the European Community:

The Simonet Plan of 1976 has been followed by the Davignon Plan of 1977 setting mandatory minimum prices for some steel products (reinforced steel bars for construction) and indicative prices (as in the Common Agriculture Policy) for others. Thanks to these measures—or perhaps to good luck—European prices have kept up rather better than many producers expected and the Community has taken at least some of the credit.[12]

With some justification, it is also claimed privately in Brussels that the only real foreign policy that the Community has been able to follow just recently has been in steel. It has built up successful and active "contact groups" with other countries, including the Soviet bloc countries, and though lacking the big sticks the Americans wielded against Japan, a Community delegation to Tokyo last winter successfully persuaded Japan to initiate voluntary restrictions and price increases to help European steel producers survive the economic recession. This is a new low profile, sometimes an almost invisible kind of industrial diplomacy. The terms Japan agreed upon in response to European appeals, for instance, have never been published in any detail. But it is also the same as with the Economic Community textile policy—essentially short-term and pragmatic, and consequently unpredictable and precarious. On top of the inherently unstable and cyclical character of the steel industry, therefore, there has developed a ramshackle political structure of *ad hoc* diplomatic relations between the United States and Japan, Japan and the European Community, the European Community and the United States, these triangular links being supplemented by bilateral relationships between each of the major actors and a series of minor ones. Growing interdependence, meanwhile, adds to the potential sources of conflict among national governments and to their mutual sensitivity in inflation policy, balance of payments policy and industrial employment policy.

Ships

With ships, the conflict has appeared more bilateral than trilateral, between Europe and Japan, with the LDCs waiting offstage and hoping soon to grab a bigger share of the much-shrunken world market. The United States appears only behind the scenes in the great, continuing Euro-Japanese shipbuilding row. It is able to do so because (as I have explained elsewhere)[13] it has evolved, over a fifty-year period, a package of policies (government procurement, cargo preference rules, tax concessions, crewing restrictions, safety regulations, preferential financing arrangements) which allow U.S. shipping operators, whether flying the U.S. flag or flags of convenience, to hold onto a substantial share of world sea transport, and which allow U.S. shipyards to keep open on the basis of a limited but very secure and protected share of the ship-building business. Both operators and market share have consequently been far better insulated against the shocks of the post-OPEC collapse first in the tanker and then the dry cargo freight market and finally in the market for new ships. The full force of this major shock to the world economy—a shrinkage of demand to *one-third* the 1974 level of 34 million g.r.t. and of new orders from 73 million tons in 1973 to only 13 million tons in 1976—is thus mainly borne by European and Japanese shipbuilders, who between them account for about two-thirds of the world capacity (excluding China and the Soviet bloc countries). The initiative in market-sharing negotiations in this sector, therefore, has come from the Europeans. It was they, last autumn, who delivered a brutal and unheralded ultimatum to Japan at the OECD, demanding that Japan agree to a 50-50 share-out of the the burden of surplus shipbuilding capacity or face even greater restrictions on their sales to European buyers. Thus, although the picture in shipbuilding is far more cyclical than it is in steel (and a great deal more violently so than in textiles), the issues of who cuts and by how much are still basically the same. But precisely because of the cyclical character of the demand for ships, the latitude for argument and disagreement is even wider.

Japan's successful conquest of this world market has been far more thorough and rapid than anything the LDCs have achieved in textiles. Its shipbuilding capacity has increased ten times in five years, from 1.7 million g.r.t. in 1970 to 17 million in 1975; its share of the world market for new ships, from 22 percent to 50 percent in the same short half-decade. Already supplying something like 90 percent of the demand for bulk carriers, the Japanese are heading for a position of dominance over production for a sector of the world economy comparable only to the dominance of the United States in aircraft or that of OPEC countries in crude oil. In consequence, the choice of a base year on which market shares could be permanently agreed by all the producer countries concerned is likely to prove impossible.

Nor is it a simple matter, as economists might suppose (and as the Japanese, with costs some 40 percent below European costs and a good deal lower still below U.S. costs, might argue), of "leaving it to the market." The market itself is so distorted by government interventions, supports, and subsidies that analysis, let alone agreement, is inconceivable.

And just as the conflict over steel is inevitably affected by the impact or different perceptions of vital national interests, so it is in shipbuilding. The Japanese, for instance, can argue rather more convincingly than their opponents that the general international interest (including that of developing countries dependent on world markets for bulky commodities) most nearly coincides with their own as an island economy heavily committed to foreign trade. Both Japan and the developing countries want cheap sea transport, whereas a carve-up such as the Europeans propose would inevitably raise freight costs as well as new-ship costs. But behind the Europeans are the United States and the Soviet Union, and indeed the OPEC nouveau riche as well, all determined for political reasons of national security (which override questions of relative economic costs) to maintain sizable national merchant marines and with them a shipbuilding and ship-repairing base industry. Like the Russians, the Europeans still protest that they enjoy less than their fair share of the sea trade generated by their own economies. Providing no less than 40 percent of the world market for shipping, Europe has only 22 percent of the market for ships.

"Fair shares," moreover, can be calculated in all sorts of ways. If everyone were to agree to take a standard percentage cut in shipbuilding capacity (or in numbers employed, though that would be trickier), there would still be the problem of defining capacity and choosing the date. For the Japanese and Swedes (and especially the Japanese) can now argue that they alone have taken precautionary action in good time to adjust to reduced demand while some other countries—notably Britain, paralyzed by an impending but vaguely conceived nationalization plan—have done nothing much but shut their eyes and hope for the best. Others, like France and the Netherlands (as well as Britain) have responded only with increased national subsidies, mergers, and easier export credits. And still, the Japanese maintain, their order books would keep shipyards busy only for another 1.2 years, against an average expectation in European yards of 1.9 years.

Indeed, the crunch in the struggle over surplus shipbuilding capacity is probably still to come—probably sometime in 1980, when order books run out for European shipyards, while Brazil, South Korea, and other newcomers get ready to expand production. The resulting tensions will mount not only between states but within them. And as one may deduce from the British case, where Clydeside and Belfast will be competing for government favor with Tyneside and Merseyside, the outcome is much more likely to be determined by the location of marginal constituencies than by relative production costs, or even unemployment rates.

Objective indicators, to judge by the older market-sharing negotiations in the other two sectors, are going to cut no more ice internationally than they do nationally. The *Financial Times* shipping correspondent has compared the European Community's threats to Japan to the barking of a suburban terrier—less likely to deter intruders the longer it goes on without actually biting. [14] And it certainly seems that as the European countries become more nationalistic in shipbuilding, so their collective bargaining power is weakened by internal conflicts and divisions. The EEC is deeply divided at UNCLOS on fishing limits and regulations and on the UNCTAD code of conduct for liner conference. The general opinion seems to be that less credence should be placed in an EEC shipbuilding plan than in the Davignon steel plan.

The evidence of this growing nationalism, following the bad example set by the United States, is undeniable. Just recently, the chairman of Lloyd Register of Shipping made this categoric prediction: "I expect the shipbuilding industry to lose some of its international character, each sector tending to become polarised to the shipping needs of the country to which it is indigenous and with the export orders going only to the best equipped and technically advanced yards." [15]

Once again, the situation seems to favor the emergence of a strong trade association as an important nongovernmental actor in international negotiations. In shipbuilding, the Japanese shipbuilders' association found itself confronted by the Association of West European Shipbuilders (AWES), which includes the Scandinavians and Iberians as well as the EEC countries. The attempt to convert Intertanko into a new multilateral stabilization arrangement under the imposing title of the International Maritime Industries Forum (IMIF) with a rationing and ingenious system of sticks and carrots to ease the market of its overload of unwanted shipping capacity came to nothing: it lacked both the backing and cooperation of the U.S. government and of the major U.S. oil companies.

Conclusion

Summing up, it is hard to believe from the evidence briefly reviewed here that we have been witnessing, in these recent discussions and negotiations about the management of surplus industrial capacity, only a kind of post-OPEC hiccup in the gradual liberalization of the world economy. The trend throughout towards protectionism and away from liberalization, and towards bilateralism instead of multilateralism, seems unmistakable. Perhaps most important of all has been the third trend encouraged by the first two: the trend away from the market economy— what Heilbroner calls the "business civilization" [16]—and towards the greater involvement of the state in business and the greater dependence of business on government. In each of the three sectors considered, and in many others as well, there has been a quite remarkable increase in the involvement of European and American governments in economic matters supposedly belonging to the private sector. Often, there has been a marked increase in the political role of trade associations or producers' organizations, both within the state and in international economic diplomacy. As a kind of syndicalism has come in by the front door, nondiscriminating multinationalism in trade policy has gone out by the back door. Moreover, the sense of responsibility which Western governments have displayed has not been to the global community, still less to any vision of a new international economic order. It has been to their own people and to the powerful pressure groups within national economies. In short, the solution which Keynesians found to the contradictions of national capitalism (including among Keynesians all those New Dealers and others who learned demand management the way the early pilots learned to fly—by the seat of their pants) seems automatically and logically to rule out the use of the same solution to the contradictions of an interdependent world economy.

The way things are going, international organizations will function more as arenas of conflict than as executive instruments for the management of interdependence and the administration of guidelines and codes of conduct. The bargains struck within states, between groups of states like the European Community, or between the United States and other industrialized countries will be too fragile to evolve into a coherent "regime." An increase in activity, therefore, at the headquarters of international organizations like the OECD must not be mistaken for an increase in their influence over the patterns of development in the world economy.

Stability in that economy may not, therefore, be regained with recovery from recession. It is not difficult to predict that the argument in the years ahead will be not so much over Japan's right to a share of the North American and European markets as over the developing countries' rights to a share in the Japanese market. In shipping, where Japanese efficiency has been proverbial, there was a recent episode that may be a straw in the wind. A contract for ships for Nigeria went, not to Japan, but to South Korea and Yugoslavia. Yet it is hard to imagine Japan's willingly making much room for LDC exports if the Americans and Europeans continually close their doors on Japanese exports. From the Japanese point of view, the international trade game must look more and more like a no-win version of musical chairs against the United States. As fast as one chair is sat on, the music starts up again and a new one has to be secured in the nick of time. And the pace at which Japanese industry has to find new sectors to conquer seems to have accelerated, suggesting progressive damage to the stability of international economic relations.

It is this loss of stability displayed in the negotiations over the management of surplus capacity which may prove the most damaging threat to the global community of the future—at least as damaging as the perceptions, so widespread, of its inherent inequity.

Notes

1. *Economist,* 2 July 1977, p. 68.

2. Gerard Curzon and Victoria Curzon, "The Management of Trade Relations in the GATT," in vol. 1 of *International Economic Relations of the Western World, 1959–1971,* ed. Andrew Shonfield, 2 vols. (London: Oxford Univ. Press, 1976).

3. Joseph Nye and Robert Keohane, *Power and Interdependence: World Politics in Transition* (Boston: Little, Brown, 1977).

4. For wheat, bacon, dairy products, broiler chickens, and canned fruit; the quotation is from T. K. Warley, "Western Trade in Agricultural Products," in Shonfield, *International Economic Relations of the Western World,* vol. 1.

5. Curzon and Curzon, "The Management of Trade Relations in the GATT," p. 263.

6. This is a tricky indicator. Numbers employed may be reduced far more rapidly and effectively as a result of nationalization and modernization, substituting capital for labor to improve productivity, than by competition from foreign imports. On this basis, the import penetration of the British agricultural market has been (over a long period) something like 97.5 percent.

7. This is an important question for the LDCs. In 1974, they ran an overall *deficit* with the developed countries on all *textiles* of $1,330 million (1970, $1,130 million); but an overall *surplus* on *clothing.* The change here (thanks to foreign investment) was very rapid, increasing the surplus from $850 million in 1970 to $3,940 million in 1974.

8. The U.S. ban on exports of nylon yarn imposed in 1974 was one dramatic demonstration of such power. But on the whole, substitution in textiles is very high, and no such seller's power would be effective for long.

9. Market-sharing arrangements in chemicals—another "strategic" industry—possibly has an even longer history, the carve-up between Dupont, ICI, and I.G. Faben dating back to the 1920s, even though it later came up against the antitrust zeal of Roosevelt's Department of Justice.

10. In Raymond Vernon, ed., *Big Business and the State: Changing Relations in Western Europe* (Cambridge: Harvard Univ. Press, 1974).

11. See Michael Hudson, *Global Fracture: The New International Economic Order* (New York: Harper and Row, 1977), esp. chap. 2, "Steel Quotas Herald Protectionism."

12. *Economist,* 2 July 1977.

13. Susan Strange, "Who Runs World Shipping?" *International Affairs,* July 1979. See also Nye and Keohane, *Power and Interdependence.*

14. John Wyles, "Growls in the Euro-Japanese Shipbuilding Row," *Financial Times,* 10 January 1977.

15. *Financial Times,* 10 January 1977.

16. Robert Heilbroner, *Business Civilization in Decline* (New York: Norton, 1976).

{ 15 }

Basic Needs versus Developmental Needs: The North-South Dialogue

NAKE M. KAMRANY AND AURELIUS MORGNER

Introduction

In recent years, the traditional preoccupation with the East-West competition, focusing essentially on geopolitical, military, and economic rivalry, has given way in part to an alternative view of the world in terms of a division between the poor and the rich nations,[1] labeled the North-South division, which focuses on the political economy of sharing world resources and wealth. The significance of world income inequality is shown by Professor Henri Theil, who has pointed out that "about 65 percent of total income inequality in the noncommunist world is accounted for by international inequality."[2] This income disparity has led to a political and economic dialogue between the rich and the poor countries which is characterized by conflict and recrimination (see Table 15.1 for selected data). In the long run, world political and economic stability may be dependent upon the dialogue and the decisions reached between the relatively and absolutely prosperous North and the relatively and absolutely poorer South concerning world poverty. Thus, North-South relations have become a significant international economic issue.

The central point of the issue is that, of the 4.2 billion people of the world, around three-quarters of them live in the less developed countries (LDCs), whose average per capita income is less than one-quarter of that of the rich countries. More importantly, approximately 1.5 billion people in the Third World are seriously poor and are considered destitute. International agencies such as the International Labor Organization (Geneva) and the World Bank (Washington, D.C.), who make world income estimates, use the following per capita income as poverty lines: $90–$180 for Latin America, $59–$115 for Africa, and $50–$100 for Asia.

There are indeed hundreds of millions of people in the Third World who lack decent levels of the physical necessities of life and do not

Table 15.1. Selected Comparative Data on Wealth of Nations

Selected Countries	Per Capita GNP (1972)	Per Capita GNP Growth Rate (1965–72)	Life Expectancy at Birth	Birth Rate per 1,000 (1970–75)	Infant Mortality per 1,000 Live Births	Literacy (%)	Per Capita Energy Consumption (Kg Coal Equiv., 1971)
Fourth World (least developed)							
Afghanistan	80	0.8	40	49.2	182	8	27
Bangladesh	70	-1.6	36	49.5	132	22	n.a.
Chad	80	1.6	38	44.0	160	5–10	27
Dahomey	110	1.7	41	49.9	185	20	38
Ethiopia	80	1.2	38	49.4	181	5	32
India	110	1.4	50	39.9	139	28	186
Mali	80	1.3	—	50.1	188	5	25
Nepal	80	0.1	44	42.9	169	9	9
Niger	90	-5.1	38	52.2	200	5	22
Somalia	80	1.1	41	47.2	177	5	31
Yemen, Arab Rep.	90	2.4	45	49.6	152	10	14
Third World (less developed)							
Angola	390	5.5	38	47.3	203	10–15	157
Colombia	400	2.4	61	40.6	76	73	638
Egypt	240	0.6	52	37.8	103	30	282
Ghana	300	1.0·	44	48.8	156	25	192
Honduras	320	1.7	54	49.3	115	45	234
Ivory Coast	340	4.1	44	45.6	164	20	265
Liberia	250	4.0	44	43.6	159	9	368
Senegal	260	-0.7	40	47.6	159	5–10	129
Syrian Arab Rep.	320	3.8	54	45.4	93	35	485

Third World (middle income)							
Argentina	1,290	2.9	68	21.8	60	91	1,773
Brazil	580	5.6	61	37.1	94	61	500
Chile	800	2.2	63	27.9	71	84	1,516
Mexico	750	2.8	63	42.0	61	78	1,270
Peru	520	1.1	56	41.0	110	61	621
OPEC countries							
Kuwait	4,090	−1.3	67	47.1	44	47	7,888
Iran	654	7.2	51	45.3	139	23	895
Libyan Arab Rep.	1,830	8.1	53	45.0	130	27	571
Qatar	2,600	6.1	47	49.6	138	10–15	2,025
United Arab Emirates	3,220	16.2	47	49.6	138	20	802
Industrially advanced countries							
Australia	2,980	3.1	72	21.0	17	98	5,359
Austria	2,410	5.0	71	14.7	24	90	5,231
Belgium	3,210	4.6	73	14.8	17	97	6,116
Canada	4,400	3.2	72	18.6	17	98	9,326
France	3,620	4.8	73	17.0	16	97	3,928
Germany, Fed. Rep.	3,390	4.1	71	12.0	20	99	5,223
Japan	2,320	9.7	73	19.2	12	98	3,267
Sweden	4,480	2.5	73	14.2	10	99	6,089
United States	5,590	2.0	71	16.2	18	98	11,244
Socialist countries							
Chinese People's Rep.	170	2.6	62	26.9	55	25	561
Czechoslovakia	2,180	4.5	69	17.0	21	100	6,615
Poland	1,500	4.0	70	16.8	28	98	4,374
Romania	810	6.7	67	19.3	40	98–99	2,975
U.S.S.R.	1,530	5.9	70	17.8	26	99	4,535
Yugoslavia	810	5.5	68	18.2	43	80	1,608

Source: International agencies.

meet their "basic needs." The actual physiological needs of men, as shown by the case of primitive man, are minimal. Basic needs, which are our interest here, reflects cultural imperatives if people are to function effectively in their existing milieus. Income needed to meet the basic needs is roughly defined by international agencies as that income that would purchase the most important items necessary to support human life at an acceptable level of activity. Essentially, the basic needs are defined according to four indices of well-being: (1) caloric intake, (2) access to health care and life expectancy at birth, (3) housing needs, and (4) access to education. Obviously, it is difficult to quantify precisely the dollar value of basic needs, since subjective values enter into what these needs are. A team of economists at the World Bank has alternatively defined the poverty line as the income level of the 40th percentile in India in 1975. This definition of the poverty line is more conservative than other estimates. Using the "Kravis dollar," which is adjusted for purchasing power, the World Bank economists set the poverty line at $250 in 1970 prices. By this standard, almost 40 percent of the population of the developing countries live in absolute poverty defined in terms of income levels insufficient to provide adequate nutrition. The authors conclude: "If the countries in our sample continue at historical rates of growth of GNP there is virtually no prospect of abolishing poverty by the year 2000."[3] More than 30 percent of the population in the low income group will remain below the poverty line, and the absolute number of people in poverty will be the same as in 1975.

One of the central issues concerning global poverty is the distinction between basic needs and development needs.

Basic Needs. There has been a growing recognition both in the rich and the poor nations that efforts at development are not trickling down to the poor; in fact, they are bypassing the poor and not improving their conditions with respect to employment, income distribution, and alleviation of basic poverty. Specific measures directed at the poor are needed. The rich nations appear to be sympathetic to this issue. For example, the American Aid program has placed increasing emphasis on projects that directly improve the welfare of the poor in terms of nutrition, sanitation, and housing. An important aspect of the basic needs argument is the *perception* of "poverty" as conceived by the leaders and the nonleaders of the less developed countries themselves as well as the perceptions of rich countries and the international community. Although the "revolution of rising expectations" has been spreading among the poor of the world for more than two decades through modern communication, the international community appears only recently to have become more sensitive, concerned, and vocal about the issue of poverty.

Development Needs. Leaders in the less developed countries are concerned principally with the overall rate of development as they have experienced it over the past decade. They do not wish to continuously struggle with the basic needs requirements. Instead, they wish to alter drastically the manner in which development occurs—that is, the old relationship of minority dominance between the rich and poor countries. They wish to alter the relationship in such a way as to enable them to attain *self-sustaining growth.*

Thus, part of the North-South debate centers on how the priority for international aid should be set by the rich and the poor nations. Should it be directed at addressing (1) the basic needs of the very poor, or (2) the development needs of poor countries, or (3) some combination of both?

Representatives of the less developed countries do not wish to see a dichotomy made between basic needs and development needs, since such a dichotomy, they feel, creates alternatives which are inconsistent with their aims. They feel that if supporting basic needs is advanced as an alternative, their objectives for self-sustaining growth will suffer. Besides, the amount of resource transfer from the rich to the poor countries is substantially less than the amount needed to meet those specific growth targets which would free them from dependency upon the rich countries. The LDCs argue that at certain annual growth rates (6-8 percent per annum) of their economies combined with some internal redistribution, both objectives—basic needs and development needs—would be met. Their basic argument for development needs is that achieving a state of self-sustaining growth would free them from dependence upon the "rich" countries for continued aid. In other words, they argue for a new order, a North-South accord that would eventually abolish the North-South distinction altogether. An aid strategy to satisfy the requirements of the basic needs concept alone is considered a continuation of the old order—a dominant-minority rela-tionship. In fact, some argue that aid for basic needs amounts to an extension of *social welfare work* from the rich to the poor countries.

If both needs are combined, the result will be either a strategy of directing aid to meet basic needs in the short run and simultaneously achieve self-sustaining growth in the long run, or a strategy of concen-trating on development needs (as has been the case in the past) with basic needs being met as a result of the growth process. The latter strategy has always sounded most plausible in an economic sense; how-ever, there is now ample evidence that in some rapidly growing eco-nomies (e.g., Mexico and Brazil), basic needs of the poor have not received a fair share of increased national income.

Past Performance Growth: Aid and Results

The growth performance of the less developed countries as a whole has been quite substantial over the last two decades. The issue of poverty (failure to meet basic needs) in the medium- and high-performing

LDCs emanates in large part from the failure of distributional mechanisms, while the issue of poverty in the low-performing LDCs emanates almost wholly from growth failure.

After a quarter century of experimentation with economic development in the poorest of the LDC countries, the disarray and in some cases the calamitous results are so obvious that a reexamination of traditional assumptions, methodologies, theories, and policies is in order. Certainly, it is not necessary to argue this point at length, since both supporters and critics of the record of economic development of the very poor countries agree on the need for reappraisal. If we divide the LDCs into three income levels, the growth record of the countries in the lowest income group (India, Pakistan, Afghanistan, the Sahel countries, etc.) amounted to only 3.7 percent, or 1.3 percent per capita from 1960 to 1975 (see Table 15.2). Yet this group has received probably more than 70 percent of all aid. Only Korea and Taiwan can be said to have been favorably affected by aid. The rest of the LDCs in the middle- and high-income groups have enjoyed impressive growth rates by virtue of foreign investment, favorable international trade development, and internal growth. These facts suggest two significant needs: (1) the need to improve drastically the growth performance of the low-income-group countries, and (2) the need for a redistribution strategy at all income levels in all the LDCs.

While economic growth performance of the upper and middle LDCs has been satisfactory over the last three decades, changes in structural, institutional, social, environmental, and distributional matters have become of growing concern, especially as they relate to justice, equity, and the overall well-being of the masses of population. It is now widely believed that there is no inherent compatibility between growth and contemporary social objectives. The poor record of income distribution in the past three decades point to some trade-offs between growth and equity. Given this increasing concern, international development institutions such as the World Bank have begun to shift their attention from activities which are purely growth-oriented to those which attempt to strike a balance between economic growth and equity.

Despite concerted effort by economists to discover the causes of

Table 15.2. Annual Percentage Rate of Growth for Less Developed Countries by Income Group, 1960–1975

	GNP	GNP per Capita
Low income	3.7	1.3
Middle income	5.0	3.3
High income	6.3	3.5

Source: World Bank.

increasingly unequal income distributions, and to devise policies to offset present trends, there is little consensus as to causes. Policy has therefore been *ad hoc*, aiming for "solutions" which may not be solutions at all but merely attempts to eliminate glaring problems in the short run. The relationship between growth and distribution factors is not well understood. A study examining income distribution and growth in eight countries using the Gini index came up with the following results:

1. Rapid growth (Korea, Taiwan), increasing equality in distribution;
2. Rapid growth (Brazil, Mexico), decreasing equality in distribution;
3. Slow growth (Sri Lanka, Costa Rica), increasing equality in distribution;
4. Slow growth (India, Colombia), decreasing equality in distribution. [4]

This mixed record of the trickling-down effect of growth has led a number of international agencies to separate the cost of meeting the basic needs as opposed to meeting development needs.

Cost Estimates

A number of estimates have been made of the costs of meeting worldwide basic needs (i.e., 2,400 calories per person, basic health provisions, basic housing, and universal primary education). According to a World Bank estimate, the annual cost for investment and recurrent costs between 1980 and 2000 would amount to $40–$60 billion per year for all developing countries and $32–$39 billion for low-income developing countries alone.

How much of the above cost estimates will be met by international resource transfers? If we assume that the international resource transfer will cover 70 percent of the capital costs and 50 percent of the recurrent costs, the amounts will vary between $18.4 and $21.9 billion to assist the low-income countries and between $28.3 and $33.3 billion for all developing countries. These figures obviously will vary depending on the assumptions made for the share of capital and recurrent costs which will be borne by the developing countries themselves.

Various estimates for the cost of development needs have·also been made. The investment and import requirements to meet the growth targets point to the need for international resource transfer. In a recent MIT study, the amount of foreign aid required between 1975 and 2000 for six countries in the Sahel zone of Africa (Chad, Maritania, Mali, Niger, Senegal, and Upper Volta) to achieve a 5 percent growth target

was $5 billion under the assumption of high export performance, and
$9 billion if the export performance is relatively modest.[5] The World
Bank team reports that if appropriate measures of accelerated growth
and distribution are combined, it would be possible to abolish poverty
by the year 2000. They point out that action in the traditional areas of
trade and aid policies could enhance the growth rate of the LDCs to
exceed their base case projections. In order to accelerate the GNP
growth rate by one percentage point, an additional aid flow of $3.0
billion per annum would be required. This additional amount would
require a substantial movement toward the 0.7 percent of GNP target
for aid.[6]

Competing Positions: The Politics of Wealth Transfer

The magnitude, composition, and transfer of aid has become a
major point of contention between the rich and the poor countries.
The continuing impasse of the North-South dialogue pointedly illustrates
the complexity and difficulty of determining what must be done to
reduce substantially, if not solve, the problem of world poverty. Despite
the progress of many LDCs in relative terms, income disparity between
the DCs and the non-oil-rich LDCs is more severe now than in the
past. The resentment of the LDCs over the unshared growth of affluence
of the past three decades has become increasingly serious. The mode
of interaction between the poor and rich countries has changed from that
of cooperation and partnership for progress in the 1950s to that of adver-
sary bargaining in the 1970s, as exemplified in the recent deliberations of
GATT (Kenya), the North-South Dialogue (Paris), Conferences on
Population and Food (Rome), and a number of conferences held by
the poor countries (for example, in Manila). The complementary and
competing positions of the various sectors will yield solutions with
varying degrees of stability and instability. Consequently, the future of
the world economic condition may range from a world of harmony,
prosperity, peace, and hope to one of conflicts, stagflation, wars, and
despair. While debate, bargaining, and dialogue will center on equitable
distribution, no theoretical framework now exists that would produce an
optimal result. In place of the old East-West struggle of the 1960s for
influence through aid rivalry, new actors and new issues have evolved
on the international scene, reflecting the bargaining positions and the
utility function of the various groups discussed below.

The OPEC Position. As an oligopoly, the OPEC countries will raise
the price of oil insofar as it appears profitable to do so. It will attempt
to get the Organization for Economic Cooperation and Development
(OECD) to agree on some indexation scheme. Its upper bound for
price at any time will be influenced by considerations of the aggregate

demand for oil, the slowing down of the rate of economic recovery of the West, fear of stagflation, the possibility of rapid development of substitutes, the alienation of the West, and the possibility of provoking military response. OPEC will try to counter the impact of the price hike upon the poor countries by providing aid and by negotiating for more concessions from OECD. The long-run concern of the OPEC countries (assuming that the cartel lasts) is to devise a strategy to establish self-sustaining economies before the exhaustion of revenue from oil—an exhaustible resource.

The North's Position. Rather than an American strategy we now have a strategy of the North, guided principally by the United States, but including the OECD countries. Its objectives are to spread responsibility for aid, to organize the oil-importing countries (hence the Washington Energy Conference of February 1974, and the formation of the International Energy Agency), to break the OPEC cartel, to preserve the pre-OPEC market system and its institutions, to gain time through conferences (Conference on International Economic Cooperation—the North-South Dialogue), to reduce dependency upon oil and other imports, to retain certain monopolistic powers relative to LDCs, especially in regard to technologies, and to minimize the influence of the Soviet Union upon both the LDCs and the newly rich oil-exporting countries, while maintaining the old trade relations.

The Socialist Position. The socialist aid strategy, with both the Soviet bloc and the Chinese bloc socialist countries, has been predominantly political and military. In 1976, Soviet aid to less developed countries amounted to 0.21 percent of its GNP—by far the least relative amount as compared to other donor countries. This declining trend in Communist aid commitments has continued, as evidenced by its decline in 1977 to its lowest point in nearly a decade—only $875 million in new credit. The most precipitous drop was in the Soviet program. Moreover, the socialist assistance programs of the Soviet Union and of China are directed exclusively to socialist-directed or socialist-tending LDCs who have either created geopolitical points of pressure or have the potential for creating such points of pressure in the future. There is no evidence that the socialist countries have in any way modified their political-military objective as the basis for aid.

The South's Position. The LDCs aim for higher commodity prices (inflation for OECD) and indexation, debt relief, greater access to markets in the developed nations, more transfer of technologies, worldwide dialogue on international economic matters, a common fund for commodities, fuller access to capital markets, and easier import terms for manufactured goods and oil imports. In the absence of any substantive power, the strategy of the LDCs has been to work through the United Nations, making use of their majority vote to create specialized agencies which are sympathetic to their cause—such as the Conference on Trade and Development (UNCTAD, 1964), the Industrial Development Organization (UNIDO, 1966), and the International Development Strategy (1970)—and to pass supporting resolutions in the United Nations General Assembly.[7]

A New International Economic Order

These issues of the North-South relations have drawn international deliberations. In 1974, the United Nations General Assembly's "Charter of Economic Rights and Duties of States" heightened the positions of the South and endorsed the following proposals:

1. Price support and indexation of LDC commodities;
2. Transfer of 0.7 percent of the GNP of the developed countries to LDCs in the form of official aid;
3. Linking the standing drawing rights of the International Monetary Fund to development aid;
4. The "right" of primary producers to form cartels.

The issue of the New Economic Order has also received considerable attention from many scholars. Professor C. Fred Bergsten's contributions and the publication of the proceedings of many conferences provide a wealth of materials on these major policy issues.[8] Moreover, the seminal contributions of Emile Despres have been the precursors of many of these recent efforts, whose aims are to transform the conventional, narrow, self-centered policies now being pursued into a system of world prosperity and respect for human dignity in the poor and rich lands.[9] Moreover, the seven reports of the Tripartite Association (European Community, Japan, and North America) have made major contributions toward policy formulations concerning the New Economic Order.[10] The uncertainty surrounding the direction of the New Economic Order is clearly expressed in one of these reports:

As reflected in debates in the United Nations, relations between the industrial and the developing countries seem to have deteriorated sharply. It is too soon to know whether these and related developments will halt or reverse the earlier trend toward closer international economic cooperation or whether the response rather will be to expand the multilateral understandings and institutions that have been created to support world economics integration. In this sense the world economy is at a transitional point.[11]

In view of a continuing shift in the distribution of power and a multipolar competition, the management of these issues is no longer the responsibility of a single nation or bloc of nations; it must be the shared responsibility of the world community at large. It follows that the problems as well as the incentives of the various participants need to be taken into account. In response to these issues, some Europeans have advocated models of autarky. The European economists perceive the world economic relations as a zero-sum game. They reflect the aura of pessimism that has set in, especially in Europe, just as the world is beginning to find new ways for at least a portion of the LDCs (those of OPEC) to pay their own way for economic development. Self-sufficiency and autarky are advocated as a means of economic survival. In the less developed countries the apparent trend toward autarky has been interpreted roughly as follows:

When the prices of commodities, materials, and energy are kept low, a system of free trade was advocated by rich countries. Now that energy prices have been increased due to the emergence of OPEC (the champions of the Third World) and the probabilities of other oligopolies have been created for other commodities and materials with the possibility of better prices (indexation), a system of autarky is being proposed. Such a system, if adopted may slow down the rate of growth of selected LDCs *and* the living standards of the advanced countries, especially those of Western Europe. It can also create major political and military upheavals, the costs of which would be enormous. [12]

In one sense, world economic relations do constitute a zero-sum game. Clearly, it is not feasible to increase simultaneously the *relative* share of world income for all countries or for a bloc of countries. It is possible to increase the absolute size of income of each country, although the rate of increase for some countries may be faster than for others, and the relative gaps may diminish and/or shift. But even this modest aim will require a good dose of enlightened self-interest.

Moreover, there is a need not only for better perception, or new visions, but also for an improved theoretical and methodological framework on the part of social scientists for the understanding of these problems.

The Dynamic Structure of Development

For nearly a quarter of a century, the economic development of the LDCs has been studied from the traditional economist's "positive" view, with the assumptions that the behavior of the decisionmakers, both leaders and nonleaders, are based on economic rationality, are consistent with complete and fixed preferences, and tend toward equilibrium. In reality, economic actors base their decisions on partial information, adapt to internal and external conditions using suboptimal strategies, and have development paths that are not smooth or optimal. As Professor Richard Day has stated, crises "often involve situations in which unforeseen crises emerge out of formerly advantageous changes and patterns in

which some segments of a population—or some whole countries—
become worse-off while others become better-off. ... People, as well as
nations, however, are often inconsistent, the economy appears frequently, if not always, to be more or less in disequilibrium, and improving conditions for some at the expense of worsening conditions for
others is a commonplace occurrence, with economic competition producing losers as well as winners." [13]

There is indeed a need to understand and explain how development
problems and crises emerge from the dynamic structure of the development system. Sufficient study of development from this point of view
may help identify the policies which can anticipate potential crises and
moderate or eliminate them by preventive action. Moreover, it is in this
context that the LDCs could arrive at realistic policy options concerning their internal policies and external bargaining positions. The LDCs
need to better assess their rights and resources and the international
institutions necessary for conflict resolution.

International Distribution of Rights and Resources. Events of the
recent past have made it increasingly clear that the distribution of
wealth among nations and the distribution of the gains from trade is a
function not only of markets and initial resources, as in the classical
theory of international trade, but also of the power of the nations
involved. The OPEC cartel was able to use an embargo, and the threat
of future embargoes, to shift the distribution of economic rents from
the oil-consuming countries to the oil-producing countries, i.e., from
production and consumption of petroleum. This display of economic
power has served as an example to other producers of primary products
and has caused them to consider the possibility of similar actions to
shift the distribution of the gains from trade. The North-South dialogue,
détente, increases in world population and its concentration in poor
countries, and the proliferation of nuclear power are among other
major developments which underscore the importance of power in
changing or maintaining the distribution of wealth among nations.
There is a need for the development of a general equilibrium model
that addresses the allocative process of the role of power in an explicit
theoretical framework, including bargaining and learning behavior,
with its practical implications to address such issues as cartel behavior,
trade agreements, and the structure of the international monetary
system. [14]

International Institutions. One of the important requirements of
international conflict resolution and international progress is an institutional framework and institutions that could effectively serve that purpose. The majority of the development agencies—including the World
Bank, the International Monetary Fund, the United Nations Develop-

ment Program, and others—were established to manage the development process under the old world economic structure. And a majority of the secretarial staff of these agencies were former colonial administrators whose ideas were embedded in acceptance of a system of exchange between the privileged and the nonprivileged whereby the bargaining positions were totally lopsided in favor of the rich and the powerful. In the absence of any other power base, the LDCs capitalized on whatever limited advantage their numbers could gain for them. (In 1955, the United Nations had 59 members; as of mid-1978, the number had increased to 150 members, two-thirds of them from the LDCs.) The establishment of the United Nations Conference on Trade and Development (UNCTAD) in 1964 provided a forum for the LDCs to articulate their position for trade instead of aid, especially under the leadership of its first director, Raul Presbisch. The establishment of the United Nations Industrial Development Organization (UNIDO) in 1966, and the United Nations International Development Strategy for the Second Development Decade in 1970, extended the scope of discussion to industrial development and the issues of food and population, environmental pollution, and related subjects. Since the formation of OPEC, however, the strategy of the LDCs has shifted to a call for reform of the existing order and a demand for an integrated and comprehensive approach to cope with the essence of poverty, as spelled out in the United Nations "Charter of Economic Rights and Duties of States" (December 1974, Resolution 3362; passed in September 1975, to negotiate compromises). One of the crucial questions concerning the North-South dialogue is the suitability and effectiveness of the existing international institutions and their administrations, bureaucracies, and the overall framework.

Dr. John Pattison and Professor Fratianni have pointed out that these international institutions do not represent a proper correspondence between the systematic needs of the world economy and institutional capability, either in terms of the allocation of tasks to organizations, or of nations as members of these bodies. The inadequacy of these institutions make the formulation and implementation of reform difficult. Pattison and Fratianni recommend that consideration of equity and efficiency determine the optimal number of members in an organization, and that there should be an understanding of how an international institution could effectively function as it relates to voting, budgets, staffing, and its incentive system. [15]

Conclusion

In summary, the issue of global poverty is complex and presents a major challenge to the ingenuity of the human race. The economic behavior emanating from the competing positions of the North and the South may be characterized as a system of multilateral bargaining or oligopoly whereby each actor tries to optimize his position. Each major bargaining group assumes a zero-sum game situation and attempts either to hold onto an advantageous relative position or to improve its relative position. A major breakthrough in the impasse will require a revolutionary departure from the existing perception of the dichotomy between the "poor" and the "rich" and of the relationship of the world's wealth and man's ability to create enough to meet the basic needs and go beyond towards fulfillment. It will take both altruism and self-interest to bring these competing positions into closer convergence. This will be possible if we break away from the traditional dismal view of economics to a vision of the possible, remembering that the cost of meeting basic needs is relatively small. A reallocation of only 5 percent of the world's annual military expenditures ($400 billion) for basic needs would be sufficient.

Notes

1. N. M. Kamrany and J. E. Elliot, "The North-South Dialogue," in *The New Economics of the Less Developed Countries,* ed. N. M. Kamrany (Boulder, Colo.: Westview Press, 1978).

2. H. Theil, "World Income Inequality and Its Components," Department of Economics, University of Chicago, 1979.

3. M. S. Ahluwalia, N. G. Carter, and H. B. Chenery, "Growth and Poverty in Developing Countries," World Development Report, Background Paper no. 6, World Bank, September 1978.

4. W. Loehr, "Economic Growth, Policy, and Income Distribution," in Kamrany, *The New Economics of the Less Developed Countries.*

5. N. M. Kamrany, *International Economic Reform* (Washington, D.C.: Univ. Press of America, 1977).

6. Ahluwalia, Carter, and Chenery, "Growth and Poverty in Developing Countries."

7. Several U.N. resolutions have been passed in support of the International Development Strategy. See United Nations publication A/AC 176/2-3, September 1975.

8. See C. F. Bergsten, *Toward a New World Trade Policy* (Lexington, Mass.: Lexington Books, 1975), and many additional publications by Bergsten. Also, for a broader treatment see Helen Hughes, ed., *Prospects for Partnership* (Baltimore: Johns Hopkins Press, 1973).

9. G. M. Meier, ed., *International Economic Reform: Collected Papers of Emil Despres* (London: Oxford Univ. Press, 1973). Also, for a significant contribution to the reform of the international commercial system to be pursued in the context of liberalization of world trade, see H. Corbert and R. Jackson, eds., *In Search of a New World Economic Order* (New York: Wiley, 1974).

10. The seven reports published by the Brookings Institution are as follows: *Reshaping the International Economic Order* (1972); *Reassessing North-South Economic Relations* (1972); *World Trade and Domestic Adjustment* (1973); *Toward the Integration of World Agriculture* (1973); *Cooperative Approaches to World Energy Problems* (1974); *Trade in Primary Commodities: Conflict or Cooperation?* (1974); and *The World Economy in Transition* (1975).

11. *The World Economy in Transition* (Washington, D.C.: Brookings Institution, 1975).

12. Kamrany and Elliot, "The North-South Dialogue."

13. R. H. Day, "Cooperative Dynamic and Development Policy Analysis" (Paper presented at the International Development Conference, Madison, Wis., 1975).

14. D. L. Brito and M. D. Intriligator, "International Power and the Distribution of World Wealth," in Kamrany, *The New Economics of the Less Developed Countries.*
15. J. C. Pattison and M. Fratianni, "International Institutions and International Progress," in ibid.

Selected Bibliography

Cassen, R. H. 1976. "Population and Development Survey: A Survey." *World Development,* October–November.

Dyson, T.; Bell, C.L.G.; and Cassen, R. H. 1978. "Fertility, Mortality, and Income— Changes Over the Long Run: Some Simulation Experiments." *Journal of Development Studies,* Special Number on Population.

Ghai, D. P.; Khan, A. R.; Lee, E.L.H.; and Alfthan, T. 1977. *The Basic Needs Approach to Development: Some Issues Regarding Concepts and Methodology.* Geneva: ILO.

International Labour Office. 1976. *Employment, Growth, and Basic Needs.* Geneva: ILO.

Kamrany, N. M., ed. 1977. *International Economic Reform: Issues and Policies.* Washington: D.C.: Univ. Press of America.

Kamrany, N. M., ed. 1978. *The New Economics of the Less Developed Countries: Changing Perceptions in the North-South Dialogue.* Boulder, Colo.: Westview Press.

Leontief, W., et al. 1977. *The Future of the World Economy.* New York: United Nations.

McHale, J., and McHale, M. 1977. *Basic Human Needs: A Framework for Action.* New Brunswick, N.J.: Transaction Books.

OECD. 1977. *Development Cooperation: 1977 Review.* Paris: Development Assistance Committee, OECD.

Sheehan, G., and Hopkins, M. 1978. *Basic Needs Performance: An Analysis of Some International Data.* ILO World Employment Programme Working Paper. Geneva, January 1978.

{ 16 }

Contemporary Issues in Development Economics

JEFFREY B. NUGENT

The developing countries—or less developed countries, as they are alternatively called—collectively comprise more than two-thirds of the world's people, but earn only a small fraction of its income. Although developing countries have probably received more attention in the academic and professional community in the last thirty years than in the previous thirty centuries, we are left with an accumulating number of questions about all facets of how, why, and under what conditions such countries develop. Some of these questions or issues are very fundamental, suggesting that even those questions which have been assumed to have been satisfactorily answered are in fact still open, and therefore that much of the conventional wisdom may be misleading.

The purpose of this chapter is to outline some of these issues and the grounds for thinking that a major shift in orientation in this particular field will be required if satisfactory explanations to the growing list of paradoxes and problems are to be obtained.

Definitional Issues

The first issue that must be faced in development economics is, What is "development"? Although noneconomists have never been happy about it, economists have strived for simplicity and have sought to avoid wasting time on semantics and definitions. Hence, economists traditionally have defined development in highly operational terms, most often as gross national product (GNP) per capita. This index has the benefit that estimates of GNP and population are available for virtually every country in the world; it allows countries to be indexed unambig-

The author gratefully acknowledges that many of the views expressed here have developed out of long discussions and years of joint research with Pan Yotopoulos.

uously and cardinally with respect to both levels of development and rates of development. The measure is also more comprehensive and perhaps less culturally biased than most other single indicators one could imagine. For example, consumption of dairy products per capita would favor those societies which have a preference for dairy products over other products; housing expenditures per capita would favor those societies in cold climates, where walls have to be thicker, insulation and heating equipment more sophisticated. Usually, the GNP per capita is conceived of as a suitable index of potential welfare, indicative of welfare that people are capable of obtaining.

Gradually, economists have become persuaded that development cannot really be measured appropriately and solely in terms of GNP. For example, studies have cited numerous examples wherein GNP statistics went up, even on a per capita basis, but not much changed; these have become known as examples of "growth without development". The initiatives of environmental concerns in the industrialized world have also made it increasingly clear that higher GNP per capita may often be associated with somewhat more subtle and difficult-to-measure environmental and other changes which worsen the quality of life and therefore make it quite possible that higher GNP per capita is inconsistent with the achievement of higher levels of potential welfare. Then, too, there has been increasing concern that the GNP per capita index is deficient because it ignores distribution. If an equitable distribution is either a natural consequence of the development—i.e., the GNP—increasing process—or at least is taken care of by appropriate tax and subsidy policies, there should be no reason to doubt the validity of GNP per capita as an index of development even if the achievement of an equitable distribution of income is considered an essential aspect of development. The signs are becoming increasingly obvious, however, that this is not the case. As GNP per capita increases, its distribution becomes less equal rather than more equal.

While comprehensive and operational measures of development in the sense of the quality of life remain, at best, at the frontier of the field and not fully operational, the call for at least supplementing GNP per capita with measures of distributional equality, or more precisely, with separate statistics on income for specially selected target groups like the poor, is now unmistakable. Moreover, there is a growing concern that, given the very substantial market imperfections and dichotomies which characterize most developing countries, even the attainment of higher incomes for the poor as well as for the rich will not be sufficient for development. Instead, there is increasing recognition of a further need to be concerned with the attainment of the various specific basic needs of target groups, such as their housing needs, health needs, nutrition and educational needs, and so on, not all of which may be attainable even with higher incomes.

Methodological Issues

The second big set of issues in development economics concerns how to go about seeking explanations for the levels and rates of development that differentiate countries and groups within countries. As a corollary of the view that GNP per capita is a homogeneous and comprehensive index of development, analysts have traditionally conceived of development as a gradualistic, continuous, and universal process. Different countries at any point in time merely represent different positions along the same continuum. From this it follows that the explanations for development can be sought in two different but complementary ways: (1) by comparing different characteristics and forms of behavior of different countries at any given point in time, i.e., international cross-section analysis, and (2) by using historical case studies. Even though in the contemporary context developed countries (DCs) may be very different from developing countries (LDCs), since they represent different points in the same continuum, one can always identify periods in DC histories which are relevant to analyzing any contemporary development problem or issue in LDCs. Detailed time series of DCs have been thought of as a very useful and valid way of supplementing international cross-section analyses, and vice versa. Many of the classic works in development economics—such as the books and articles of pioneers like Simon Kuznets, Walter Rostow, and even Irma Adelman—emphasize such methods.

The trouble is that empirical evidence has been mounting that the growth processes of developed countries historically and those of contemporary developing countries are different in several fundamental ways. Their starting points in terms of initial endowments were very different, institutional conditions were different, technological changes were very different, external conditions and the relationships with trading partners were very different, and so on. Also, as LDCs do the things that DCs do (or did), the consequences are in many cases very different. For example, as incomes go up in LDCs, so as to become more on a par with those in DCs, the distribution of income need not, and in fact generally does not, become more equal, like that of DCs. Historical processes even in DCs have not turned out to be uniform. This has led to pessimism as to what has been and can be learned from those methods that have come to constitute the tool kit of development economics. The result has been identification of such a variety of "special" cases, that the notion that there is a "general" case becomes dubious indeed (see, e.g., Ranis 1978).

One important new methodological approach is to salvage the existing methodology by trying to identify the appropriate typologies of development, i.e., the different developmental paths which different types of countries pass through. If this challenge can be met, it would essentially allow development economists to strike a compromise between assuming that the development process is uniform and that it is completely heterogeneous, if not random. It is by no means assured yet that such typologies exist and thus that the traditional methods can be retained, at least in modified form.

A second approach is to undertake historical studies of LDCs themselves. This approach is certainly commendable, but it is severely hampered by the scarcity of historical information on LCDs.

Third, the increasing interdependence of the world has led to the suggestion that the internal development of any economy cannot be properly understood without understanding how that economy is embedded in and constrained by that of the rest of the world. The modeling of the advantages and disadvantages of various forms of "dependence" that may be thought realistic from this perspective is certainly no easy task, making this alternative approach a treacherous though potentially very important one.

Finally, the fact that development is multidimensional and involves numerous trade-offs among its different dimensions suggests the relevance and importance of general (dis)equilibrium analysis that would seek to understand the extent to which and why the behavior and incomes of different groups are different, yet interdependent. The modeling of growth and distribution has been limited primarily to simple fables based on traditional theory relating growth and factor accumulation to the functional distribution of income. It has become painfully obvious that even the best of fables getting one to the functional distribution of income are of very limited use in explaining the personal distribution of income, especially in the long run, where simplifying assumptions like that of given factor endowments are no longer relevant or appropriate.

With the traditional methods of the field being subjected to increasing disbelief, but the alternative methods difficult if not impossible to implement, we are left in the unenviable position of needing to know much more but faced with considerable uncertainty about the best way to proceed.

Theoretical and Empirical Issues

Despite the accumulating evidence that development is a much more complicated and nonuniform process than it had traditionally been conceived to be, there are still all sorts of questions about the validity of the "special" cases, and some of the negative conclusions which have been drawn. Will histories of LDCs really yield different implications than those of DCs? Do poor people really become worse off in the process of development, justifying the concern for distribution and basic needs; or is it only that relative inequality as measured by conventional indexes increases while the poor actually become better off? If the latter is closer to the truth, the need for reform both in measuring development and in the methods to be used may not be as great as has been suggested above (see Fields 1977). Another query along these same lines is how real the alleged differences in behavior between LDCs and DCs or between different types of LDCs are. Perhaps when the institutional and environmental conditions are better understood and/or such understanding can be better converted into analytical models, more definitive studies will show that behavior of LDCs is really more similar to that of DCs than it has generally been thought to be.

If the presumed differences and special cases of LDCs do in fact hold up to this closer scrutiny, a second generation of theoretical issues arises from the need to fill the void. The assumption of the similarity or uniformity of the development process gave rise to the view that theory could simply be transferred from DCs, where it originated, to LDCs, where it is needed. But if it cannot be transferred, what theory is there? Where does one start? What is the nature of the required new theory? If, as has been suggested above, such theory should include specification of dependence relations as well as of general interdependence between and among local groups and actors, the task of building a new type of theory is prodigious indeed.

Unhappily, laboratory conditions by no means prevail, especially in long-term development, making it more difficult to specify and then test theory in development economics than in most other fields. While it has become common to simplify matters by separating cyclical movements and determinants from long-run ones, the fact is that LDCs are subject to greater income instability than DCs. Business cycles are both more frequent and typically more severe. Can demand factors therefore be excluded? If not, what kind of macrodynamic theory is appropriate for LDCs, given that the assumptions of both Keynesian and monetarist theories do not seem to fit LDC conditions?[1]

A third generation of theoretical issues arises from the necessity of designing theory that is more fitting to the informational and market imperfections typical of contemporary LDCs. Another range of issues derives from the need to better portray and explain what seems to be the ongoing disequilibrium of the development process. It is one thing to talk about vicious circles, low-level equilibrium traps, and the need for "big pushes" and "critical minimum efforts"; it is a very different and far more difficult thing to make such concepts operational and to articulate them into an overall theory of developmental disequilibrium. The difficulty of such a task is no doubt one reason why economists have gone to such lengths to make traditional theory work, to keep trying to patch it up, and even to try to undermine the evidence contradicting the traditional models. But even such a process continually raises new theoretical issues: each new paradox has to be explained and, in order to keep from "throwing out the baby with the bath water," so to speak, requires ever more sophisticated (convoluted) theoretical arguments.

Is It Time for a Paradigm Change?

Recent years have witnessed a remarkable growth in the number and nature of paradoxes in the traditional neoclassical theory of development. The paradoxes take many forms. For example, those who migrate do not seem to be the marginal or the unemployed, who cannot manage to operate in their place of origin, but rather the better educated, more ambitious people, who consider themselves more likely to get ahead in the cities.[2]

No paradox is probably so fundamental and persistent as the finding that development is uneven, that it does not spread internationally and internally the way it would be predicted to, despite the alleged spreading effects of the trade, exchange, and factor movement mechanisms which operate. Mainstream economics has emphasized the difficulty of achieving takeoff, but once takeoff is achieved and development is on the turnpike, its trickling down and spread were thought to be automatic. The fact that income inequality has been increasing in most LDCs at the very time that growth has been accelerating is, therefore, perhaps the most important paradox for orthodox development theory. It leads to the issues of measurement and definition, methodology, and theory and empirical analysis that have been outlined in previous sections.

Admittedly, the recent literature in development economics has begun to own up to these failures and paradoxes by pointing to exogenous factors such as inappropriate government policies, market imperfections, and information costs. Such an approach may, however, be too timid and fall short of the mark. It is the purpose of this section to suggest as an alternative explanation that the processes which generate the backwash effects of development are endogenous to the system. In this sense phenomena such as unemployment and inequality during development are not paradoxical, but, rather, may be the logical, although not exclusive, consequences of excessive reliance on the market mechanism during the early stages of development. Should this analysis be correct, the appropriateness of the market as an important foundation of orthodox economics for the context of the LDCs must be called into question.

Three interrelated ideas, which are part and parcel of the body of theory known as neoclassical economics, have had a profound influence in shaping the orthodox economics of development. These ideas have provided the theoretical building blocks for the study of development economics and have outlined the kind of policies appropriate for achieving economic development.

The first idea is that development is a gradual, continuous, and cumulative process which can effectively rely on marginal adjustments. Equilibrium positions are thought to be stable, and the price mechanism serves as the beacon for summoning the required adjustments and thus becomes, in itself, an important device for promoting economic development. The corollary of this view is that static, partial equilibrium techniques are sufficient for analyzing economic development.

Second is the idea that order is created out of conflict and selfish drives through operation of automatic, equilibrating mechanisms—the neoclassical counterpart of the Invisible Hand of classical theory. These mechanisms guarantee that development generally benefits all major income groups. In the ruling paradigm of a harmonious world, rich and poor, capitalist and laborer all work together for increased output to mutual advantage.

Third is the optimism concerning the future possibilities for continued development and its spread among groups and across nations. Exchange is capable of leading to a Pareto-optimum position that benefits everybody, at least in the sense that the gainers have the potential to compensate the losers. The neoclassical theory of international trade is an even more definite statement of the proposition that free exchange will spread the benefits of development across the world through specialization and the division of labor.

Neoclassical economics is a house of many mansions, and any brief outline of a few basic ideas inevitably is more like a caricature than a sketch. Beginning with Marshall, moreover, the advocates of the theory have provided for numerous exceptions and generous modifications. Yet, the three salient ideas I have just described portray the essential characteristics of orthodox development economics; they are the red thread running through the ruling paradigm of the field. Any description of neoclassical development economics, for example, that omitted the gradual adjustment features which make the application of the marginal calculus possible would be grotesque. Likewise, any approach providing for automatic and persistent departures from equilibrium would be inconsistent with orthodox analysis. Equally inconsistent with it would be hypotheses predicting that the same (class of) people will stubbornly remain at the periphery of development and at the bottom of the income distribution ladder.

The ruling paradigm of the economics of development rests on the classical-neoclassical view of a world in which damage is gradual, marginalist, nondisruptive, equilibrating, and largely painless. Incentives are the bedrock of economic growth. Once initiated, growth becomes automatic and all-pervasive spreading among nations and trickling down among classes so that everybody benefits from the process. This view is analogous to the communicating vessels of elementary hydraulics: the pressure in the vessel with higher initial endowments leads to raising the water level in the other vessels. The mechanism that trips off change and restores equilibrium is the pressure created by nonidentical endowments. Its impulse is transmitted through the pipeline that connects the vessels. Analogously, development is initiated by incentives arising from inequality and is promoted by the market mechanisms that connect the rich and the poor. According to this paradigm, therefore, what is required for development is to create the proper incentives, to perfect the market mechanisms, and thereby to initiate the changes that lead to self-propelled takeoffs. The incurably optimistic payoff is the general spread of development and the homogenization of the rich and poor to the extent that they become indistinguishable—at least up to exogenous factors like the quantity of talents they possess or their tastes for risk-taking.

This is one, but certainly not the only, possible scenario. Contrast this paradigm with another borrowed from physics in which the Second Law of Thermodynamics holds center stage. The moving force in this case is not the Invisible Hand, which strives to bring order out of disorder, but entropy, which represents disorder, loss of information, and unavailability of energy. The Second Law of Thermodynamics states that the universe is constantly and irreversibly becoming less ordered than it was. A cup that is resting on a tray, left unto itself, will land on the floor more fluid and disordered than it was before. Work, the expense of energy, represents an attempt to generate order out of disorder or to counter the entropy of the universe, which is constantly increasing (Georgescu-Roegen 1971; Commoner 1976, chap. 2).

While the neoclassical paradigm views development as a cumulative process ruled by equilibrating mechanisms and centripetal tendencies, an application of the entropy law emphasizes the centrifugal forces, the jolt and backwash effects of development. Instead of the optimistic mechanisms of the melting pot or of the communicating vessels which lead to uniformity and homogenization, the disequilibrium paradigm suggests that economic development, at least in its early stages, acts like the suction principle in inducing biformity. It nourishes the towering heights of *polarity* at one extreme at the same time it creates *marginalization* at the other extreme. Just as cream rises to the top, development trickles up for a while to benefit those who are well-endowed; and as sediment becomes mired at the bottom, the victims of development are crowded into the periphery.

Which paradigm fits better and which will be more fruitful? The issues raised above with respect to the definition of development, its methodology, and its theoretical and empirical problems seem to fit somewhat more securely with the alternative disequilibrium paradigm than with the traditional neoclassical one. Indeed, one could agree that it has been the paradoxes arising from the application of the traditional paradigm that have focused such issues to be raised. But since the alternative paradigm has yet to be fully articulated, it has a long way to go before it might be said to be more useful or fruitful than the traditional one. Nevertheless, my prediction would be that its articulation and development will hold center stage as a critical issue in the development economics of the next decade or so.

Notes

1. For criticism of traditional macrodynamic theory for LDCs and some suggested simple alternatives see Nugent and Glezakos 1977.
2. For further examples of such paradoxes and analyses of those mentioned here, see Nugent 1977 and Nugent and Yotopoulos 1977.

References

Commoner, B. 1976. *The Poverty of Power.* New York: Knopf.
Fields, G. S. 1977. "Who Benefits from Development? A Reexamination of Brazilian Growth in 1960's." *American Economic Review* 67 (September): 570–82.
Georgescu-Roegen, N. 1971. *The Entropy Law and the Economic Process.* Cambridge: Harvard Univ. Press.
Nugent, J. B. 1977. "Momentum for Development and Developmental Disequilibria." *Journal of Economic Development* 2:1, 31–52.
Nugent, J. B. and Glezakos, C. 1977. "Expectations, Inflations, and the Phillips Curve in Latin America." Research Paper in Economics, no. 7708, University of Southern California.
Nugent, J. B. and Yotopoulos, P. A. 1977. "What Has Orthodox Development Economics Learned from Recent Experience?" Paper presented to the American Economic Association, New York, December 1977.
Ranis, G. 1978. "Equity with Growth in Taiwan: How Special Is the 'Special Case'?" *World Development* 6 (March): 397–410.

Selected Readings

General

Alchian, A. A., and Allen, W. R. 1969. *Exchange and Production Theory in Use*. Belmont, Calif.: Wadsworth.

Branson, W. 1972. *Macroeconomic Theory and Policy*. New York: Harper and Row.

Chase, R. X. 1977. "Why Economists Disagree." *American Journal of Economics and Sociology* 36 (October): 429–32.

Crandall, R. W., and Eckaus, R. S. 1972. *Contemporary Issues in Economics*. Boston: Little, Brown.

Galbraith, J. K. 1977. *The Age of Uncertainty*. Boston: Houghton Mifflin.

Heilbroner, R. L., and Thurow, L. C. 1975. *The Economic Problem*. Englewood Cliffs, N.J.: Prentice-Hall.

Hunt, E. K., and Sherman, H. J. 1972. *Economics: An Introduction to Traditional and Radical Views*. New York: Harper & Row.

Johnson, H. G., and Weisbrod, B. A., eds. 1973. *The Daily Economist*. Englewood Cliffs, N.J.: Prentice-Hall.

Lipsey, R., and Steiner, P. 1978. *Economics*. New York: Harper & Row.

McConnell, C. R. 1975. *Economic Issues*. New York: McGraw-Hill.

McKenzie, R. 1978. *Modern Political Economy*. New York: McGraw-Hill.

Mundell, R. A. 1968. *Man and Economics*. New York: McGraw-Hill.

North, D. C., and Miller, R. L. 1978. *The Economics of Public Issues*. New York: Harper & Row.

Ott, A. F., et al. 1975. *Macroeconomic Theory*. New York: McGraw-Hill.

Phelps, E. 1970. *Microeconomic Foundations of Employment and Inflation Theory*. New York: Norton.

Puth, R. C. 1977. *Current Issues in the American Economy*. Lexington, Mass.: D. C. Heath.

Samuelson, P. A. 1976. *Economics*. New York: McGraw-Hill.

Shapiro, E. 1974. *Macroeconomic Analysis*. 3rd ed. New York: Harcourt, Brace and Jovanovich.

Shultz, G. P., and Dam, K. W. 1977. *Economic Policy beyond the Headlines*. New York: Norton.

Stokey, E., and Lechauser, J. 1978. *A Primer for Policy Analysis*. New York: Norton.

Sutton, H. 1976. *Contemporary Economics*. New York: Praeger.

Tucker, J. E. 1976. *Current Economic Issues and Problems*. Chicago: Rand McNally.

Issues in Welfare, Distribution, Opportunity, Discrimination, and Justice

Andur, R. 1977. "Global Distributive Justice: A Review Essay." *Journal of International Affairs* 31 (Spring): 81–88.

Becker, G. S. 1957. *Economics of Discrimination.* Chicago: Univ. of Chicago Press.

Bendman, Z. T. 1977. "Why We Need to Get Poor." *The Futurist,* August, pp. 210–13.

Budd, E. C., ed. 1968. *Inequality and Poverty.* New York: Norton. See especially the articles by Milton Friedman, Harry Johnson, and George Stigler.

Friedland, R. 1976. "Class Power and Social Control: The War on Poverty." *Politics and Society* 6, no. 4: 459–89.

Galper, J. 1978. "What Are Radical Social Services?" *Social Policy* 8 (January): 37–41.

Goldman, A. H. 1977. "Limits to the Justification of Reverse Discrimination." *Social Theory and Practice* 3 (Spring): 289–306. Reply by A. Jagger, ibid. 4 (Spring 1977): 227–37.

Harrison, B. 1974. "Ghetto Economic Development." *Journal of Economic Literature,* March.

Hollander, S. 1977. "Adam Smith and the Self-Interest Axiom." *Journal of Law and Economics* 20 (April): 133–52.

Jensen, H. E. 1977. "Economics as Social Economics: The Views of the Founding Fathers." *Review of Social Economy* 35 (December): 239–57.

Kain, J. F., ed. 1969. *Race and Poverty: The Economics of Discrimination.* Englewood Cliffs, N.J.: Prentice-Hall.

Kenya, G. 1978. "Scarcity and Strategy." *Foreign Affairs* 56 (January): 396–414.

Kohler, H. 1966. *Welfare and Planning.* New York: Wiley.

Lairvant, K. R. 1978. "Poor Countries and the Rich: A Few Steps Forward." *Dissent* 25 (Winter): 43–53.

McConnell, H. M., and Yaseen, D. S., eds. 1972. "Revolutionary and Counter-Revolutionary Theory in Geography and the Problem of Ghetto Formation." *Perspectives in Geography,* vol. 3.

McCracken, P., et al. 1977. *Towards Full Employment and Price Stability.* Paris: OECD.

McCrone, D. J., and Hardy, R. J. 1978. "Civil Rights Policies and the Achievement of Racial Economic Equality." *American Journal of Political Science* 22 (February): 1–17.

Mbatia, E.L.O. 1978. "Economic Effects of Fair Employment Laws on Occupations: The Application of Information Theory to Evaluate Progress of Black Americans." *Journal of Black Studies* 8 (March): 259–78.

North, D. C. 1966. *Growth and Welfare in the American Past.* Englewood Cliffs, N.J.: Prentice-Hall.

Ranis, G. 1969. "Economic Dualism at Home and Abroad." *Public Policy* 18: 41–54.

Salamon, L. M., and Siegfried, J. J. 1977. "Economic Power and Political Influence: The Impact of Industry Structure on Public Policy." *American Political Science Review* 71 (September): 1026–43.

Sales, W., Jr. 1978. "Capitalism without Racism: Science or Fantasy?" *Black Scholar* 9 (March): 23–34.

Scott, K. H., and Wilson, C. Z. 1977. "Economic Evaluation of Social Programs: Problems and Potentialities." *Education and Urban Society* 9 (August): 509-40.

Wilkins, R. 1977. "Toward a Single Society." *Crisis* 84 (June): 300-302.

William, K. T. 1970. *The Political Economy of the Black Ghetto.* New York: Norton.

Issues in Economic Cycles and Stagflation

Board of Governors, Federal Reserve System. 1974. *The Federal Reserve System: Purposes and Functions.* 6th ed. Washington, D.C.: Federal Reserve.

Burns, A. 1969. *Business Cycles in a Changing World.* New York: National Bureau of Economic Research.

Duboff, R. B. 1977. "Full Employment: The History of a Receding Target." *Politics and Society* 7, no. 1: 1-25.

Fels, R. 1977. "What Causes Business Cycles?" *Social Science Quarterly* 58 (June): 88-95.

Flemming, J. 1976. *Inflation.* Oxford: Oxford Univ. Press.

Friedman, I. S. 1973. *Inflation: A World-Wide Disaster.* Boston: Houghton Mifflin.

Friedman, M. 1977. "Inflation and Unemployment." (Nobel Lecture.) *Journal of Political Economy* 85 (June): 451-72.

Friedman, M., and Heller, W. W. 1969. *Monetary Versus Fiscal Policy.* New York: Norton.

Friedman, M., and Schwartz, A. 1963. *A Monetary History of the United States, 1867-1960.* Princeton: Princeton Univ. Press.

Gordon, L. 1965. *Readings in Business Cycles.* Homewood, Ill.: R. D. Irwin.

Gordon, R. A. 1974. *Economic Instability and Growth: The American Record.* New York: Harper & Row.

Gordon, R. J. 1977. "Can the Inflation of the 1970's Be Explained?" *Brookings Papers on Economic Activity,* no. 1, pp. 253-79.

Griffins, B. 1975. *Inflation: The Price of Prosperity.* New York: Holmes and Meier.

Juster, F., and Wichtel, P. 1972. "Inflation and the Consumer." *Brookings Papers on Economic Activity,* no. 1, pp. 71-121.

Ledachman, R. 1973. *Inflation: The Permanent Problem of Boom and Bust.* New York: Random House.

Lindsey, L. 1977. "Politics of Inflation: An Unorthodox Perspective." *Social and Economic Studies* 26 (March): 86-95.

MacRae, C. D. 1977. "A Political Model of the Business Cycle." *Journal of Political Economy* 85 (April): 239-63.

Morley, S. A. 1971. *Economics of Inflation.* New York: Holt, Rinehart and Winston.

Morrison, R. S. 1973. *Inflation Can Be Stopped.* Cleveland: Western Reserve Press.

Phelps, E. S. 1972. *Inflation Policy and Unemployment Theory.* New York: Norton.

Stein, H. 1969. *The Fiscal Revolution in America.* Chicago: Univ. of Chicago Press.

Stein, J. L. 1974. "Unemployment, Inflation, and Monetarism." *American Economic Review* 64 (December): 867-87. Reply by R. Van Order, ibid. 67 (September 1977): 741-46.

Issues in Energy

Abelson, P. H. 1975. *Energy for Tomorrow.* Seattle: Univ. of Washington Press.

Davis, D. H. 1974. *Energy Politics.* New York: St. Martin's Press.

Dox, S. A. 1977. *Energy: A Critical Decision for the U.S. Economy.* Grand Rapids: Energy Education Publishers.

Environmental Information Center. 1973. *Energy Index.* New York: Environmental Information Center.

Erickson, E. W., and Waverman, L. 1974. *The Energy Question: An International Failure of Policy.* Buffalo: Univ. of Toronto Press.

Hausman, J. 1975. "Project Independence Report: An Appraisal of U.S. Energy Needs up to 1985." *Bell Journal of Economics and Management Science,* Autumn, pp. 517-51.

Henderson, L. J. 1977. "Energy Policy and Socioeconomic Growth in Low-Income Communities." *Review of Black Political Economy* 8 (Fall): 87-103.

Hoffman, K. C., and Jorgenson, D. W. 1977. "Economic and Technological Models for Evaluation of Energy Policy." *Bell Journal of Economics and Management Science,* Autumn.

Hummel, C. F. 1978. "Perceptions of the Energy Crisis: Who Is to Blame and How Do Citizens React to Environment Lifestyle Trade-offs?" *Environmental Behavior* 10 (March): 37-88.

Johnson, W. A. 1976. *Competition in the Oil Industry.* Washington, D.C.: Energy Policy Research Project.

Knowles, R. S. 1975. *The American Oil Famine: How It Happened and When It Will End.* New York: Coward, McCann and Geoghegan.

Medvin, N. 1974. *The Energy Cartel: Who Runs the American Oil Industry?* New York: Vintage Books.

Miller, R. L. 1974. *The Economics of Energy: What Went Wrong?* Glen Ridge, N.J.: Thomas Horton.

Odell, P. R. 1975. *Oil and World Power: Background to the Oil Crisis.* 3rd ed. New York: Taplinger.

O'Toole, J. 1975. *Energy and Social Change.* Los Angeles: Los Angeles Center for Future Research, University of Southern California.

Pindyck, R. S. 1978. "OPEC's Threat to the West." *Foreign Policy,* no. 30 (Spring), pp. 36-52.

Rand, C. 1975. *Making Democracy Safe for Oil.* Boston: Little, Brown.

Sears, D. O. 1978. "Political System Support and Public Response to the Energy Crisis." *American Journal of Political Science* 22 (Fall): 56-82.

United California Bank. 1977. *The Energy Crisis: Its Implications for the U.S. ... Its Impact on California.* Los Angeles: Research and Planning Division, United California Bank.

Werner, R. A. 1977. "Oil and U.S. Security Policies." *Orbis* 21 (Fall): 651-70.

Yager, J. C. 1974. *Energy and U.S. Foreign Policy.* Cambridge: Ballinger.

Issues in International Economic Relations

Aliber, R. Z. 1973. *The International Money Game.* New York: Basic Books.

Askari, H., and Cummingo, J. T. 1977. "Future of Economic Integration within the Arab World." *International Journal of Middle Eastern Studies* 8 (July): 289-315.

Baldwin, R. E., and Richardson, J. D., eds. 1974. *International Trade and Finance: Readings.* Boston: Little, Brown.

Browne, R. S. 1977. "Demands for a New International Economic Order." *Review of Black Political Economy* 7 (Spring): 309-16.

Cole, S. 1978. "Scenarios of World Development." *Future* 10 (February): 3-20.

Einzig, P. 1970. *The Euro-Dollar System.* 4th ed. New York: St. Martin's Press.

Gupta, J. Das. 1977. "Nation, Region, and Welfare: Ethnicity, Regionalism, and Development Politics in South Asia." *American Academy of Political and Social Science Annals,* no. 433 (September), pp. 125-36.

Hyman, S. 1978. "International Politics and International Economics: A Radical Approach." *Monthly Review* 29 (March): 15-35.

Kamrany, N. M., ed. 1977. *International Economic Reform.* Washington, D.C.: Univ. Press of America.

————,ed. 1978. *The New Economics of the Less Developed Countries.* Boulder, Colo.: Westview Press.

Kenen, P. B., and Lubitz, R. 1971. *International Economics.* 3rd ed. Englewood Cliffs, N.J.: Prentice-Hall.

Kindleberger, C. P. 1963. *International Economics.* Homewood, Ill.: Richard Irwin.

Kindleberger, C. P., and Herrick, B. 1977. *Economic Development.* New York: McGraw-Hill.

Morgenthau, R. S. 1977. "Developing States of Africa." *American Academy of Political and Social Science Annals,* no. 432 (July) pp. 80-95.

Pinder, J. 1977. "Reform of International Economic Policy: Weak and Strong Countries." *International Affairs* 53 (July): 345-63.

Rood, F. R. 1973. *International Trade and Investment.* 3rd ed. Cincinnati: South-Western.

Snider, D. A. 1966. *International Monetary Relations.* New York: Random House.

Todaro, M. P. 1977. *Economic Development in the Third World.* London: Longman.

Volkov, M. 1977. "Third World Countries: Problems of Economics and Ways of Solving Them." *International Development Review,* no. 3, 17-20.

Wilcox, C. 1976. *Economies of the World Today: Their Organization, Development and Performance.* New York: Harcourt, Brace and Jovanovich.

Yotopoulos, P., and Nugent, J. 1976. *Economics of Development: Empirical Investigations.* New York: Harper & Row.

Issues in Technology, Productivity, and Growth

Brown, E.H.P. 1973. "Levels and Movements of Industrial Productivity and

Real Wages Internationally Compared, 1860–1970." *Economic Journal* 83 (March).

Denison, E. F. 1967. *Why Growth Rates Differ.* Washington, D.C.: Brookings Institution.

———. 1974. *Accounting for United States Economic Growth, 1929–1969.* Washington, D.C.: Brookings Institution.

Denison, E. F., and Kendrick, J. 1972 . Hearings before the Subcommittee on Priorities and Economy in Government of the Joint Economic Committee, 25, 26, 27, April 1972, in *Improving National Productivity.* Washington, D.C.: GPO.

Eads, G. 1974. "U.S. Government Support for Civilian Technology: Economic Theory vs. Political Practice." *Research Policy,* vol. 3.

Eads, G., and Nelson, R. 1971. "Governmental Support of Advanced Civilian Technology." *Public Policy,* Summer.

Fuchs, V. R. 1968. "Medical Case," a part of Chapter 5 of *Productivity in the Services: Three Case Studies in the Service Economy.* New York: Columbia Univ. Press.

Kendrick, J. 1944. *Postwar Productivity Trends in the United States, 1948–1969.* New York: National Bureau of Economic Research.

Kendrick, J. 1961. *Productivity Trends in the United States.* Princeton, N.J.: Princeton Univ. Press.

Kuznets, S. 1971. *Economic Growth of Nations.* Cambridge: Harvard Univ. Press.

Mansfield, E. 1971. *Technological Change.* New York: Norton.

Mansfield, E., et al. 1977. *The Production and Application of New Industrial Technology.* New York: Norton.

Marimont, M. L. 1969. "Measuring Real Output for Industries Providing Services: OBE Concepts and Methods." In *Production and Productivity in the Service Sector Industries,* ed. V. R. Fuchs. New York: Columbia Univ. Press.

Mark, J. A. 1972. "Concepts and Measures of Productivity." In *The Meaning and Measurement of Productivity,* Bureau of Labor Statistics, Bulletin 1714. Washington, D.C.: GPO.

Meadows, D., et al. 1972. *The Limits to Growth.* Washington, D.C.: Potomac Associates.

Mishan, E. J. 1973. "Growth and Anti-Growth: What Are the Issues?" *Challenge,* May, pp. 26–42.

———. 1976 *Technology and Growth: The Price We Pay.* New York: Praeger.

Nordhaus, W. D. 1972. "The Recent Productivity Slowdown." *Brookings Papers on Economic Activity,* no. 3.

Perry, G. L. 1971. "Labor Force Structure, Potential Output, and Productivity." *Brookings Papers on Economic Activity,* no. 3.

Rostow, W. W. 1971. *The Stages of Economic Growth: A Non-Communist Manifesto.* 2nd ed. New York: Cambridge Univ. Press.

U.S., Department of Labor. 1973. *Productivity and the Economy.* Bulletin 1779.

Windus, M. L. 1973. "Regulatory Influences on Technological Innovation." Office of Nationa R & D Assessment staff working paper, May.

The Authors

Joseph Bisignano is a senior economist on the research staff of the Federal Reserve Bank of San Francisco. He received his Ph.D. degree in economics from Stanford University.

David M. Chereb is a research associate in the Program in Productivity and Technology, University of Southern California. He is director of research, Applied Economic Analysis. He received his Ph.D. degree in economics from the University of Southern California.

William A. Cox received his Ph.D. degree from Princeton University and is currently an economist with the Joint Economic Committee, U.S. Congress. He has been associated with the United Nations Industrial Development Organization, Vienna, Austria, and he has taught international economics and economic development at the University of Maryland and the University of Southern California.

Richard H. Day is a professor and chairman of the Department of Economics, University of Southern California. He received his doctorate from Harvard University and served on the faculty of the University of Wisconsin from 1963 to 1976. A pioneer in the development of recursive programming models and adaptive economic theory, he is co-founder and co-editor of the forthcoming *Journal of Economic Behavior and Organization.*

Michael DePrano is an associate professor in the Department of Economics, University of Southern California. He received his Ph.D. degree from the University of Illinois. His fields of interest are monetary theory, money and banking, and macroeconomic theory.

Jay W. Forrester, Germeshausen Professor at the Massachusetts Institute of Technology, directs the System Dynamics Program in the Alfred P. Sloan School of Management. Professor Forrester was a pioneer in early digital computer developments and holds the basic patent for invention of random-access, coincident-current magnetic storage which became the standard memory device for digital computers.

John P. Hardt is associate director for senior specialists and senior specialist for Soviet economics at the Congressional Research Service. He is also a member of the faculty of economics and of the Institute of Sino-Soviet Studies, George Washington University.

Michael D. Intriligator received his Ph.D. degree from M.I.T. and is now a professor of economics at the University of California, Los Angeles, where he teaches economic theory, mathematical economics, and econometrics. He is associate editor of the *Journal of Interdisciplinary Modeling and Simulation*, and of the *International Journal of Applied Analysis*.

Nake M. Kamrany is adjunct professor of economics and the director of the Program in Productivity and Technology at the University of Southern California. He has previously held faculty and research positions with M.I.T., Stanford Research Institute, the World Bank, and the University of California, Los Angeles.

Michael W. Keran is officer in charge of research of the Public Information and Bank Relations Department, Federal Reserve Bank of San Francisco. He is also an associate economist for the Federal Open Market Committee and is the author of many articles on domestic and international finance and stabilization policy.

Arthur B. Laffer is a professor of business economics at the University of Southern California. He is also closely associated with the editorial page of the *Wall Street Journal*, a member of the policy committee and the board of directors of the American Council on Capital Formation (Washington, D.C.), and editor of Marcel Dekker, Inc., series on Economics, Finance, and Business.

Edwin Mansfield is a professor of economics in the Wharton School of Business, University of Pennsylvania, and has also taught at Harvard University and Carnegie-Mellon University. His research includes econometric studies of technological change and innovation.

Aurelius Morgner is a professor in the Department of Economics and the School of International Relations, University of Southern California. He holds the Ph.D. degree from the University of Minnesota. His fields of interest include international trade and finance, the economics of development, and the history of economic theory.

Jeffrey B. Nugent, who received his Ph.D. degree from the New School for Social Research, is a professor of economics at the University of Southern California. His fields of interest include development economics, macroeconomics, and international economics; and his publications include *Economics of Development: Empirical Investigations* (with Pan A. Yotopoulos), 1976.

Robert S. Pindyck is currently an associate professor at the Sloan School of Management, M.I.T. He has served as advisor to the Republic of Tunisia, the Federal Reserve Board, the Federal Energy Administration, the Development Research Center of the International Bank for Reconstruction and Development, and other agencies.

Susan Strange is on the faculty of the London School of Economics. She is a noted scholar in the field of political economy, with extensive publications on the major issues of international economy.

Lester C. Thurow is a professor of economics and management at M.I.T. He is one of the leading social scientists in the field of economic reform, welfare economics, and the quality of life. He has been on the faculty or staff of Harvard University, the Council of Economic Advisors, and various other governmental and private groups. He is currently associate editor of the *Quarterly Journal of Economics* and the *Review of Economics and Statistics*.

Index

Library of Congress Cataloging in Publication Data

Main entry under title:
Economic issues of the eighties.

    "Based on a series of lectures presented at the University of Southern California in
1977 and 1978 as a part of the Department of Economics' colloquium 'Contemporary
economic issues.' "
    Bibliography: p.
    Includes index.
    1. Economic policy—Addresses, essays, lectures. 2. Economic history—1945-
—Addresses, essays, lectures. I. Kamrany, Nake M., 1934-   II. Day, Richard H.

HD82.E286   330.9'048   79-16772
ISBN 0-8018-2248-3
ISBN 0-8018-2271-8 pbk.